Dear John

Dear John

THE
JOHN
LLOYD
AUTOBIOGRAPHY

pitch

First published by Pitch Publishing, 2022

Pitch Publishing
A2 Yeoman Gate
Yeoman Way
Worthing
Sussex
BN13 3QZ
www.pitchpublishing.co.uk
info@pitchpublishing.co.uk

ISBN 978 1 80150 109 5

Typesetting and origination by Pitch Publishing
Printed and bound in Great Britain by TJ Books, Padstow

CONTENTS

My book dedication is to my children
Aiden and Hayley.

You were wonderful children, and now
you are amazing adults.
I am so proud of you.
Every day I think of you and every day
you make me smile.

Love you always,
Dad.

FOREWORD

I AM happy to finally have this book in my hands.

It will bring back so many memories and I hope everyone will enjoy it as much as me.

John and I have been friends for 50 years.

It is time to go back to Memory Lane ...

Bjorn

Legendary Swedish player Bjorn Borg won 11 Grand Slam singles titles, including Wimbledon five times in a row from 1976.

ACKNOWLEDGEMENTS

TO THE Lloyd family and all my nieces and nephews, thank you for all your love and support.

To Phil Jones, thank you for your unwavering belief in our project despite the many bumps in the road. Your writing skills are incredible, and I have so enjoyed our time together collaborating on our book.

Thanks to all my colleagues that I have worked with at HBO and BBC. I have been so fortunate to have spent time with so many talented and wonderful people.

Thanks to my fellow competitors from all over the world who I either partnered or played against on the tour.

I have been so fortunate to have so many incredible friends in my life. To all of you, I am extremely thankful and grateful.

Many thanks to everyone from Pitch Publishing who had faith in our book.

MUM, DAD AND A
TENNIS-MAD SCHOOLKID

A letter from the John Lloyd of today to his former self as he embarks on life in the green blazer of Southend High School for Boys.

Dear John,

Get an education. The dream is to become a professional tennis player. It's one you have had since you were five, when batting a ball against a tiny wall in the backyard was the daily ritual.

You believe you have the talent to succeed and you certainly have parents to back you all the way. But the chances of making it to the top are slim. Plus, one serious injury and it can all be taken away from you in a heartbeat.

Without an education, there will be nothing to fall back on. So, don't skip school on a whim. Your sore rear end will thank you for it. Attend and learn. Pass your exams. Then, when the worst befalls you at the start of your tennis career, you will have options and not just the worry of potentially shattered dreams. Just get an education.

John

MY MOTHER and father were amazingly selfless people. Many parents are, of course. The best mums and dads always put their children first. But the sacrifices my parents made weren't so they could proudly wave their children off to university, with the promise of careers as city professionals. No, they gave up so much in their lives to keep their boys' sporting dreams alive. Elder brother David, younger brother Tony and myself all wanted to make it as professional tennis players. We all dreamed of playing in the Wimbledon Championships. Thanks to Mum and Dad, those dreams came true for all of us.

My father Dennis was from a wealthy background in the south of England, while my mother Doris grew up in a mining family of 12 in the north-east. She lost one of her brothers in a mining accident: a terrible tragedy amid an early life of hardship.

We used to visit my grandmother in the old terrace Mum had grown up in. How so many people squeezed into that tiny brick house I could never understand. The streets resembled those used in the film *Billy Elliot*, about the child dancer from mining stock. The only bathroom – and its big old tub – was downstairs, the toilet was outside. There was a coal fire and no heating anywhere else in the house. Tony and me had to share with Gran. Even in winter, she would have the window open and just a single sheet to cover her in bed. It was bloody freezing. But they were made of sterner stuff in that mining community, fuelled no doubt by liberal mounds of suet pudding made in a handkerchief and drizzled with Lyle's Golden Syrup. I loved it. But I would be so full and bloated afterwards. 'This must be what it feels like to eat a football, whole.'

It was rough up there, but the locals were great people, so warm and welcoming. They were tough, though. By virtue of her upbringing and surroundings, so was Mum.

Doris met and fell in love with Dennis during the Second World War. My father was from money in Essex: big mansion of a house in Chingford, complete with its own tennis court, and all. The contrast to their respective lives in their formative years could not have been greater. Mum must have thought she had hit the jackpot when she married into that kind of wealth, with the promise of a life of luxury. Unfortunately for her, that's not how it panned out. Luxury, in Mum's case, was not for life.

When my grandfather on my Dad's side died of lung cancer, he left everything in two equal measures to his two children. My father was suddenly a very wealthy man. He decided to plough all his money into a retail clothes business in London. I was too young to know what was happening in Dad's work life. I just remember we had it good back then. The business was an apparent success.

Unfortunately, my father was too trusting of people. He was probably too nice for his own good. When a partner persuaded him to open up another arm of the business in Birmingham, it was the beginning of the end. He was, to put it bluntly, screwed out of his fortune. He lost everything and was left with massive debts.

What he did next was a wonderful life lesson for me. He didn't go bankrupt and carry the stigma of that through life. He took two jobs and paid all his creditors back in full, penny by penny. It took him 25 years, but he was never declared bankrupt. I always admired Dad for that. He told me: 'If you make a deal, you honour it. It's that simple.' That line about honour has always stayed with me.

Our family of six – Mum, Dad, sister Ann, brothers David and Tony and me – downsized into a three-up, two-down house on Woodfield Road in Leigh-on-Sea, which is a borough of Southend-on-Sea just to the north of the Thames Estuary. It wasn't much bigger than the house my mother grew up in and there was still an outside loo. That was an experience and a half in the middle of winter, I can tell you. Using the toilet for the first time and sitting on what felt like a large doughnut of ice, with the passing rag 'n' bone man shouting 'any old iron', is a memory never to fade.

Leigh-on-Sea's historical claim to fame was its minor involvement in the Norman Conquest of 1066 and its mention in the *Domesday Book*. My brothers and I had hopes of creating our own history for Leigh ... on the tennis courts. And to that aim, our father's misfortune would – strange as it may sound – help us. That's because he took one job as manager of a friend's newly opened store, HW Stone's Sports shop, and a second job as tennis coach at the local club.

David was six years older than me and had hit many a ball against the wall at the back of the house. I wanted to be like my big brother, so copied him. Tony, in turn, copied me. It's where we hit our first volleys. A coal shed took up a quarter of the space in the tiny garden, so there wasn't much room to play tennis. But I was only four when I started practising against the wall, so I didn't need much space either. Every day after school, I would bat the ball against the small shed wall, imagining I was taking on some great tennis champion. It was my favourite part of the day: that and being first to the milkman's horse cart when he delivered one of those bottles with the cream on the top. That was just the best on my cereal,

14

and if I could get to it before the rest of the family it was a little victory.

When my father had his business in London, he was in the city six days a week. We didn't see much of him. Now things were different, especially at weekends. We would all join Dad at the Westcliff Hardcourt Tennis Club, where he coached part-time. It was a family club about half a mile from our house, not too far from the sea front. During the summer, we spent all day there. The kids would play football on the field there, have a game of hide-and-seek or go down to the beach, while the adults played tennis. Mum brought lunch down for us all and then, in the afternoon, we youngsters would get time on the courts. It was such a healthy way to grow up. My best friends were made at the club. Certainly, some of my best days ever were spent there. These were innocent, magical times.

Mind you, looking back, it was ever so antiquated. There were no indoor courts, so playing in winter – when it was dark from about 3 o'clock – required a floodlight that was pointed at just one of the courts. The net posts had spikes at the bottom. We'd use those to crack the ice on the courts in freezing temperatures. There was no way a bit of frost was beating us. I would think back to these days when I was about 16 and first playing in America. I was at the Orange Bowl in Miami, where all the world's best juniors gathered. The Americans I talked to – at least those based in hot states like Florida – had been able to play three or four hours a day, every day after school whatever the season. My rivals had probably spent 50 times more hours on court than me, maybe more. That's why in those days British players had a reputation for maturing late: they had talent but not enough court time on the clock.

When I first started playing tennis, as an infant really, my brother David was already ranked in the top ten in the country in the under-12s. He was doing well in local tournaments and was considered a top prospect. He always inspired me: always gave me something to target. Seeing him succeed is probably why I had the unshakeable belief I was going to be a professional tennis player. There was no doubt in my mind.

That, in turn, is one of the main reasons why I never gave a damn about school. What use was education to me? I was going to play tennis for a living. I was going to play at Wimbledon.

I passed my 11-plus exam to earn a place at Southend High, the grammar school for boys. That in itself was some kind of miracle. I had learning difficulties, which would be diagnosed quickly enough nowadays but weren't acknowledged back then. Unless there was repetition of a task or an experiment we were meant to carry out, there was something in my brain that prevented the information from sticking. It's hard to describe, but it had a damaging impact on my schooldays. In a class of 32, I was hardly about to receive special treatment. Visual stimulus I could respond to, but the lessons were unimaginative and as dreary as white chalk on black board. Again, no wonder I believed school wasn't for me.

This downer on school and learning was stupid in the extreme, of course. The chances of making it in tennis were slender and there was no money in the game. My goal wasn't kept secret. I didn't care who I told. Most people patronised me or thought I was plain daft. They thought tennis only happened properly two weeks a year, at Wimbledon. Anything else was a circus sideshow. When my father took me to Wimbledon as a 12-year-old, when I wandered the grounds in some permanent state of bliss, I gazed at great champions like Lew Hoad and John Newcombe, I smelled the grass, I saw the new white balls brought from their boxes and thought: 'How fantastic. How glamorous.' This was for me. Somehow, I was going to make it happen. It never crossed my mind for even a solitary second that I might need qualifications to fall back on.

My headmaster was a 6ft 4in giant of a man, Mr Price. He was expressionless and looked for all the world like Lurch from *The Addams Family.* He didn't like me even before he met me. That's because he loathed my brother David, who had attended Southend High before me. David was always in trouble, picking fights with prefects and generally giving Frankie Price and his staff the runaround. David was a frequent visitor to the head's office – and not to collect badges of honour. But I didn't expect to maintain the family tradition quite so soon. My first run-in with Lurch came as early as day one.

The morning had already started badly because Mum had made the mistake of sending me to school in short trousers. Just two other mothers out of around 150 hadn't read the memo either on 'long trousers only' and made the same costly error. Costly because it drew even more attention to the new kid, leading to more teasing and possible beatings. Later, the English teacher – who, I was to learn, also hated my brother David – sent me to the head's office for something I hadn't done, as if to rekindle the family grudge. Lurch stared down at me from about ten feet in the sky and scared the living crap out of me. My only thought: 'I've got to stay away from this bad place called high school.'

That's what I did, as much as conceivably possible. I bunked off at every opportunity, usually climbing out of windows and threatening prefects to say I had been in school when I so obviously hadn't. By lunchtime, I was normally out of there. I would save money from my paper round to play pinball machines at transport cafes. I became so good that a couple of shillings could see me through two hours of play. If it was good weather, I would go sunbathing on the cliffs. If I was particularly flush with cash, I would head to the cinema for an afternoon matinee. As long as I was out of sight and filling the afternoon, most pastimes would work to drown out school. My sister Ann wrote a few 'John can't attend school today because ...' letters. They were a big help. But my attendance record was so bad – and when I was there, I was late nine times out of ten – that I couldn't escape punishment forever. A caning every now and then was inevitable.

The first time Lurch caned me was a monumental shock to my system. He lectured me for about ten minutes, then pointed to the cupboard in the corner. That's where he kept his collection of canes. I had to bend over his desk. He lifted my blazer to expose the hitting zone, then whacked me twice with full force. It was seriously painful. Lurch was such an expert with the cane that he managed to criss-cross his 'design' on my arse. Where the red raw lines met, he drew blood. He would lecture me some more before I could leave his office, doubtless knowing my backside was stinging. Then I would run to the toilets, fill a basin with cold water and sit my bare bum in it. I would leave it sizzling in there for a while, before planning my next escape. It was a battle of wills. We despised each other. I took gratification in knowing my class had the worst overall attendance record in the five years I was connected to Southend High.

Lurch had his petty revenge. When I was only 11, I was playing on the school's under-15s tennis team, thanks to an invitation from an older boy named Trevor Stone. I was better than the older kids and being outmuscled was less of an issue at tennis than it was at rugby or football. Nonetheless, this was a big deal and pretty much unheard of. In many ways, it was a stupid thing for me to do. I had to give up my Saturdays to play on terrible potholed courts with threadbare nets and balding tennis balls against lads I could beat playing left-handed. But at the end of the first year on the team, we were awarded what were known as 'half colours'. That's to say a gold letter 'T' for tennis could be sewn on my blazer pocket as a mark of honour. Lurch had to begrudgingly present it to me at an assembly of around 500 students, so that in itself was probably worth the Saturday sacrifice. The year after, I was due to receive 'full colours'. This was gold braid stitched to the sleeve of each arm of a school blazer. No 12-year-old had ever enjoyed this distinction. I wasn't about to become the first. Lurch told me he was not giving me 'full colours' so as not to make me stand out from my peers. When I told my father, he immediately pulled me from the team and I never played for my school again.

Dad was remarkably supportive. Throughout all my truanting ways, my father was never on my case. Okay, so he hadn't seen all my report cards strewn with Ds and Fs because I had thrown them out of the train window. But all else considered, he was more than forgiving. He accepted it because he knew tennis was in my blood. He was also seeing tennis opportunities opening up for David.

With just our one floodlit court at Westcliff, playing during the week in winter was increasingly difficult. Dad asked Lurch if he could take me out of school on one afternoon a week to play at Queen's Club in London, where I had been accepted to practise alongside other promising British juniors. Lurch said: 'I've never heard of anything so stupid.'

'If you don't grant permission,' said my father, 'I'll take him out of school anyway and move him elsewhere.' The headmaster reluctantly agreed, although how foolish of him to miss his chance to ditch me and improve the school's attendance record in one fell swoop.

So, on Wednesdays, I would leave school at midday, ride my bike the 20 minutes to my house, collect my packed lunch from Mum, head to the station and climb on the train to Fenchurch Street, eat half my sandwich on the 50-minute journey, walk to Tower Hill tube station and travel to Barons Court. I would arrive at Queen's Club about two.

The indoor courts there were made of fast, hardwood boards. Water sometimes leaked through during winter and we would have to throw down sawdust. There was no heating. It was freezing cold. But these were like five-star facilities to me, especially the big hot baths at day's end. There was no annoying knocking on the door to hurry up or battling for hot water like there was at home. Most important of all, I was able to play three to four hours at a time with players of my ability, watched over by a top coach.

My return journey started around rush hour. I would get a seat on the tube train at Barons Court, no problem. But it was packed out from Earl's Court onwards. The polite thing – and expected thing for a youth back then – was to vacate one's seat for a woman or an elderly person. I pulled down my bobble hat, pretended to be asleep and counted the number of times the train stopped to judge when to get off. I would get some dirty looks as I clambered from my nice, comfy seat; but hey, I had been playing tennis all afternoon. A boy needs his rest.

There was no pretending on the train from Fenchurch Street back home. I would eat the other half of my sandwich and then genuinely fall asleep, usually drooling on an unsuspecting stranger's shoulder. I would often get a nudge from the porter at the end of the line and have to head to the opposite platform to go a couple of stops back the other way. Even then, I would climb the hill to home and would be through the door by eight.

And all this, every week, on my own, at the age of 12. What innocent times.

My schooldays were finally over at the age of 15. I counted down the weeks until I could concentrate solely on my chosen profession. Exams were not for me. I left without an O level to my name. The mock exams had shown how futile even sitting them would have been. I sat the mock mathematics test over three days, starting with arithmetic. I took one look at the paper and decided that, on a good day, I would do well to get 30 out of 100. 'Why bother?' I thought. I signed my name where requested on the exam paper, then raised my hand.

'I'm finished, Sir.'

'You can't have finished, Lloyd. You only started two minutes ago.'

'Can I leave now, Sir?'

'No, you have to sit there for the next three hours.'

Next day, I learned from the error of my ways. This time, I signed the algebra paper and, rather than draw attention to myself by asking to leave, simply rested my head for a good, long nap.

My friends found all this very amusing, of course. But the headmaster did not.

'Nought out of 200!' he barked. 'Is this your sum knowledge of the last five years here? You are a disgrace to the school. All you have written is your name.'

It crossed my mind to say: 'Can't I at least have a mark for getting that right,' but I thought better of it. Lurch still had one eye on the cane cupboard. It was no less painful to be thrashed at the age of 15.

'Show me more effort in the geometry exam or you know what's coming to you.'

When I sat that test, I filled the pages with all kinds of triangles and theories, plucking something about Pythagoras from my memory banks. X equalled Y when multiplied by Z was one of my creative answers. Up went my hand for more paper. My friends were looking at me as if to say: 'What's happened to Lloyd? Has he gone mad?' Three hours later, I had shown more effort as requested. But the fact I had made it all up meant I scored another big fat zero. Let's just say the powers that be at Southend High were not pushing me to sit the proper examinations at the end of term. Instead, I was able to leave three weeks early. It was tennis time.

I moved to London and stayed in a YMCA. It was so cold in winter that I had to sleep with two tracksuits on. I did part-time jobs to pay my way, like washing cars, and simply lived to practise at Queen's Club or play in tournaments that would bring my childhood dream closer to reality.

Then, aged just 16, I received the shock of my life and the dream started to unravel.

Torquay was the venue for an indoor event I had entered. My habit, whatever the weather, was to hit the courts cold. It could be snowing outside and I still wouldn't warm up properly.

Straight away, I would think I could smack down big serves. Boom, I hit one serve. Crunch went something in my arm. I was in excruciating pain. For the one – and I think only – time in my career, I had to default. My arm was bent out of shape. I had done some worryingly bad damage.

My godfather was a lovely man by the name of Alan Murley. He was my father's best friend and, fortunately for me, one of the top bone specialists in Oxford. Alan examined me and told me, in his forthright manner, 'You've got a severe case of golfer's elbow. You've got the ligaments and tendons of a 40-year-old. To be quite frank, with an injury that bad, I'm not convinced that you are ever going to have a career in tennis.'

It was a devastating diagnosis. Here I was at 16, without any qualifications and with the prospect of my tennis career being over before it had even started. Perhaps the best I could now hope for from tennis was to coach in some capacity. That would not have been the end of the world, but right there and then it felt like it.

Alan explained: 'I'll try to help you with some exercises. But you can't – and absolutely must not – hit a tennis ball for six months.'

The exercises felt impossible at first. I couldn't even lift a glass of water with my injured arm. But they took effect in time. I could even work for a family friend's electrical business, helping two big bruisers lug fridges around. I was getting my strength back. But could I hit a tennis ball pain-free?

It was the scariest thing, that first day back on the tennis court. Had I rested my arm long enough? Would I be able to strike the ball without fear? It was difficult to forget the agonising pain of that serve six months earlier. 'Deep breath, John – here we go.' I hit a forehand: no pain; then a backhand: no pain; then a serve: still no pain. The relief washed over me that I wasn't washed up at 16.

My godfather saved my career, I'm certain of it. If I had seen another doctor who had been less blunt and had sugar-coated the condition, I might have returned too soon and done irreparable damage. I respected Alan so much that what he said was gospel. I would never have gone against his advice or wishes. He put the fear of God into me, actually. With another doctor, who knows?

Alan might have saved my career, but the two men to nurture it were my father and a great friend John Barrett, for so long the voice of tennis on the BBC. My mother was a huge influence, too, of course. She was the organiser-in-chief, a proper tennis mum, not just to me, but all her sons. On the playing side, though, Dad and John were my earliest mentors.

How blessed was I to have a father who had no ego when it came to coaching me? He knew that at a certain level I would pass him by – that I would need to get advice from people who had played or coached at a higher level than Dad. He just wanted me to be the best player I could be. He didn't need to be front and centre, taking credit for producing a player with world-class potential.

It could have been so different. I could have been the son of a father who wanted the glory of manufacturing a champion: part of some kind of sporting experiment.

Stephen Warboys was a fellow Essex lad and one of my peers on the junior scene. Long before the careers of the Williams sisters and Maria Sharapova were dreamt up by ambitious fathers, Stephen was the first prototype for a wonder-kid turned champion. His father was a former British player, Jack

Warboys, a multi-millionaire with enough cash and clout to employ Wimbledon champions Rod Laver and Pancho Gonzales as his son's hitting partners. Stephen had an advanced nutritional regime, he was advised to sleep for a minimum of 11 hours a night, he wasn't allowed to watch television and he was home-schooled from the age of 11.

I was drawn to play Stephen in a competition sponsored by London's *Evening News*. The match took place on a court at his father's mansion, which also boasted a running track, a boxing ring and indoor swimming pool. When I saw the house and compared it to my family home, where we were packed together like sardines, there was a certain amount of envy. But it didn't last long. As soon as I realised there were no televisions in the house, my green-eyed monster was killed.

The 'Warboys Experiment' worked for a while. Stephen was just eight when he won the Under-15s Open Championship, only 13 when he became the youngest player in the Wimbledon Junior Championships of 1967 and was runner-up in that event four years later. For a while, he was probably the best junior tennis player in the world.

But by 1974, Stephen had fallen out with his father and would eventually relocate to Canada. He had been turned into a loner through no fault of his own. When the rest of us were partying at tournaments – just doing regular teenage stuff – he was stopped from joining in by his father. The older Stephen got, the more he must have resented that and wanted to rebel. He had been denied a normal childhood. There was nothing to envy in any of that. Thank heavens for a dad like mine.

Jack Warboys was 20 years ahead of the times. Many more parents have since tried to create tennis champions. What they all failed to grasp is that in the vast majority of cases it doesn't work. Even if their children have success on the court, it usually comes at the cost of a lost relationship off it. I have seen examples of parents mortgaging their homes to pay for coaching in Florida. Imagine the pressure that puts on the child, even more so if they become the expected breadwinner at 14 or 15. Pathetically, it is usually a case of frustrated parents wanting to live their lives through their children.

When you look at it, when you get down to the very basics of it all, you could lose your precious relationship with your child over hitting a yellow tennis ball across a net. It's so ludicrous. Jack Warboys paid that price and I can't imagine anything more expensive.

While Stephen was being shackled, my father was letting me run free. Not only was I allowed to travel on my own to Queen's Club every Wednesday from the age of 12, but I was also given permission to stay overnight in London once a week to practise on the indoor courts at Wimbledon from a similar age. This was all courtesy of the fine gentleman that is Mr John Barrett.

John was a tennis pioneer, developing British talent with the help of his Barrett Squad – an elite group that trained together. John knew my brother David and was kind enough to take time to see me play. He saw my potential and, without asking for anything in return, agreed to help me progress. Every Friday after school, I would head to south London to stay at the flat John shared with his wife Angela Mortimer, the former Wimbledon champion. On Saturday morning before breakfast, we would run two to three miles around Wimbledon Common. We would then play a few hours on Wimbledon's indoor courts in the morning,

I would demolish several plates of food at lunch, before another few hours of tennis in the afternoon.

The first time we played, there were tennis balls strewn all over the court after practice. I left them there and went to sit down. John, pointing to the balls, said: 'What do you think you're doing?'

'My dad normally picks up the balls,' I replied in all innocence.

'No, no, not anymore. You do that. Pick up every one and don't say anything like that to me again.'

John was right, of course. I was a lazy sod. That had such an impact on me that, to this day, I pick up all the tennis balls wherever I play, even at things like corporate events, for fear of retribution. It's ingrained in me, just as the greatest kindness and consideration is ingrained in John Barrett – just as the very essence of decency was ingrained in my father.

Dad had one shot he loved more than any other. He called it the drag volley. It was a forehand or backhand volley at the net, where you had to cut the ball to create spin and an acute angle. Even if Dad lost a set, he was happy if he could come away saying he had hit a drag volley. Tim Henman was one of his favourite players and one day, after a victory for Tim, my father said: 'You hit two gorgeous drag volleys today.' Tim didn't have a clue what he was talking about, so I explained. Thereafter, Tim always asked after my dad – 'How's Dennis? Ask him how his drag volley is shaping up.'

A couple of years before Dad died, he was bedridden and no longer had good eyesight. But he could still enjoy listening to my commentaries on television. One player hit what I decided was very much like a drag volley. My co-commentator asked: 'What the heck is that?' I took great delight in pointing out: 'This is a Dennis Lloyd speciality – my father's own brand of shot. I'm going to tell him to patent it, in fact. It should be in teaching manuals, with his name alongside it.' Dad loved hearing this and it apparently perked him up no end.

My head was always too big for caps and hats, so any I was given often ended up worn by my father while he coached. In his later years, when he was still only charging £8 an hour for a lesson and loving every minute of it, a woman in her mid-50s – not blessed with any particular talent, but a trier – was hitting some mid-court shots Dad's way. She connected with one at Mach 5 speed. It was on course for his head. His reactions weren't what they once were. He couldn't get his racket up in time. So, he used one of my caps – at least the peak of it – to flick away danger and probably injury. Dad loved telling me these stories. Even in some small way, the fact he wore my caps all the time he taught his beloved tennis kept us connected.

Dad was still coaching until he was 88; still listening to members claiming they had hit the legendary drag volley; still insisting he would not believe them without hard evidence – 'With all due respect, just a select few can hit a shot like that, you know … just a select few.' Only a couple of untimely falls and an insistent doctor put paid to his life on the courts.

We lost Dad in 2014 at the age of 94, four years after Mum's passing. Their spirit lives on in four children and tens more grandchildren and great-grandchildren. Dad remains the oldest playing member Westcliff ever had. He did always say: 'Tennis is a game for life.'

My parents sacrificed so much for us. We had the occasional holiday at Butlins, but there was nothing more glamorous for them. All their money most summers went on funding our travels to tennis tournaments in other parts of England. Dad would stay home to work; Mum would come with us. That's just the way it was. We were having great fun at their expense. Many years later, when we boys started to make some money from tennis, it was fantastic to be able to pay for their more extravagant holidays and give them some kind of overdue reward.

But it was only the smallest of paybacks in the whole scheme of things, because how can you truly repay anyone for a childhood so extraordinary that inspired the fulfilment of a dream?

Dear Mum & Dad,

One of the biggest thrills of my life was winning the mixed doubles title at Wimbledon in the early 80s, looking down from the Royal Box presentation ceremony and seeing your smiling faces. That meant the world to me. I knew what you had sacrificed to get me there.

I love that I'm a life member of Westcliff Hardcourt Tennis Club, the place where we spent so many happy times together and where you were honoured with the unveiling of a commemorative plaque a decade ago. That was some speech that day, Dad. But then why should I be surprised that the man who led the club's annual pantomime productions could command the stage in such a manner?

Thank you for supporting me, for believing in me and for giving me the freedom to dream big. I hope I made you proud.

Your loving son,

John

SPECIAL SIBLINGS

A letter from the John Lloyd of today to his former self, offering wisdom on family investments and book deals to avoid.

Dear John,

Here are two crucial pieces of advice that will prevent you living with that most unhealthy of companions called regret.

I positively encourage you to plough money into brother David's brave new world. His radical proposal to change the face of British tennis will make you rich.

But do not plough headlong into a foolish book deal with Margaret Thatcher's daughter. You will not be in the right frame of mind to make sensible, rational decisions on a story that directly involves your then wife, Chris Evert. It's a bad idea. Don't do it.

John

MY ELDER brother David stood wearing his hard hat in a field in the middle of nowhere on a cold and rainy British day and announced this is where he would revolutionise indoor tennis in the country. I concluded he had lost his marbles.

This desolate expanse of land in Heston near London's Heathrow Airport was the site of the first David Lloyd Leisure Club. I didn't say anything to him at the time but, as I tried desperately to tap into my brother's vision, I thought: 'You must be nuts. You've got no shot here … not in a million years.'

Some mornings, I wake up banging my head against the wall because I know if I had invested just 50 grand in David's ambitious plan, I would have become a multi-millionaire. Who's nuts now?

When David left the professional tour, he worked at a tennis facility in Canada and saw how a top-class leisure club should be run. His reaction was: 'Wow! This really works. People love it.' That was the start of his dream to transform the tennis landscape in the UK. And my word, did it ever need transforming.

We had Queen's Club in London, but the indoor facilities there were cold and uninviting. Wimbledon's indoor courts were inadequate, and elite places like the Vanderbilt, where Princess Diana used to play, were archaic. Plus, these places weren't exactly freely available to the general public unless you had serious money or considerable clout. David could not understand why Britain didn't have more centres like the one he was heading up in Canada.

It wasn't just me who thought my brother might be a bit delusional. I know others couldn't envisage the British public paying good money to visit a club that combined tennis with restaurants, saunas, gyms, hair salons and Jacuzzis. We lived in a country where people were still content to play in the park, on tired shale courts, across broken nets, with no clubhouses and no bathrooms … where it cost them next to nothing to have a quick hit.

David mortgaged his house to get his project off the ground and sought out investors. At that point, I was married to Chris Evert. I was making good money, Chrissie was doing even better, and it would have been no problem to put in £50,000, even £100,000. It wouldn't have been any kind of risk. But I wasn't thinking about the future. I was on the road, playing tennis, living very much for the day. Invest? Invest in what? That wasn't in my DNA, unlike my brother.

David always had that ability to make £5 out of one. He used to do things like buy tennis racket gut from India and sell it for several times the amount. He had a paper round and bought a machine to string rackets, then invested that money to buy rackets which he sold in Germany when the Deutschmark was strong. He always loved doing a deal: it's where he got his highs.

When David asked if I wanted to put some money in, I said: 'Yeah – whatever you want.' But deep down, even though he was naturally a very confident guy, I don't think he knew if his project was going to work out. History wasn't in his favour. He knew he was taking a punt. I ended up investing £10,000.

When the leisure club was completed, it was damn impressive, but I still thought: 'How are you going to get the punters in?' David was clever to build the first one near the airport and initially to keep it open 24 hours a day. Airport workers would use it before and after shifts, some even playing tennis in the early hours of the morning. Gradually, word spread about just how great a facility this was and the club took off.

David's centre was a place you could take the whole family. Queen's members started to go there, in turn making Queen's

Club up its game. It couldn't be quite so complacent and stuffy anymore. In fact, the only thing Queen's had going for it in comparison was its postcode.

The Heston club was David's pride and joy, but the venture was set to grow. He soon had planning permission for another leisure centre, then another, then another. Princess Diana officially opened the Raynes Park club amid great fanfare. When my brother was up to seven centres, the company went public. If I had invested £50,000 at the outset, I could have made £6–7 million when it was floated on the London Stock Exchange in 1992. Now you know why I do a bit of head banging against the walls.

Three years later, there were 18 David Lloyd Leisure Clubs when Whitbread bought the company for somewhere in the region of £200 million, which was a record in the City at the time. After that, my brother and his son Scott created Next Generation fitness clubs. Incredible success followed incredible success. All the family were so fantastically proud of David's achievements. If only the same could be said of the establishment.

It is staggering to me that he has not been recognised with an OBE or an MBE. This is a man who not only revolutionised British indoor tennis, but who helped Britain to a Davis Cup Final and later led the team. This is a lifetime of achievement across so many levels and it is disgusting he has not been honoured.

I lay a great deal of that blame at the door of the Lawn Tennis Association, the governing body for tennis in the UK. David should have been the chief executive there 20 years ago or more.

David has been very open and honest about wanting the job. He has even been quoted, in spite of all his successes, as saying he 'failed' because the job he wanted most was to run the LTA.

He knew he could put tennis back on the map, have more people playing in parks, schools and universities and lift it from being just the seventh-ranked participation sport in the country.

But it was like straight-talking Brian Clough with the England football manager's role. His face, his views, did not fit with the governing body's safety-first policy. Likewise, David knew he would never get the top job in tennis. The LTA was too bureaucratic and didn't want anyone outspoken. David would not only have ruffled a lot of feathers, he would have cut away a lot of the fat. Why appoint someone who might take away your job? The LTA were afraid of him.

David triumphed against the odds in the corporate world, so he is better placed than most to give this verdict. He says that if the LTA of old was a corporation, it would have been bankrupt many times over. The fact he was never in charge, he calls 'the biggest failure in his life'. The only failure is that of the LTA.

Of all the ironies, David's son Scott was named chief executive of the LTA in the summer of 2017 and formally took up the position in January of 2018. At last, the LTA had seen the light. Scott is not a cosy fit, not by any means. He is very much his own man, with an outstanding business career and passion for tennis. Finally, the LTA had made a bold appointment.

At the time of the appointment, LTA chairman David Gregson said: 'Scott … has a deep understanding of the British tennis landscape and a clear commitment to our strategy of focusing on grassroots tennis in communities – from schools to clubs to parks. After a rigorous search process … Scott was the unanimous choice of the LTA's Recruitment Committee.'

Okay, Scott is my nephew, but putting all bias aside, I believe the LTA had at last got it right.

David was always an inspiration. He was a little more than six years older than me and already a highly ranked junior player in Britain when I was batting the ball against the coal shed wall in my backyard in Leigh-on-Sea. He was my role model, someone to look up to.

As he developed his career and made it on to the professional circuit, I knew that was what I wanted as well. My brother was a tough act to follow but he made the dream seem like an attainable reality. I wasn't watching a stranger achieve these things on television or having to imagine any of this as I lay in bed at night. He was right there in front of me, my very own big brother, achieving the goals I one day hoped to emulate.

It took me a few years to catch up because of the age difference, but once I was on the circuit as well, we had the privilege of playing alongside each other on the British Davis Cup team. He was fiery and patriotic and would always stand his ground if the opposition started to get in his face. I recall some of the tastier altercations in the Davis Cup chapter of this book, but I should point out he wasn't shy at also having a pop at me. I remember in a fierce contest in Rome against Italy's Adriano Panatta and Paolo Bertolucci that David was shouting at me and cussing me during changeovers to steel me for the battle. If I'd had just a bit of that tenacity, I would have been a much better player. I needed some of David's inner pugnacity.

He is very opinionated and that would lead to a few barneys with team-mates on Davis Cup duty. Paul Hutchins, the GB captain at the time, and Mark Cox were both Wimbledon club members. Buster Mottram, David and me were not. My brother wanted to analyse just why that was. Debates on class, public school privilege and social equality would be heated and commonplace. While they were going at it hammer and tongs, I would take myself off to my room. I never did like confrontation. David was fuelled by it.

My younger brother Tony was the most mild-mannered of the tennis-playing brothers and the most modest. He was also the best player. He would never admit to this, but I have no doubt he was the most talented of the three of us, with just a beautiful game and incredible hand-eye coordination. That's not just my opinion. There were many other experts who believed that, too.

A couple of things counted against him. He had a degenerative back condition that forced him to sit out the game for months on end. Plus, he didn't like all the travelling associated with being an aspiring tennis pro.

In those days of the early 1970s, when you were trying to forge a career on tour, you had to play in some horrible places. European communist countries were especially grim, with shockingly poor facilities, terrible hotels and unpalatable food. If you didn't get sick you were doing well. Tony struggled with life on the road and decided it wasn't for him.

And yet he had so much ability. Tony made it to the main singles draw at Wimbledon in the centenary year of the Championships in 1977. All three brothers were in the singles that year, in fact: an extraordinary family achievement.

We teamed up in doubles at Wimbledon as well, twice reaching the third round. Tony lost in the first round of the doubles there in 77, playing alongside another Briton Chris Kaskow. In partnership with me two years later, we had the daunting prospect of opening up against the number two seeds Wojtek Fibak and Tom Okker – and it was on one of the big show courts, Court One. Tony was so nervous, we couldn't get him out of the bathroom. Tournament referee Alan Mills had to give him the hurry-up in the end.

When play got underway, I was trying too hard initially. I was playing my brother's protector. It was a role I had first adopted in primary school. If anyone picked on him, I would jump to his defence. There was only a year and a few months' difference in our ages, but I was very much the big brother. We shared a room and couldn't have been closer. Hurt Tony, and my gang would hurt you right back. Yes, I led the John Lloyd gang: a very young band of tiny tearaways. We weren't into knocking over old ladies on our bikes or anything like that, but we would join forces to help a brother in need.

I was the elder brother with the higher ranking and greater experience. There was no way I was going to let the second-best doubles team in the world bully my brother into submission in front of the world's glare. I was darting this way and that, trying to cover more of the court than it was my duty to do. We lost the first set 6-2.

Suddenly, the lights went on in Tony's head. He started playing unbelievably well. My little brother was all grown up and didn't need protecting anymore, least of all from me. He was the best player on the court that day as we won in five sets, knocking out the second seeds. We eventually lost in four close sets in the third round to 12th seeds John Alexander and Phil Dent. The following year, we again reached the third round. Not too shabby for a couple of brothers from Leigh-on-Sea, whose idea of success as kids was snaring crabs in a pool of water near our local beach.

Those seaside days were paradise to us. When the tide went out, we could walk about three quarters of a mile – wearing flip-flops so cockle shells wouldn't cut our feet on the journey – to an area where water had become trapped in a bay known as The Ray. This is where we would put tempting morsels on the end of lines and tempt crabs to take the bait, before collecting them in buckets. When I took my own children there for the first time, they thought it was the best thing ever, even though they were being raised on Californian beaches. They loved running on the sun-baked mud, building mud castles, throwing squelchy mud and snagging the odd crab or two. The tide didn't go out like this in America. It was magically mind-blowing for them.

One time, on a beautiful summer's day, we ran into my old swimming teacher Bill Giddings, who was performing voluntary lifeguard duties. He said: 'John, you can keep your Australias, you can keep your Caribbeans, there's nothing like a sunny day down in Southend on The Ray.' I thought the sun might have adversely affected him. But actually, he had a point. That muddy beach did possess something special for me, too, if only in the collection of cherished memories there, especially those with my little brother.

We were a pair of wanderers on the football front, too. Even though we lived close to London, we didn't choose to support Arsenal, Chelsea or Tottenham. No, it was Wolverhampton Wanderers for me ... Bolton Wanderers for Tony. For more than 50 years, we have followed both clubs through thick and thin. We have seen them both slump to the lowest level of English league football and climb all the way back to the top again. You won't find two more ferocious supporters of their clubs.

Tony married and became father to three children. He put his abundant tennis skills and remarkable technical knowledge to use as a coach. He never looked at the playing careers David and I enjoyed with envious eyes. There isn't a jealous bone in his body. He supported David and me throughout and we have stayed close, to the point we talk – from one side of the Atlantic to the other – several times a week.

My sister Ann chose not to pursue any kind of tennis life, although she did play at the local club where our father coached part-time and she could hit a decent ball. When my mother and father were working or taken away from home, Ann would take on the matriarchal role and kept her brothers under her supportive wing. She saved me from a severe school beating or two by writing notes to extricate me from trouble, without Mum and Dad finding out. Without Ann, I would have felt the full force of the headmaster's cane on many more occasions. I adored her for protecting me in that way.

Ann married journalist and all-round good guy Bob Hammond, who wrote about football and tennis for Thomson Newspapers for many years. They live overlooking the courts at Westcliff Hardcourt Tennis Club, where we grew up playing and where our father coached well into his 80s. David bought Mum and Dad a gorgeous bungalow nearby, just yards from the beach. That close proximity meant Ann and Bob were so important to my parents in the last years of their lives. They were with them every day and, after my mother passed away, couldn't have been more supportive of my father. Dad was a traditionalist, who was used to having meals cooked for him and laundry done for him. He struggled to make a piece of toast without burning it. Buttering his bread with big lumps of butter was about his limit. Cholesterol. What's that?

Ann made sure he was looked after at the house he knew and loved. I can only imagine how much hard work they were putting in and yet they had not signed up for this marvellously selfless caring role. I felt really guilty about it – being an ocean away in

America and unable to offer practical help. I have nothing but the utmost love and respect for all they did for Mum and Dad.

Ann told me how our father became obsessed with telling one particular story in his last months and days. It involved me and my first foray into the literary world. The book was *Lloyd on Lloyd* and the author was Margaret Thatcher's daughter, Carol.

I was in a bad place in my marriage, my tennis and my life in general at the time and got suckered into taking part in this frankly terrible idea. I went with the flow, when it was actually such a stupid thing to do. My ranking had slumped, I was half-retired, thinking I should support Chrissie's career and loathing myself for letting my career go when in my prime years. What a ridiculous time to enter into a book deal.

My then wife Chris Evert was the other Lloyd in the title. We offered our opinions on each other, married life and tennis. It was very much a pro-Chrissie book: it didn't portray me in a favourable light at all. Friends, picking up on some of the rubbish written about me, commented: 'How did you allow that to be said about you?' I had no answer. I honestly didn't know why. That's about as much as I can remember from the book. Even though it sold in decent numbers and had some positive reviews, I have tried to obliterate it from my memory.

The only positive thing to come out of the whole sorry saga was that my mother and father were able to visit 10 Downing Street and meet the Prime Minister of the day, the formidable Margaret Thatcher. For my dad especially, this was a dream come true. Winston Churchill and Maggie were his two political idols. Both my parents adored her and were only too delighted to join Chrissie, Carol Thatcher and me for a visit the week before the book was launched. Mrs Thatcher was amazing to Mum and

Dad, making them feel so at home and personally taking care of the historical tour of the property.

This triggered something in my father's brain because, in his final days, he would tell visitors to his bedside that the book was due for re-release. He would say: 'You know, John's book was a bestseller and it will be a bestseller again.' There was I trying to pretend the damn book didn't exist, while he was bringing it up the whole time. It can only be that the meeting with Margaret Thatcher at Downing Street must have created such a happy memory – one of the most momentous occasions of his life – that he was tapping into the pleasure area of his mind in his dying days and coming up with this fabrication about the book. My sister Ann was there with him until the end.

The rich fabric of our lives was crafted in that tiny corner of Leigh-on-Sea we called home. The stitching was so strong that the family bonds are, too. We have had our ups and downs, though. What families haven't? And certainly, David and I have not always seen eye-to-eye. We may not always be in each other's lives, but there's no denying we have quite the family history.

Dear Ann, Tony and David,

Writing this book has given me plenty of pause for thought and it has been a delight tapping back into childhood memories from in and around that cramped house we shared.

Can you believe it even now? The three Lloyd boys all played the main draw at Wimbledon in the same year and were supported all the way by their big sister. How many other families can even get close to that?

Thanks for the memories,

John

THE PRESSURE PRIVILEGE

A letter from the John Lloyd of today to his former self as he takes his unquestioned talent into a string of Wimbledon Championships in the 1970s and 80s. One tournament in particular almost cost him his life.

Dear John,

As you take to the Wimbledon courts, with attention never more focused on you and expectation weighing you down, think on this line from the legendary Billie Jean King: 'Pressure is a privilege.' Just four words. Four words that can make your Wimbledon career.

You walked these fabled grounds as a child with your father. You dreamed of playing at Wimbledon. You made that dream come true. What's to fear now? Don't make pressure the thing to fear.

Your playing career will go so quickly. You will wake up one day in your 30s, the end in sight, and wonder where all the time went. A career in tennis is a privilege. Playing at Grand Slams is a privilege. Appearing at Wimbledon is, for a British player, the greatest privilege of all.

You are lucky to be doing this, so just go out there and put yourself on the line and embrace every second of it. Enjoy the pressure. Repeat to yourself: 'Pressure is a privilege. Pressure is a privilege.'

Now, go play,

John

WIMBLEDON WAS the place I almost died. Before you say it, I know I died many a time out there on court in the men's singles. No, I'm talking about the literal meaning of dying: losing your life, taking your last breath on earth. Wimbledon was the place I almost died aged just 21. Wimbledon was the place I almost drowned. Yes, drowned.

The 1976 Wimbledon fortnight had just begun. The sun was shining brightly, just not for me. In the first round, I had drawn the big-serving American Phil Dent: a man born on Valentine's Day but who showed little love for me at the end of a long, gruelling five-set match. It was a tough draw. Phil – who you might know also as the father of a more recent US player Taylor Dent – was a highly accomplished grass-court player. It was a hot day in London: 80 degrees-plus. The heat always felt more intense at Wimbledon. The air seemed to get trapped there and the humidity was high.

We both serve-volleyed, but nonetheless had some lengthy points and that added up to hours on court. Phil had the annoying habit of consistently lobbing me and making me run for my points that day. I ran, I retrieved – a lot – and I found myself serving for the match at 5-3 in the deciding fifth set. Match point was mine at 40-30. This would have been an important win for me: for the home boy against a man who had beaten the great Bjorn Borg en route to making the 1974 Australian Open final. I had lost in the Wimbledon first round the previous two years. This would have been big.

I say would have been big, would have been important, because that's not the way it ended. As I bounced the ball on match point and pushed back to serve, my left leg locked and went into a full and agonising cramp. I walked back from the baseline, hitting my leg with my racket hoping to loosen the muscle. Soon, the umpire was urging me to play on. I limped back to the line to serve. Phil Dent could smell blood. I served, he returned the ball somewhat more delicately than usual. A drop shot, in fact. He knew I couldn't run. The bastard. It was the perfect tactic. He broke back and I didn't win another game, losing the decider 7-5.

More than four hours on court was quickly followed by an indecent amount of time facing the media, with me still dripping in sweat. Unlike today, you usually did whatever press duties were asked of you. There were no agents and tour press officers giving you options of an early out. You didn't have the luxury of picking and choosing – or at least we didn't know any better. Nowadays at Wimbledon, the top players are obliged to do a press conference of maybe 15 minutes and then select what television or radio interviews they will (or won't) do at a maximum three minutes a pop. There'll be a shower and a massage before facing the press, a quick 'see you later' and some sushi. If that had been the pattern that day after the Dent match, I might have been saved the trauma that followed.

I eventually got to the locker room past nine o'clock. There was no one else there. There were maybe two physiotherapists on hand most days, but they had buggered off. No sign of Phil Dent, either. I decided to run myself a hot bath. When you have just had serious cramp, it's not the smartest thing to do. But bear in mind, this is an era when we fuelled our bodies not with pasta or gluten-free products, but with steak, chips and a couple of cans of Coke. Stretching? That was something you did when you first got out of bed and were yawning. Bjorn Borg, perhaps the greatest athlete ever to play tennis, never stretched before going out to play. It just wasn't done.

The Wimbledon baths were huge. You could almost swim in them. Still sweating buckets, I lowered myself into the steaming hot water. I was angry and upset, going through all the crucial points of the match and wondering how I could have lost the damn thing. Eventually, I thought I had better wash and get out of there. I reached for the soap. My hand cramped. It looked like I had a claw. The cramp moved like an agonising wave through my body. My stomach muscles, right under my heart and chest, went into spasm next – followed by both my legs and my other hand and arm. I was suffering the most excruciating full-body cramp … and I was screaming. I don't know if a forest tree makes a sound when it falls if there's no one around to hear it. But trust me when I say a fully cramping British tennis pro most definitely does make a noise, even when there is no one around to bear witness. Therein lay my problem. I could scream and shout for help all I liked. There was no one there.

Every part of my body was in spasm. The bath was too big and deep for me to roll out. I was sliding down into the water. I was sinking. I was going to bloody well drown in the Wimbledon bath.

It's funny what goes through your mind at such moments. My life should have been passing before my eyes. That's what's meant to happen when you're about to die, right? Not me. My ego took over and I started to imagine the headlines in the newspapers the next day: 'BRITISH PLAYER COMMITS SUICIDE IN BATH AFTER DEVASTATING LOSS'. I even thought the British government might be called upon to start an inquiry as to why too much pressure was being applied to home players at Wimbledon. I cried out one last time before going under.

The next thing I knew, I had two arms underneath me and I was being hauled out of the water. Aussie Bob 'Nails' Carmichael, a former top-ten player, had been to a Wimbledon cocktail party and was several sheets to the wind. He was bursting for a pee and looking for a toilet. There were urinals near the baths and he knew it. Thank f*** for that. I lay on the ground for a good hour after the rescue, received the help I needed and got away from Wimbledon alive. Losing a first round five-setter suddenly took on a whole new perspective.

A few clever dicks have since asked me: 'Why didn't you just do this?' and 'Why didn't you just do that?' Irritated, I tell them: 'You go into a full-body cramp, have nothing to prise yourself up on and see if you can "just do" anything. You can't. You're screwed.'

Cramp was an occupational hazard back then. We just weren't armed with the right knowledge on food, hydration and conditioning. Electrolytes were the stuff of sci-fi. Hell, we didn't even know that a banana would have helped. I suffered a lot after matches, but not as badly as after the Dent match.

The only remedy then was to take salt tablets, but they made me feel nauseous. Players like former World No.5

Harold Solomon and the fast-serving Aussie Colin Dibley were particularly bad 'crampers', especially in the humidity of the American summers. They would roll up like pretzels. Drinking pickle juice in between changeovers was what they resorted to, but it made me throw up. So, I would continue to cramp at inopportune times, usually in restaurants when I would suddenly and violently knee the underside of a table. A few curious looks were flashed my way.

You know, I'm still paranoid about cramp to this day. I won't swim out too far from the shore for fear of my leg seizing up and me drowning. Bob removed me from the bath that day at Wimbledon but no one has ever been able to remove the mental scars ... the fear of drowning.

In fact, Wimbledon has scarred me in more ways than one. The first wound was inflicted when I was just ten. My dad was a tennis fanatic and took me to Wimbledon to soak up all the magic and majesty. I was in complete awe of the place. It was easier then than now to get a grounds pass. Once through the gates, we would walk around the outside courts for hours. We could smell the grass. It was a special scent, a unique place ... something I can bring to mind quite vividly more than half a century later. I carried my autograph book with me, just in case we bumped into any of my heroes, and, this day, Dad spotted the American player Frank Froehling. Nowadays, Froehling builds tennis courts in my current home state of Florida. That day he was about to bulldoze my innocence. I was a shy lad but Dad encouraged me to approach Froehling for his autograph. There I was, this small, timid boy looking up at this giant of a man, seeking a scribble on a piece of paper to complete my day. 'Not now, sonny,' came down a booming American voice from what seemed like the heavens. I jumped back. Then the rejection hit me and I started to well up. My lesson for the day: some heroes are not so heroic after all. Later, I cut him some slack thinking he might have just finished a match, maybe even lost that match, and didn't want to be bothered by the likes of me. But I've never forgotten how the 'no' made me feel, so I've always tried to sign autographs whenever I can in a kind of lifelong retaliation. As for how marvellous I felt wandering the Wimbledon grounds with my dad, Frank Froehling – nor an army of autograph resistors – could never take that away from me.

Playing on the Wimbledon lawns was something I so wanted to do. I dreamed of little else. Some dreams do come true. And yet the way I played at Wimbledon was the worst part of my career in many ways. Somewhere along the way, I allowed the dream to turn nightmarish.

My first year in the main men's singles draw at the All England Championships was 1973. I had tried and failed to come through Wimbledon qualifying the previous two years but now, as an 18-year-old, I had made it by right. I had played at the club before, in juniors and as a guest of my mentor John Barrett, who later had a long and distinguished commentary career with the BBC. But this was something else. The promised land. Not that there was much promise at first in my debut performance. It started badly. First round, French left-hander Jean-Francois Caujolle across the net, and I found myself two sets to love down. This was not in the screenplay of my Wimbledon premiere, the one I had viewed in my head. A quick rewrite was required. Three sets later, I was victorious. My first win in the main draw at Wimbledon and one I would like to say I remember vividly and cherish fondly. Cherish, yes, in a way. Remember, no, not at all. I'm not great at recalling my tennis matches. I can remember every girl I ever dated. But every opponent? No. Monsieur Caujolle's name and the situation I found myself in were brought back to mind only after a search through the Wimbledon results archive. Thank you, Google.

I read that Australia's Keith Hancock was the man I beat in straight sets in the second round. Then it was India's Vijay Amritraj, an opponent I do remember well (we actually teamed up in the doubles one year) and a match I *can* recollect. I again came from two sets down, only to lose the decisive fifth set 7-5. A big disappointment, but an encouraging debut. I had to make the most of those two debut wins, though, because I wouldn't taste triumph in another men's singles match at Wimbledon for four years. In fact, I would win only 14 more games in defeats to Sweden's Leif Johansson (thanks again, Google) and champion Jimmy Connors in the following couple of years, before that punishing five-set defeat against Phil Dent in 1976.

Now this one, I do remember. My biggest and best singles victory at Wimbledon came against American Roscoe Tanner in four sets on Court One on the opening day of the centennial Championships in 1977, when he was fourth seed and being talked about as a possible Wimbledon champion. I was an unseeded 22-year-old. He had been a semi-finalist there the previous two years and had won the Australian Open on grass earlier that season. A tremendous upset, caused by yours truly. That was what I was actually capable of.

So, it wasn't all bad in singles. I even got revenge on Phil Dent for almost killing me when I beat him, again in a five-setter, in the first round in 1981. Other Wimbledon memories would linger a lifetime, like those tied up in playing men's doubles there with my brothers David and Tony. You can't put a price on that. And the two mixed doubles titles I won there with Australia's Wendy Turnbull in 1983 and 84 – such fantastic occasions. Making it on to the Championships' roll of honour is an achievement to treasure. Thanks to the All England Club's tradition of not changing names on its victory roll even after divorce, my name is even there twice on the singles honours' board. Okay, it was my ex-wife Chrissie who did the actual title-winning, but it twice reads Mrs J.M. Lloyd nonetheless. When I walk past it, I visualise it without the 's' in Mrs. You take your victories where you can.

But if I am brutally honest, overall, for the ability I had, my Wimbledon performances were pathetic. I never got beyond the third round there in singles. I was in awe of the place but most definitely not awe-inspired. It affected me in a bad way. My last men's singles match at the All England Club was in 1986 when I was 31. I lost in the first round. In fact, in 14 consecutive years in the Wimbledon main draw, I fell at the first hurdle nine times. That didn't make good reading when I was searching the archives. But I didn't need to see the results in black and white to know the truth of it. If I could ever go back in time and change anything about my career, it would be the way I played and performed at Wimbledon.

That's what I've always admired about first Tim Henman and then Andy Murray: their ability to embrace the British crowd and the pressure that goes with being a leading Briton at Wimbledon. In their case, they were British contenders and title hopefuls at the most prestigious tournament in the world. I went the opposite way.

I played better at tournaments abroad, like the US Open and especially the Australian Open where I reached the final in 1977, only losing in five sets to the gifted American Vitas Gerulaitis. Overseas, I just felt like another player with no added attention or expectation. I never adjusted to that glaring light or invasive scrutiny at Wimbledon.

It didn't help that we players did almost everything for ourselves. We weren't surrounded by managers, agents and coaches in a kind of supportive entourage that, in the modern era, acts as a cocoon of comfort. It would have been the height of luxury for me to worry about nothing but hitting tennis balls when Wimbledon came around: a luxury not afforded me.

Instead, I found myself playing such distracting roles as ticket collector. It is amazing how many long-lost relatives I suddenly had when Wimbledon came around. I would make phone calls for hours the night before matches, trying to hook 'family' up with tickets. No texts or emails back then; no managers to do it for me. 'I'm coming down from Newcastle. Can you get me two tickets for Court One?' came the request. 'Oh yeah, I'll pull 'em out of my arse,' came my reply.

How tiring all that ticket-hunting became when I was already contending with playing a tournament as massive as Wimbledon as a home player. But I felt compelled to do my best for family – whether or not I had ever heard of them. Foreign players would have their wives or girlfriends with them and, with so little money around back then, they weren't able to fly in extended family and friends. That's how it was for me when I played abroad. But in my home country it was so different. At Wimbledon, it was a pressure I could have done without.

There's another form of Wimbledon pressure I wish I had been able to conquer, maybe even savour. The on-court pressure. It was after my playing career was done that I heard Billie Jean King, one of the game's all-time legends, deliver my favourite tennis line ever: 'Pressure is a privilege.' That quote separates the great players from the good players – and it teaches an insightful lesson I learned too late in life. The greats embrace pressure. I ran away from it. I only wish I had had a team in place to help me discover that privilege.

When I shared the court in men's doubles or mixed doubles, I was fine. But on my own I was all too aware of the groans from the crowd when I missed a ball or fluffed a shot. Rather than say: 'Okay, I'll show you what I'm about. Next point I'm gonna have you cheering for me,' I let it adversely affect me. That would ratchet up on the big show courts. Centre Court is a special place, scene of so much drama and brilliance down the decades. But truly, I kind of froze on Centre Court. I remember asking the Wimbledon referee not to put me on Centre Court or, for that matter, No.1 Court. They never complied, of course: I didn't have that kind of power. But I didn't want to be showcased like that. I would rather have been more anonymous, out on Court 7 … out on court nowhere. What it would be to have the chance to go back and embrace the pressure. The fact I never did has to be the greatest regret of my tennis career.

Dear Bob Carmichael,

Thank you for deciding to attend that Wimbledon cocktail party. Thank you for filling your bladder to bursting point. Thank you for knowing your most convenient of Wimbledon conveniences. Thank you for the most immaculate timing. Thank you for saving my life.

We laughed about the incident whenever we ran into each other. You playing the rescuer to my stranded whale. I hope you are looking down and having another chuckle right about now.

God Rest Your Soul,

John

'WIMPLETON'

A letter from the John Lloyd of today to his teenage self, offering the advice he wishes he could have been given as he tackled a fastidious tennis referee with a military air.

> *Dear John,*
> *He will be arrogant and pompous. You will feel you are being scolded like some kind of naughty schoolkid. Much as you want to, knocking his block off is not an option. Taking him on in a battle of words won't work either. This is a case of one rule for a frightening specimen of a Romanian and another rule for young upstart you. You can't win here, so take what the caricature of a captain has to say, take your Wimbledon wild-card and enjoy making your debut at the All England Championships.*
> *Don't do something you'll make me regret.*
> **John**

HERE'S A quick quiz question. Name the most famous and historic tennis tournament in the world. Here's a clue, it's played on the lawns of SW19. Those of you crying out 'Wimpleton', see me after class. Actually, don't bother. I'm all done with correcting you.

If you want to call the greatest tennis show on earth 'Wimpleton', knock yourself out.

It has always astonished me – and amused me – that around 90 per cent of the people I talk to in the States refer to the famous fortnight in such a way: replacing the 'd' with a 't' and occasionally throwing in a 'p' for a 'b' for no apparent reason. This mispronunciation once caught out a contestant on the long-running US game show *Jeopardy!* – a show in which the answers are given in the form of a question.

When host Alex Trebek asked about the first women's champion at an 1884 tennis tournament, a Nebraska native by the name of Reid Rodgers replied: 'What is Wimbleton?'

'Correct,' said Trebek. Reid banked $400 and the game moved on, but not for long. Trebek was soon told to issue a correction to Mr Rodgers and enlighten the nation, saying: 'I'm informed that you very clearly said Wimble-TON not Wimble-DON a few moments ago.' They stripped the poor bloke of his $400 and he finished second.

Getting the pronunciation of the place wrong sounds downright amateurish. But then, that wouldn't be altogether out of place with the Wimbledon of old – and I'm not just talking about the era of amateur players. For so long, the place was trapped in some kind of time warp, the club members especially. Wimbledon had its traditions, quite rightly. It still does. But when I first started playing there in the early 70s, it felt mired in a bygone era it was reluctant to change.

The fact it was the tournament every aspiring player wanted to appear in – and ultimately win – was in spite of, not because of, its old-fashioned members, who regarded us as interlopers who happened to inconveniently swing by for a couple of weeks every year. We were like dirty bathwater: to be poured away as soon as possible.

A time warp is where you will find the tale of the colonel, the captain and the gentleman farmer. Just before my time there, the referee at Wimbledon was Colonel John Legg. A military man doling out the discipline: there's perhaps some logic in that. The referee had the final word when a player questioned an umpire's ruling, as well as having responsibility for arranging qualifying events, organising the order of play and coping with weather interruptions. There's also the occasional breach of security to contend with. Colonel Legg once escorted a protestor named Helen Jarvis off Centre Court during a 1957 visit from the Queen. Jarvis climbed over the courtside wall during the men's doubles final, campaigning for the 'Life, Love and Sex Appeal Party' – and a new UK banking system. Refereeing undoubtedly has its vagaries.

Colonel Legg was succeeded by his son-in-law Captain Mike Gibson, who was chief referee from 1962 to 1975. He liked to use his army title because 'it made it easier for the players and I liked them calling me captain'. He was an even stricter disciplinarian, a man Romania's Wimbledon finalist Ilie Nastase once referred to as 'the worst referee in the world. He thinks he is God … or a little higher.' And there's no question, he was a terrible referee who had no idea about the game of tennis. The ATP and WTA would eventually come along to take charge of the men's and women's games respectively. But until then, Captain Gibson ruled Wimbledon. He was fond of a drink, his brogues, twirling his moustache and dictating with an iron fist. So stiff was his hairy upper lip, it would have made a good place to hang my dry cleaning.

Back then, there were no rankings to determine our place in tournaments. We had to fill in our results on an entry form and send it in by post, hoping to be accepted into the draw. Gibson was the man behind such decisions. One year, he kept me out of the main draw and forced me to play the qualifying event instead – all because I had dared to stand up to him at another tournament he refereed in Bournemouth. It was a clay-court tournament in the British spring: bloody freezing in other words. I reached the final of the under-21s tournament there and, chilly as it was, kept my tracksuit on. I had earlier seen Gibson watch the big, intimidating Romanian Ion Tiriac play in his tracksuit in the main draw and thought 'what's sauce for the goose has to be okay for this British gosling'. The surly captain approached me and I wrongly assumed he was about to congratulate me on my success.

'Lloyd,' he bellowed in his upper-class accent. 'Don't you ever wear a tracksuit in my presence again. Do you understand?' Then, he stormed off.

I was only a teenager but I thought, 'I'm not gonna have this.' I cornered him in the players' lounge. It turned out to be a costly mistake on my part.

'Excuse me, Captain Gibson.'

'Yes, Lloyd.'

'I'm trying to understand why you gave me such crap when you allowed Tiriac to wear a tracksuit in the quarter-finals of the main event.'

'Are you coming out against my authority?'

'I'm just making a point.'

'Not a good point, in my opinion.' He turned his back to me.

When Wimbledon came around, everyone believed I should have been given a wild-card into the main draw. Well, almost everyone. Gibson dumped me into the pre-Wimbledon qualifiers as punishment for my 'stand' against him and I was knocked out in the last round. My Wimbledon Championships debut would have to wait.

In later years, I swear Gibson was a danger to players. Many of us believed his attitude to rainy conditions was: 'Carry on until the ball floats.' He would walk on to a wet Wimbledon court, with competitors pleading for play to be stopped, test the grass with his brogues, give the conditions a cursory glance and say: 'Play on!' If this inspection was taking place in the late afternoon, or early evening, he would already have consumed one too many beverages. There wasn't the player-power we see today, so we had no choice but to play on and risk injury. These orders, by the way, came from a man I had never heard of playing a single game of tennis in his life. For him to be in charge of such a prestigious tournament says all you need to know about the Championships at the All England Club at the time. He reigned supreme from 1962 to 1975.

Then, in all its brilliance, Wimbledon appointed a gentleman farmer from Lincolnshire as referee. Maybe the club thought he had spent so much time standing in fields that few others were better qualified to oversee its lawns. His name: Fred Hoyles. His claim to fame: botching it when John McEnroe was having his 'you cannot be serious' rant in 1981.

McEnroe was playing fellow American Tom Gullikson in a first-round Wimbledon match when he served what looked like a perfectly good ace. The linesman called it out, then quickly corrected his error. Umpire James Edwards went with the original call and, in so doing, unleashed Mac's monster within.

'You can't be serious, man. YOU CANNOT BE SERIOUS!' shouted Mac, navy-blue headband possibly preventing his head from exploding. 'That ball was on the line! Chalk flew up! It was clearly in! You guys are the pits of the world.' Superbrat was born.

McEnroe was docked a penalty point for insulting the umpire, then another for calling the referee a shit, but he won the match and went on to win his first Wimbledon title by beating Bjorn Borg in the final. Truth is, Mac should have been kicked out of Wimbledon. I love John, I'm a fan of what he brought to the game, but he should have been thrown out that day. Nowadays, of course, that kind of behaviour wouldn't be tolerated. But back then, you had a farmer in charge. Fred Hoyles was a lovely guy, perhaps too nice to handle a star player in full rant who simply dominated him. But Hoyles could and should have made a big difference in tennis history right there. The fact he didn't highlighted it was a farmer doing a tennis professional's job. It was Wimbledon at its worst.

The club finally saw sense and appointed a former player to the post in 1983. Alan Mills spent 23 years in the job: the longest term in Wimbledon history. He relied on his tennis credentials and undoubted integrity to earn respect, not a military title. He once said, referring to the age-old military referees: 'It was – how shall I put this? – slightly different in those days. The players were almost treated like the naughty schoolboy going before the headmaster. I'd much rather, if they have a grievance, that they come in and we talk it over and sort it out.' I only wish Alan had been in charge that bitterly cold day in Bournemouth.

Wimbledon was not quick to move with the times. I'm an honoured full member of the club now, but I was only a temporary member when I was married to Chris Evert, even though I had been British No.1 and represented my country on countless occasions. I suppose it was like being on perennial standby. Temporary equalled 'toeing the line': criticise the club or the courts and full membership might never be forthcoming.

When I was coaching Chrissie, she was put on one of the smaller show courts – not far from the members' balcony – for a second round at Wimbledon. Chrissie always had to have eye contact with her coach between every point, but we were so much in the spotlight in those days I was worried having me courtside at that particular venue; a tight, jam-packed court might have brought unwanted attention from the crowd and been more of a distraction for her. I asked Chris Gorringe, long-serving All England Club chief executive, if Chrissie's mother and I could watch from the members' balcony. Chrissie was a Wimbledon champion and full member, after all.

'There's no way I can watch her from the court, Chris, so if you could do me this big favour ...'

'I'll have to go to the committee,' he replied. I held back on saying: 'You've got to be shitting me.' I bided my time.

About an hour later, Gorringe returned with the news we would be allowed to watch from a decent vantage point overlooking the court, situated on the members' balcony. I had been there a thousand times, but frustratingly we had to wait to be escorted up. Most of the members were having lunch, so it was quiet when we got there – pretty much Mrs Evert and me watching Chrissie demolish her opponent. We were no trouble to anyone.

Four elderly members suddenly emerged, the youngest about 80. I turned to Mrs Evert and said: 'Here we go.' Sure enough, one of them toddled over, about 85 and with the beginnings of a beard. She prodded me in the back, then said: 'You know you have to be a member to be up here and you are not a member, are you?'

She obviously knew who I was and knew the answer to her own question.

'No, I'm not.'

'So, what are you doing here?'

My first instinct was to give her a quick shove over the balcony, but I calmly replied: 'That's my wife playing down there.'

'Yes, I'm fully aware of that. You've still not answered my question.'

'Mrs Evert and I have permission from Chris Gorringe and the committee to watch from here, just for this match.'

'Oh, I suppose that's okay then,' she said begrudgingly. She strolled away and left us in peace, though I'm sure I felt a few dagger-like looks stabbing me in the back. That's how Wimbledon was in those days: stuffy, snobby, elitist.

It drove Buster Mottram, my old Davis Cup colleague, nuts, even though his mother and father were both members of the All England Club and Buster had right-wing leanings himself. Buster was – and still is – an eccentric bloke. Even though he reached as high as World No.15 in 1983, he wasn't beloved by the British public because he never learned the art of public relations. He wanted to play his matches, make a certain amount of money and retire, which he did at an early age. Grand Slams didn't pay too much better than other tournaments then, so the whole two-week major thing annoyed him, especially Wimbledon where he disliked the grass and even more so the upper-class twits. Buster was a nutcase, but a fun nutcase ready to display his quirky nature whenever the mood grabbed him.

Faced with a first-round Wimbledon opponent on Centre Court – a match he believed there was no way he could lose – he told me he was going to see if he could serve a ball into the Royal Box and make it look like an accident. When he was two sets and a break up, confidently heading to victory, I saw that quirky look cross his face. He was looking at the sky and then almost trying to draw attention to the wind on court. I'm not sure there was even the slightest of breezes that day. But he was already building his excuse for what he was about to do. I had told some of the players in the locker room what Buster planned and they had said: 'He's just joking.'

Now I was telling the players: 'Here, watch this – he's about to do it.' I could just tell.

Buster then hit a full toss serve as hard as he could straight from his end of the court towards the Royal Box at the other end. It didn't reach its intended target, but it surely made a few bums shuffle on cushioned seats. Buster tested the wind with a raised finger, blaming that for his wild serve. BBC commentator Dan Maskell, the master of understatement, uttered the line: 'Dare I say, a mishit.' That was Buster's playful swipe at elitism.

Thankfully, things have changed for the better in the last 15 years and more. There is still an air of snobbery at times, but I no longer feel like an invader on their precious territory. It's a much better tournament as a result. Younger members have come in and energised the place. They embrace modernity: you only have to see the roofs on Centre Court and No.1 Court to appreciate that. These huge developments have arrived while maintaining the best of Wimbledon traditions. It's not perfect, there is still a way to go, but the overall atmosphere of the place is heading in the right direction.

There is a magnificence about Wimbledon that's apparent as soon as you enter the grounds. It doesn't matter how many hundreds of times I have been there, it still fills me with awe. For all my own personal gripes, I want to emphasise here and now just what an amazing place it is – unquestionably a tennis Mecca. For two weeks every year, it feels like the centre of the universe. People book holidays from work just so they can sit at home and watch the fantastic television coverage. That's truly remarkable if you really think about it. Henman Hill is awash with fans who might not have tickets for the show courts, but who are happy to watch the big screen all day from a giant mound of grass – even when the sun is beating down and turning pale skin lobster red. Where else in the world would you get this kind of dedication and devotion?

The grounds are immaculate, from the flowers of purple and white to the manicured lawns of play, and the daily excitement is palpable as I walk past the field of overnight campers hoping to make it through the famous gates on Church Road to see their heroes. It is special. I hope I never lose sight of that, even when I'm tempted to find fault. And there is fault to find, even at a more modern, forward-thinking Wimbledon, as I'm about to spell out. Nothing huge, though, and nothing that can take the shine off a tournament that remains a privilege to attend and enjoy.

The All England Club rightly sees itself as the standout venue in tennis in the way Augusta National does in golf. The hierarchy from both clubs exchange annual visits. The Masters is a wonderful tournament, but Wimbledon shouldn't ever use Augusta National as its role model. It only admitted its first two female members in 2012, for heaven's sake. And what about poor Gary McCord? He was barred from working for American network CBS at the Masters after his commentary there in 1994, when he quipped the greens at Augusta were so slick the club must have 'used bikini wax' and that the bumpy terrain looked 'suspiciously like body bags'. McCord was never to return. How dare the Masters tell the rights-holders who should be commentating. Their event is for the world, not just for the damn club. That goes for the All England Club as well, because there was a time when Wimbledon would try to enforce its will on the BBC in a similar way, asking for certain commentators on certain matches, because it was *their* product. What arrogance.

I understand the All England Club's desire to show Wimbledon is the cream of the tennis crop, just as long as its own self-importance doesn't become overly ridiculous. Making club rules for members to abide by all year round is one thing, but do some of the silly rules really need to be inflicted on the Championships every summer, just to show how much the tournament stands apart from every other?

Why can't Roger Federer have coloured soles on his shoes if he's wearing all white on every other bit of his body? Who the hell is looking at his soles when a genius like Federer is playing? And yet, in 2013, Wimbledon made Federer change his tennis shoes with an orange sole to something neutral. That's plain stupid.

Another thing: let players warm up in coloured tracksuit tops and then play the match in all white. To deny them this simple exemption makes no sense. Talk about behind the times. It's not 1949 anymore, when American Gussie Moran was accused of 'putting sin and vulgarity into tennis' by wearing lace-trimmed knickers at Wimbledon.

That reminds me. There was even a furore about coloured underwear at the Championships some years ago when Frenchwoman Tatiana Golovin wore crimson red knickers under her all-white outfit. White knickers can actually be more revealing for a woman, I would say, and as for men, at least you don't see streaks of … well, you know what streaks I'm talking about … when they wear coloured pants. I'm not being purposely indecent or gross here, it's just a fact.

More recently, Venus Williams was reprimanded for the colour of her bra. Where's Mac when you need him? 'You cannot be serious!' Wimbledon did get with the programme, explaining: 'The rules state that players can wear any colour underwear they like provided it's no longer than their shorts or skirt. Anything else must be white.' I don't believe this solves the coloured bra issue, though.

I have another suggestion for Wimbledon concerning the Royal Box, which comes from watching the Academy Awards. It's long been a bugbear of mine to see empty seats in the Royal Box on Centre Court around lunch and teatime even when there's a big name in action. While elite members and their esteemed guests are busy eating, drinking and socialising, the best seats in the house are going begging. It looks bad on television because the main camera is facing that way the whole time. People at home must be thinking: 'I thought it was impossible to get tickets for Centre Court – and yet look at all those empty seats.' It happens at the French Open, too, where the President's Box often resembles the *Mary Celeste*. It shows the sport's biggest events in a terrible light. So, my polite suggestion to Wimbledon: use seat warmers.

At the Oscars, when some A-lister sitting in one of the front rows nips off to the toilet, a person is employed to temporarily plug the gap: a seat warmer. The TV cameras, therefore, don't capture empty seats and all looks as it should. There are some C-list Wimbledon members who will never get a look-in when it comes to the Royal Box. They would chop off their right arm to get in there. Their big chance could come when the cucumber sandwiches are being served. Shove in the seat warmers, Centre Court will still look packed and everyone's a winner. Just a thought.

All this complaining might seem a good way for me to lose my All England Club membership. But as long as my brother David is still alive and kicking, I think I'm okay. Yes, I'm a full member now (if you pardon the expression). In the end, David and I were, indeed, welcomed in, although the club certainly took their time, perhaps because we were considered too controversial or critical. Wimbledon is thankfully evolving in that regard now. It is more progressive. I'm assured there has to be a unanimous vote of members to boot someone out of the club, so as long as David isn't killed off in the process of an anti-John Lloyd vote, I'm going to be hard to dislodge.

One of my biggest gripes came in the Sampras-Ivanisevic-Krajicek era when serve dominated and there were just no rallies on grass. The ball boomed down court and was not for coming back. The lawns were too fast.

'Tear up the grass courts,' I proclaimed. 'Time for a change.' I was ridiculed.

The Australian Open used to be played on grass. The US Open used to be played on grass. Both tournaments blossomed on hard courts.

'Change the surface at Wimbledon, too,' I said. 'Keep the colour green if you have to, but within a year or two no one will even remember the grass. It's not about the grass, it's about the quality of tennis.'

And the quality of the men's game in that period was terrible.

So, what happened? The All England Club only went and made their grass courts slower. Grass was the new court's nature, but its character was pure hard court. In essence, they were doing what I had suggested. The new surface has provided some of the most spectacular matches tennis has ever served up. Wimbledon now has a product to match its prestige.

For all its history and mystique, Wimbledon has become increasingly corporate. That's the way of the world, I suppose. The prize money is huge and ever-growing. Many of the people in attendance could witness Mickey Mouse taking on Goofy on Centre Court and still be in awe. The place is that remarkable. Driving there, seeing those queues of people sleeping out overnight to gain access to the grounds is something to behold. I used to think some of those people might, just might, be coming to see me play. That gave me a sense of feeling damn special. If the players of today take a step back from the game's riches and a circuit where one tournament can so easily blend into another, they will truly absorb and appreciate there is no other tournament like this and there never will be. This is Wimpleton!

Dear Wimbledon,

You are a magnificent event: the best tennis tournament in the world. You are loved by people the world over, me included. But please don't allow that to make you too cocksure, too full of yourself. You've changed for the better in the last 15 years or more. I've seen less stuffiness. But it still exists.

You work best when you are not so stuck up … when you don't take yourself too seriously all the time. So perhaps think about ditching some of the silly rules. Keep the pristine all-white kit by all means – but let the players have coloured soles on their shoes or wear coloured bras.

Maybe consider that Royal Box seat warmer suggestion of mine, too.

Even with a few concessions, you will still be the best tournament on the planet. Just a more sensible best.

Yours imploringly,
John Lloyd

FINE ROMANCES

A GREEN Rolls-Royce convertible pulled up outside my Wimbledon maisonette and out stepped American film actress Valerie Perrine, wearing a mini skirt the size of a curtain pelmet and a top not created to hide her assets. It was a hot summer's day during Wimbledon and June was bustin' out all over.

'Lovely to see you again, Valerie. You look ... well ... wow!'

'So good to see you, too, John.' There was a kiss, kiss on the cheeks, continental style.

'Unfortunately,' I pointed out, 'that's not quite the attire for the Wimbledon tea room.'

Valerie was nominated for an Oscar, a BAFTA and a Golden Globe for her portrayal of Dustin Hoffman's girlfriend Honey Bruce in the 1974 movie *Lenny*. We met a couple of years after that during the filming of an ABC television special in the States entitled *Super Guys and Super Gals*. It pitched together, in a mixed doubles competition, eight tennis professionals and eight glamorous women, including actresses Farrah Fawcett, Deborah Raffin and Veronica Hamel and models Alana Hamilton and Cheryl Tiegs. Valerie was great fun and we had a night out off the back of it, but it went no further than that at the time.

Six months or so went by and I was playing at the 1977 Wimbledon Championships. Chatting to my pal and colleague Bob Carmichael about films, I mentioned the night out with Valerie and he said, in his slow, Australian drawl: 'Oh, she's a bit of all right that one. I really like her. She's beautiful. Bit too old for you, though.' There was an age difference of 11 years between Valerie and me.

'Did you know she's right here in London, right now?'

'Doing what?' I asked.

'Filming *Superman* at Pinewood Studios.'

As a movie buff myself, I knew this big-budget film was being shot there with some unknown actor in the lead role and Marlon Brando as his father. But I didn't know Valerie was in it. I later learned she was playing Lex Luthor's girlfriend and villainous accomplice Eve Teschmacher.

'You should call her and invite her over to Wimbledon,' Bob suggested.

'No, she won't even remember who I am.'

'Of course she will. Go on … ring her.'

I didn't need much more persuading so rang Pinewood Studios, saying: 'I'm John Lloyd, a British tennis player. I'm actually playing at Wimbledon this coming week and – I know it's a long shot here – I want to contact Valerie Perrine and invite her to the tournament.' I left my details and thought that might be the end of it.

The next day, I received a call at my house from Valerie.

'John! It was such a great surprise to hear from you – and yes, I would love to see you at Wimbledon.'

'That's fantastic. Come over to my house in Wimbledon and we'll stroll across from there. I'll arrange a ticket for you.'

Valerie's visit coincided with me becoming big news at Wimbledon. Well, for a day or two at least. I had defeated one of the pre-tournament favourites Roscoe Tanner in the first round. She arrived at my place in a blaze of Hollywood glamour and flamboyance. Valerie looked amazing, but her outfit was destined only to turn heads and potentially give a few of the older club members a heart attack. 'Is this really unsuitable?' she asked, looking down at her miniscule skirt.

'I'm afraid so. Wimbledon is a very conservative place.'

'But I haven't got anything else with me, apart from this.' She showed me some kind of scarf-cum-shawl. 'Maybe I can drape this around me?'

That wasn't good enough for my mother, as things transpired. With all three of the Lloyd brothers involved in the Wimbledon singles event that year, my parents were proud attendees. When they clapped eyes on Valerie, their faces spoke a thousand words.

'Mum, this is my friend Valerie,' I said, somewhat timidly as my mother stared daggers at her. The tea room collective had never been so outraged.

The Ford Modelling Agency held a big party in town during Wimbledon and – again, after a bit of cajoling from that old rascal Bob Carmichael – I invited Valerie to join me. This was honestly more for Bob's sake than mine. I picked her up in a black cab. She had this big, dorky-looking guy in glasses with her. 'This is Christopher Reeve,' she said. 'He's going to be a major star.' He didn't seem to have much personality, so I thought: 'Yeah, right.' I had already questioned the wisdom of this *Superman* movie thing. Not only was I spectacularly wrong on that front, but I would later play tennis a few times with Christopher and discover he was the greatest guy, worthy of the superstardom Valerie had predicted.

At the function, Bob was clearly thrilled to meet Valerie. He was far more into her than I was, so I decided to discreetly back away and leave them to their conversation. I was happily chatting to a few of the models on the other side of the room – you will not be shocked to learn – when Valerie came over. 'I don't like that Bob you introduced me to. He's coming on to me and he's way too pushy. I want to get out of here.' Bob had blown his big opportunity to impress and obliterate me from the picture. As for me, I saw Valerie a couple more times after that and we had fun. She was a real character. But it was never destined to be anything long term. Sadly, her acting career didn't maintain the heights of the 70s. The last film I saw her in was the 2000 release *What Women Want*, in which Mel Gibson's character is electrocuted and can suddenly hear women's thoughts. Forget Superman, that's a real superpower … one I cannot profess to have ever possessed. More's the pity.

If I had, maybe I would not have fallen quite so hard for beautiful Maureen Nolan: one of the singing Nolan Sisters. I was playing in Eastbourne at the same time they were appearing at the theatre there. Someone from the family saw me out of a window, playing with my young nephew, and we were soon formally introduced. I went to see them perform and got to meet the extended family. They were just fabulous, including the girls' mother and father. We spent more time together after that. They were so much fun to be around. I travelled on the train to gigs with them, all the time growing more attached to Maureen. The girls could burst into spontaneous song at any point, even walking down the street. They were always in perfect harmony.

Unfortunately, Maureen and I were not. She wanted us to stay just friends. I adored her and wanted more than that. I would have found it painful to be around her knowing our relationship had no future, much as I enjoyed being in the warm company of her family. We lost touch through the years, although I looked on with great fondness as the Nolans' careers blossomed. I also felt deep sadness when the family lost Maureen's sister Bernie to cancer and when I read that two other sisters, Linda and Anne, experienced their own battles with the disease.

My profession – and a certain amount of celebrity – brought me into contact with many beautiful women in the entertainment business. I went out a few times with the stunning Canadian actress Barbara Parkins, star of the massively popular 60s television series *Peyton Place*, after meeting her at a party. Likewise, I dated British actress Susan George – star of the film *Straw Dogs* – for a short while. She was dubbed by one cinema writer of the time as a 'sexpot'. That was more to do with the roles she was given than her personal life, although she was undoubtedly sexy. It was when I attended her birthday party that I first caught a glimpse of this 'other' world, full of famous faces. Our relationship quickly fizzled out before we were ever a real item. I was on the road, she was busy with her career. It wasn't like today when you could keep in constant touch through mobiles and computers, maybe fanning the ol' flames of desire from afar.

That wasn't all bad. Quite the opposite, in fact. I didn't have to keep looking over my shoulder the whole time, wondering if someone was filming me or taking pictures of me on their mobiles. Yes, I had to deal with the paparazzi sometimes, especially when I was married to Chris Evert. But I consider myself lucky to have serial dated in that era and not this one. There wasn't as much money around in my day, either. I never found myself questioning a woman's motivation in wanting to date me and I was always honest with them in return, explaining: 'I'm in town this week, next week I'm gone. If you want to have some fun this week, then great. It is what it is. But it can't be any more than that. If that doesn't work for you, let's not start anything.' Reading that back, I appreciate it is the least romantic invitation imaginable. But at least I didn't lead any of the women on with a fresh line in bullshit every week.

Maybe that kind of carefree attitude, in my early 20s, stemmed from having been engaged at the age of just 19 to Swedish player Isabelle Larsson. We had a fantastically romantic time in Australia and New Zealand and, young as we were, believed this was it. We had each found the person we were meant to spend the rest of our lives with. I introduced her to my parents: 'Mum, Dad, this is Isabelle – my fiancée.' My mother and father were most conservative, so Isabelle and I slept in separate rooms. My parents wanted to believe I wouldn't have sex until I was married.

When I went over to stay at Isabelle's parents, I stood there with my travel bag saying: 'Point me in the direction of where I'm to sleep.' Isabelle said: 'You're sleeping with me, silly.' The next morning, her mother brought me in a cup of tea. I thought: 'I love Sweden and all its people'. I was not the only one. There was always a clamour to play the Bastad tournament in Sweden each summer, when the tennis definitely took a back seat to the beaches, the partying and the gorgeous women. Losing early at that event was no hardship, I can assure you. It meant you could stay the rest of the week without tennis getting in the way.

Isabelle scared the life out of me when I received a letter from her saying she thought she was pregnant. Again, that shows you the sign of the times. No mobile phones, no texting, no emails. If Isabelle or I went on the road playing tennis, we didn't even have a landline to call our own. Thus, the letter. I read it and thought: 'Holy shit! My life is about to end. My parents will never speak to me again for as long as I live.' Isabelle wrote that she had a doctor's visit arranged to confirm her suspicions. That meant I had to wait for another bloody letter, all the time thinking about my parents' likely reaction and my imminent ostracism. When the second letter arrived, I tore it open and read: 'Sorry John – false alarm.' I was a lot more careful after that.

Our fledgling tennis careers pulled us apart in the end. Isabelle and I saw less and less of each other and the realisation dawned: this was not our 'happy ever after'. Isabelle was ranked number two in Sweden and was destined for top spot when she was diagnosed with a hole in her heart and had to give up her playing career. She married and had children. If she is still anything like the youngster I knew and loved, they are very lucky children. It was only when I started going out with tennis superstar Chris Evert, some five years after my first engagement ended, that I once again felt marriage was not only possible but desirable. I was just 24 when I married Chris.

It is funny to look back now on how my parents behaved when it came to my love life. Puritanical is a tad strong, but not far off. In their minds, I would not have slept with Chrissie until after our big Catholic wedding. When I was engaged to my second wife Deborah, Mum and Dad came to stay with me at my condo in Palm Springs, California. I had three bedrooms. They stayed in one, Debs and me split the other two. I was respectful enough of their feelings not to share a bed with my fiancée, even in my own house. I did it for Deborah's reputation. I wanted them to like her. If they thought she was some kind of 'loose woman', winning them over would have proved difficult.

On the second day of their visit, we were gathering to watch television. Deb, in all innocence, came into the room and sat on my lap. The next day while I was on the court practising, I saw my father in conversation with my fiancée. Suddenly, she took off. 'What's wrong with Deborah?' I asked. 'She's got herself worked up over something and nothing,' he replied. When I later got in the car with her, I asked what had been said. She refused to tell me at first, but eventually relented. 'They didn't like me sitting on your lap,' Deborah explained. 'They said their other sons' partners don't do that kind of thing.' I could not believe my ears. It wasn't like we had even kissed. Deb insisted I say nothing, for fear of making matters worse. I agreed, instead deciding to give my parents the silent treatment.

After a few days, my father told me: 'I think I owe you an apology.' I said: 'Yes, you do. With all due respect, this is my house. Deb did not do anything wrong. We show our affection. That's what we do, like it or not. You have to accept it.' My mother and father never kissed in public and although they could be affectionate with their children, they were not demonstrative in front of others. I understood this was alien to them, but to be shy about showing affection was no longer acceptable to me. Once we had cleared the air, they were more relaxed about Deborah and me. They became really fond of her, even when she blurted out the due date of our first baby. Deb was pregnant when we got married but I had not told my parents and planned to keep it hidden from them. Once the date was out there, my mother quickly worked it out. They wanted to imagine we were still in the holding-hands phase until we tied the knot and the reality would have rattled their world for a while. It counted as a minor strike against Deb, not me. They could not see their boys in a negative light, not ever. Just as well they never heard me deliver my 'this is just for fun … for one week only' line back in the day.

VITAS AND OUR
FINAL SHOWDOWN

FAWLTY TOWERS is one of the most beloved British sitcoms ever. Vitas Gerulaitis thought it was garbage. But then my old friend could never be accused of being a conformist, even when he was becoming one of the best players in the world.

If I was chuckling at John Cleese's antics in *Fawlty Towers*, Vitas wouldn't laugh along just to be polite. 'You expect me to sit here and watch this?' he asked, quite obviously in a rhetorical manner. Next thing, he was gone – with his 'garbage' verdict, delivered in his best Brooklyn brogue, still hanging in the air.

Not that Vitas was lacking a funny bone: quite the opposite. This was a man so full of humour and so quick-witted he came up with one of the all-time classic tennis quotes after a rare victory over Jimmy Connors.

Vitas had defeated Jimmy in their first meeting in 1972 but then lost 16 successive times to him across eight painful years. After finally breaking that losing streak at the semi-final stage of the 1980 Masters, a reporter at the post-match press conference asked Vitas how he had pulled off this coup. With a grin, he said:

'Let that be a lesson to you all. Nobody beats Vitas Gerulaitis 17 times in a row.'

With his unruly mop of blond hair and a personality to match, Vitas Gerulaitis always played life by his rules. The tragedy is that life was cut way too short. The sadness is revisited when I remember this was the last man standing between me and my first Grand Slam singles title.

Such was our friendship, we practised against each other just 90 minutes before the biggest match of our lives.

The Australian Open moved to December from January the year I reached the final. American Roscoe Tanner won the January event of 1977, before a calendar change saw the tournament switch to December for the next decade. Tanner was never destined to become the answer to the quiz question: who won the same Grand Slam singles title twice in 1977? The defending champion was knocked out in the first round by New Zealand's Chris Lewis, a future Wimbledon finalist. Vitas was the top seed and, in the absence of Connors, Bjorn Borg and Arthur Ashe, fancied his chances of winning his first major even before Tanner's early exit. It never entered my head that I had a chance, too.

We were good buddies and spent almost all our time together during that event. We played hard on court during the day; we played hard off court at night. There were female courtesy drivers at the Australian Open that December. They weren't exactly meant to fraternise with the players, nor was it a sackable offence. Vitas and I had playboy reputations, so it felt rude not to live up to the billing. We each dated a driver and a few late nights resulted. But we were both quite capable of burning the candle at both ends. Both of us reached the quarter-finals.

Three-time Wimbledon champion John Newcombe was my opponent in front of a record crowd at Kooyong. 'Newk' was a national treasure in Australia and on a comeback after missing much of that year. Queues formed for hours hoping to catch a glimpse of him knocking out a Pom and reaching the semis. He had been telling all who cared to listen he was going to win the title, which rubbed a few of his rivals up the wrong way to the point they were telling me: 'You've got to beat him.' I did, in four sets: one of my best career victories.

The *New York Times* reported: 'Before a record crowd of 12,000 … Lloyd's speed blunted the power of the 33-year-old Newcombe.' My defeated opponent was quoted in the same report as saying: 'It was one of those days when my legs were not moving with my arms, and although I wasn't playing badly, it was hard getting everything coordinated.' I'm surprised he didn't add: 'And I'm pissed off at Lloyd cos he's basically a shit player.'

Age-wise, I had ten years on Newcombe and beat him on three consecutive occasions later in his career. Admittedly, he was past his best – but that timing wasn't my fault. Yet the defeats seemed to rile him. When he had downed a skinful at some function, also attended by my ex-wife Chris Evert and me, he told me what a shit player I was and had been. Chrissie had taken six months off but was set to make a return. He told her he had tried to make a comeback and that it 'never works out', that she should stop now. The personal criticism aimed at me was simply ordinary, but his words to Chris were beautiful. I loved it when people gave her ammunition by telling her the things she couldn't do. She took great delight in proving them wrong. Her comeback brought her another sackload of major titles. Newcombe at least later told Chrissie how wrong he had been.

And as for this shit player? Well, in the semi-finals I brushed aside an Australian qualifier Bob Giltinan, who allowed nerves to get the better of him. Even though Bob took just six games off me, he had done remarkably well to get that far after five years out of international tennis because of injury and national service in Vietnam.

I was the first British man to reach a Grand Slam singles final since Fred Perry 41 years earlier. Some of the biggest names in the game skipped the Australian Open, falling as it did through the Christmas period. But the top eight seeds were Vitas, defending champion Tanner, Aussies Tony Roche, Ken Rosewall, Phil Dent and John Alexander and Americans Stan Smith and Tim Gullikson. Add Newcombe into the mix and these guys were hardly what you would call slouches. Making a major final was a special achievement. Waiting for me in the final was my pal Vitas.

Semi-final night, as we had all tournament, we went for dinner. I didn't know quite how to bring it up, so just blurted it out in the end: 'Look, it's my first slam final ... it's your first slam final. What are we gonna do about practice tomorrow?'

Vitas replied: 'Well, what the f***. We're gonna practise against each other. Are you gonna learn something new from my game? No. Am I gonna learn something new from your game. No.'

We practised against each other just an hour and a half before the final. Can you imagine that any time in the recent past? Never in a million years.

I would have been shocked had Vitas not made the final because I had seen first-hand, from another practice session we'd had earlier in the tournament, how mentally switched on he was.

Play had been washed out this particular day. The rain kept falling, there were no indoor courts and so even a practice hit seemed out of the question, to me at least. Vitas had other ideas. He said: 'I've grabbed some tennis balls. Just bring your worst racket – we're gonna practise.'

By worst racket, he meant the one I could most afford to break. We travelled with four or five wooden rackets, all strung with gut. It's not like nowadays when players have 12 rackets all strung to perfection and can have any – or all – of them restrung at the drop of a hat at tournaments. If the strings went on one of our rackets, we could maybe have it restrung five weeks next Tuesday. If I was playing well with one particular racket, I would keep it for matches. It never came out for practice.

'The worst racket thing I can do,' I said, clambering into a taxi, 'but a practice court on the other hand ...'

'We'll find one. Trust me.'

We drove around Melbourne, the rain now abating, in search of a vacant and accessible tennis court. We spotted a perfect grass court in a park. Yes, it was vacant. No, it was not accessible: not easily, at least. It was fenced off and padlocked. 'Come on, we'll climb over,' said my adventurous American mate, while I did that unadventurous British thing of: 'We might get in trouble. What if the police catch us? We might break our necks or something. We've only just got through the first round and I had to come from two sets to one down so I don't want to risk ...' By this point in my rambling, Vitas had climbed his way in and I was honour-bound to follow him.

The grass court was saturated. The balls were soon soaked, too. Sprays of water flew off them with every stroke. 'Is this really worth it?' I foolishly asked. Vitas was in no doubt. 'We'll get some serves in, we'll do a bit of volleying. It's all good.' We practised in the wet for about an hour, after which he said: 'Now remember this. We're the only two people in the tournament who have played today. That gives us a huge psychological edge.'

To be perfectly frank, I didn't see it that way. That kind of practice session would not have entered my head but for Vitas. His attitude was one of trying to get one up on the rest and that worked for him. It carried him all the way to the final in Kooyong – that and his gigantic amount of talent and flair.

The modest grass court venue of Kooyong, in Melbourne's inner precinct, staged the Australian Open from 1972 until the tournament moved to the National Tennis Centre at the city's Flinders Park in 1988. There were two locker rooms: one for the top eight seeds, one for the rest. I was among the rest until I reached the quarter-finals, which is when I was invited into the main changing room. I said: 'I'm superstitious. I'm staying put.'

It was New Year's Eve: the day of the final. I made a nervous start. Playing my pal didn't make it any easier. Vitas won the first set 6-3. When he took the second set 7-6 on a tie-break, I might have seemed in big trouble at two sets to love down, but I was starting to read his game. My nerves had gone. I was enjoying the occasion. I knew I could get back into it. I won the third set 7-5 and I was in business.

Back then, we had a short break after the third set when we could return to the locker room. Neither of us had a coach or any kind of entourage, in stark contrast to what you see today, so weirdly we were each alone in our individual locker room. Or so I thought. Vitas actually had company in the shape of the tournament physio who was treating my opponent for cramp.

Into the fourth set, I still had the momentum. I put up a lob, Vitas reached for it and cramped up again. This, of course, was the first I had seen of his pain. As a sometime sufferer of cramp myself, I knew it all too well. I won the fourth set 6-3 to level the match, but I allowed his condition to affect me. I started playing drop shots and more lobs, trying to manoeuvre him around the court and make him run as much as I could. It was a stupid thing to do. I was already on top, I didn't need to change my tactics. Vitas was receiving treatment at the changeovers and, rather than give him the runaround, I was playing into his hands by losing my rhythm. With his cramp under control and my game plan out of control, he got an early break of serve in the deciding set and would never surrender it. He took the fifth set 6-2 and, with it his first – and only – Grand Slam singles title.

Following his victory, Vitas alluded to his belief that there might have been some divine intervention. God apparently forgives a playboy. 'Today was my lucky day and the good Lord looked down on me. The pain was dreadful and I remember looking up toward the sky in the fourth set and saying to myself I couldn't win without some sort of help. My muscles were popping out because of the cramps, which spread right through my body, but I wasn't about to give up in such an important final.'

Looking back, could I have been tougher, could I have been more ruthless when he had cramp? The answer is a definite 'yes'. Should I have won that final? Again, most definitely 'yes' – and that's a big regret. I was the better player for the majority of that match. But what's the use of could have, would have, should have? I lost and that's all that counts. At the end of a bittersweet, often exhilarating, week, I could at least say, I was pleased that if anyone had to beat me, it was a great guy like Vitas Gerulaitis. Did we go out that night? Even silly questions deserve an answer sometimes. We did, indeed. It was New Year's Eve after all.

That was just the start for Vitas. Less than two months later, he reached a career-high ranking of World No.3. He would finish inside the top ten for the next five years and reached at least the last four at five of his next six Grand Slams, making two finals.

I first played Vitas, a New Yorker born to Lithuanian immigrants, when I was 17, and even then saw how he stood out from the rest. He had charisma, a certain flamboyance, a winning swagger, athleticism and energy in abundance. Squeaky clean, he was not. Although he didn't drink, he received treatment for substance abuse and in 1983 was implicated in a cocaine conspiracy, but never charged.

He was generous to a fault, always ready to pick up the dinner tab – which is maybe why he once had the third-highest bill ever accumulated on an American Express card. The hiring of a few private jets here and there might also have helped.

He was the type of person who so lived life to the full, you felt he was indestructible. And yet, in 1994, only nine years after his retirement from the game, aged just 40, Vitas was taken from this world despicably early when he died in his sleep from carbon monoxide poisoning in a friend's guest cottage at Long Island. The tennis world went into mourning.

We made some magical memories during our friendship. There are some we might have been locked up for, that are better left unsaid. But many of the brightest and best memories came in that special Australian Open of December 1977.

It was in Australia that I truly embraced every new experience, every new adventure – even the less comfortable ones.

Travelling to Australia every December, training hard all the way through to the Australian Open and missing Christmas at home was not to every player's liking. But I loved it. People would ask me: 'Do you not miss the seasons? What about Christmas by an open fire? The snow?' I'd reply: 'Are you kidding me? Screw the seasons when you can escape the British winter for 85-degree temperatures and the beach.' I had as many as 12 Christmases away from home during my playing career.

It could take a whole day of travel to get there and, because I have never been able to sleep on planes, that was tough. There was no in-flight entertainment like today, so I became slightly more intelligent because I had to read. The long haul was worth it for six weeks of Australian sunshine.

The people there were always so welcoming. You would get the usual banter between Aussies and a Pom like me, usually about cricket: that was par for the course. I loved their national loyalty. You would see it among the players, too, when they would go to watch their fellow Aussies play. The attitude there was 'he's a mate, you support him'. In Britain, we had more of a jealous streak. I was as guilty as anyone of hoping my fellow Brits would lose because I knew it would better my career. That's the uncharitable way it was.

Australia had its downside, too: boiling temperatures, spiders … sharks.

The Australian tennis circuit started in Adelaide, where – on one of my earliest visits – I stayed with a family in a house with no air conditioning in unbelievably high summer heat. My room-mate was another British player, Robin Drysdale. We had to share digs back then. Money was scarce and hotels not an option.

I won my opening matches on the Adelaide grass, but was shattered. I wasn't getting proper sleep because of the heat. There was a fan in my room circulating hot air and I was sweating like a pig. It was like trying to sleep in a sauna. One night, when the homeowners had gone to bed, I took my pillow and a roll-up mattress into the kitchen, opened the fridge door – aah, the lovely cool air – and settled in for the night. I put an alarm clock at my side to wake me before the homeowners got up. At the end of the week, they couldn't work out why their milk was going off so quickly. 'That's a weird one,' I said, like butter wouldn't melt. Actually, in that fridge with the door open, it probably would have. But I digress. The bottom line is, I got the sleep I needed and reached the final. A good week's work.

Spiders were an occupational hazard. At one place in Melbourne – a kind of two-bed 'granny flat' at the bottom of someone's garden – an enormous creature spun from a line of silk down on to my flatmate's belly button as he lay, eyes closed, headphones on. I was passing by his door when I was suddenly transfixed by this dangling spider. When it landed on his stomach, he leapt so high he almost hit the ceiling and fell, full force, on my boom box. That was knackered. The commotion didn't deter another spider from dropping down from the air vent. If it was possible, this one was bigger.

Straight away, I was thinking: 'I've got an air vent in my room. There'll be big, ugly spiders up there, too. They must be coming down for something. It's probably to bite me.' Okay, so spider phobias bring out my irrational side. Nonetheless, some extermination was required before I could rest easy. I rummaged through the kitchen and found a wasp spray. I gave the air vent a good squirt with the aerosol and, within seconds, two spiders

– now of a size that made them worthy of a place in the *Guinness Book of Records* (again, that might have been that irrational thing kicking in) – dropped on to my bed. Splat! They were soon in that great big spider's web in the sky. Although they had gone, my fear had not. I lay there most of the night, sheet pulled over me, imagining their families were about to drop in on a revenge mission. Disturbed sleep in Australia is a definite pattern, now I think back.

In Sydney, the flirtation with dangerous wildlife took on a whole new dimension. I had gone to the beach with Frenchman Thierry Bernasconi. He was a good player but was a big guy, who carried a bit of timber and had the movement of a sloth on court. We were swimming about 40 yards out at sea when a siren sounded. The shark net had been breached. This is a realisation that will get the heart racing far more than any spider visitation. It was everyone on to shore. Well, I'm telling you, this guy Bernasconi never moved so fast in all his life. He was like a hybrid of Mark Spitz and Michael Phelps. He sped past me, ran on to the beach and continued at a pace that would have made him a world tennis champion had he replicated that on court.

These are just a few of the only-in-Australia moments that immediately spring to mind when I think back to the fun I had there through the years. It feels quite fitting that, given my love for the place, my Grand Slam final debut should come there. I should have sensed the potential for that to happen because, in the weeks leading up to my trip to Australia, I beat some quality players to reach the Swiss Indoor final in Basel and London's prestigious Benson & Hedges Championships final at Wembley, losing to the great Bjorn Borg on both occasions. After reaching the Australian Open final, my ranking soared.

John Barrett, my long-time friend, mentor and tennis guru, told me then: 'You can do one of two things here. You can either go full steam ahead and work even harder to build on what you've achieved … or you can enjoy the fruits of your labour and stay roughly where you are.'

Of course, me being me, I took the second option. I was enjoying myself too much. Plus, I always thought there was another year and another opportunity. So what if I've lost in one tournament; next week there's another and beyond that another … then the next … and the next. The word 'tomorrow' offers a seemingly endless stream of invitations. Then, suddenly, one day you wake up having turned 30 and find there are far fewer tomorrows.

I know deep down there were only a couple of times in my career I worked to my capacity. One of those phases came while working with coach Bob Brett towards the tail end of my playing career, when I reached the 1984 US Open quarter-finals and my ranking climbed again. The rest of the time I was cruising. My game was better than my mind. I will always regret that. I tell young guys coming through now how important it is to work as hard as you can: to never have to live with regret on that score.

After taxes, I came away with around US$ 12,000 from reaching the Australian Open final. In my 12 years on tour, I made about $850,000 in total. Twenty-year-old Naomi Osaka made almost $0.5million more than that from one event when she won her first women's singles title at the 2018 Indian Wells tournament. That's simply staggering. So, when people ask me do I envy the money available to players nowadays, it's difficult to say: 'Absolutely not … I'm 100 per cent fine with it.'

But I do like to point out, there are friendships that came from my playing days that are priceless and will last forever. I'm not sure many of the current crop will be hanging out with each other in the decades to come.

I also like to point out that I maximised my enjoyment of life on tour. They might win more money nowadays, but I absolutely guarantee they are not having as much fun as I did. Not in a century of Saturday nights.

CHRISSIE

A letter from the John Lloyd of today to his former self as he is about to tie the knot with Grand Slam tennis great Chris Evert.

Dear John,

Even though getting married was always part of the plan, something inspired no doubt by the relationship played out so successfully before your eyes by Mum and Dad, no one ever prepared you for a celebrity union. You know what it is to be famous yourself in Britain, but that is about to shoot to a whole new level when you tie the knot with one of the most famous women on the planet. You need to appreciate very quickly just how big this is or risk being swallowed up by it.

This relationship, this marriage, will bring you some of the happiest, headiest days of your life. But if you are not focused on your own goals at times, as well as those of your wife, you will lose a sense of who you are along the way and self-respect will be hard to find. That path can only lead to the emotional end to something once so exhilarating.

John

THE BEGINNING of the end came in New Zealand.

'Chrissie is having an affair with Adam Faith,' he announced.

My good friend David Schneider was reading aloud from a newspaper as we sat eating breakfast on the other side of the world.

Chrissie was my wife: tennis superstar Chris Evert-Lloyd.

Adam Faith was the 1960s pop star turned actor: the first British artist to have his first seven singles reach the top five in the UK charts. He was a friend.

'Nah … that's a *National Enquirer* story,' I said, knowing the report David was reading had been picked up from an American gossip rag known for sensationalistic fiction and fabrication.

It wasn't fictitious or fabricated, as things turned out. It was fact.

Right there in Auckland, the disintegration of my marriage to one of the world's greatest sportswomen began in earnest.

I rang Chrissie. She denied the story. But the truth would eventually surface. There were troubles ahead and already, even at this pretty early stage in our time together, the realisation was dawning that our marriage was unlikely to work.

Chris Evert was already a seven-time Grand Slam singles champion when we started dating during Wimbledon 1978. She was in her fifth year as World No.1. She had been a household name since the age of 16. She was a megastar.

We had different circles of friends so, although I admired her career from afar and undoubtedly fancied her, it never entered my head we could ever become close. That was until Swedish player Ingrid Bentzer, who was friendly with Chrissie, approached me in the Wimbledon players' tea room, saying: 'John, why don't you go up and have a chat with Chrissie?'

'Why would I do that? She doesn't know me.'

'I just think it would be a good idea,' said Ingrid.

'But why?' I couldn't understand this sudden suggestion, thinking that to randomly bother the great Chris Evert was not the done thing. When Ingrid nudged me a third time and became ever more insistent, the penny dropped for old numb-nuts here. She was trying to fix me up.

My heartbeat, my blood pressure, everything was probably going up as I sauntered over, trying to maintain my outward cool. We started chatting. It felt right. If I had known Chrissie at all – known the incredible professional and champion I would later learn all about – there is no way in a million years I would have asked her out at that point. But I didn't know any better, so I suggested a date that very night. She agreed. Again, it was only later I would learn just how lucky I was Chrissie had said 'yes' to a night out during a tournament as big as Wimbledon. That was far from the norm for her. For me, it was a different story. I didn't play by the rules which said you had to be in bed early and rest up well. If someone suggested to me I should be in bed by ten, I would say: 'Who with?'

In deciding where we should go on a first date, I made the idiotic choice of Tramp, the UK's number one nightclub at the time, which had been founded nine years earlier by Johnny Gold. Chrissie and Jimmy Connors had broken off their engagement, but were still in touch. They both won Wimbledon in 1974 and it was a summer love match that made many column inches in the papers. The engagement might have been short-lived, but their relationship was very much an on-and-off affair in the following years. I didn't know where things stood, but knew discretion was essential as we started out. If Chrissie and I were ever to keep our date quiet, we needed to be low-key. There was nothing low-key or discreet about Tramp. It was a stupid move, but we somehow got away with it.

The evening went well – at least, well enough for me to ask for another date and for Chrissie to agree. We talked things through and decided to go completely under the radar this time, so I booked a London restaurant called Newtons, assuring her it was private. About 20 minutes into dinner, I heard this booming voice and laughter. I recognised it as that of Bjorn Borg's coach and mentor Lennart Bergelin. He had taken a bunch of Swedish press there for a meal. Chrissie must have been thinking: 'Private, John? Oh yes – we're so anonymous here.' Thankfully, Lennart was tucked away in another part of the restaurant, to be heard but not seen. We got away with it … again.

After that, the safest option was to take late-night strolls in Hyde Park near Chrissie's hotel under the cover of darkness. I would later discover that Chrissie going for a walk at 11 at night while she was still contending for a Grand Slam was again so out of character. Her mother was the only other person 'in the know' about our secret meetings.

Chrissie beat defending champion Virginia Wade in the semis to reach the Wimbledon final, having lost to the best of British at the same stage the previous year. Virginia never beat Chrissie again, later being quoted as saying: 'The worst thing you can do to yourself is to beat Chris because the next time she plays you, she goes out of her way to make it her business to really show you who's boss.'

In the final, Chrissie faced Martina Navratilova, who was playing her first Ladies' Championship title match. Chrissie won the first set 6-2 and was a break up in the second – only to unravel and lose that set. Chrissie then strangely lost her way from 4-2 up in the decider. Again, I would later learn she just never fell away in a match like that: it just didn't happen. This day, it had, and it was almost beyond belief. As I watched with my old friend Martin 'Arnie' Hill I said: 'So much for my date with Chris tonight. There's no way.'

I saw Mrs Evert soon after the final and said: 'I know Chris won't want to go out tonight so please say bad luck to her for me.' Mrs Evert replied: 'No, no – she told me to tell you she'll be down in about 20 minutes.'

Date on, even after surrendering the Wimbledon title. In later years, there was no chance that would ever happen. Chrissie wouldn't speak to anyone for a week after a loss like that, least of all me. It was like a death in the family or worse. But in 1978 at Wimbledon, Chris Evert the Ice Princess had thawed.

Martina would never accept or believe this – and it sounds egotistical – but I truly think Chrissie's mind was not totally on that Wimbledon final. Our relationship, new as it was, had led to her taking her eye off the prize. This isn't ego talking. It is simply that the more I got to know Chrissie, the more I saw first-hand how she operated, the greater my conviction became that her mind had not been 100 per cent on the final in those exhilarating early days of our relationship.

Chrissie was even quoted saying as much: 'If I had been hungry, the match was mine. In the last four games, all I could think about was going out with John.'

Our romance blossomed from there. After a while, we no longer had to hide. We were a couple and proud of it. I was well known in Britain at the time, but going out with Chrissie took things to a different level. She was a big, big star, albeit that in the UK she wasn't exactly popular at the time – perhaps because she had a reputation for being a bit cold and business-like. There was more to her than that, of course, and once we were married, the Wimbledon crowd adopted her as an honorary Brit. She was pretty much adored thereafter.

It was fortunate I had enjoyed some kind of celebrity lifestyle before getting together with Chrissie because it must be a tremendous shock to the system if you marry into that lifestyle and have never experienced any of it before: people staring at you in restaurants, having to be careful what you say and where you go, photographers hanging around the house hoping for that money shot.

We married at St Anthony's Roman Catholic Church in Fort Lauderdale, Florida in 1979, and in my wedding vows I pledged not only to love and respect Chrissie but to support her career. She would return to the courts as Chris Evert-Lloyd.

There were a number of occasions at cocktail parties in the States when people would say: 'Mr Evert, your table is over here.' When you marry a superstar, you have to accept that you are not going to be the first name on the page. Check the ego at the door. If you love someone and commit to someone and each know deep down it is a 50-50 relationship, there's a chance of it working. If your ego is too big and can't accept the situation, don't get married in the first place.

There were some blurred lines, though. Before I met her, I always flew business class. Chrissie always flew first class. When we were married, did that mean I automatically flew first class, too? If it was the other way around and the husband had most of the money, his wife would be in first class if she travelled on her own. It would be a given. But with roles reversed? I don't know. It just felt awkward. Chrissie had expensive tastes and quite rightly for one so successful. But if I could afford a £1,000 ring for a Christmas gift, she would be more accustomed to wearing one ten times more expensive. If I could run to buying a Jaguar, Chrissie could afford a fleet of Bentleys. These are just silly, made-up examples, really, and nothing more than that. It is just to illustrate this was now my reality. Not that Chrissie made it an issue. While we were married, everything felt shared and she made sure it was never a problem. But it was an underlying factor for me, nonetheless.

The flip side to any negativity, of course, is that there were fantastic perks, like being able to book any table in any restaurant, secure tickets for the show of your choice, fly Concorde and get invited into the cockpit for take-off and landing, and hang out with A-list stars. I was just a lad from Leigh-on-Sea in Essex and, though I had made some decent money in the previous few years, I was catapulted into a new world. Doors just opened.

My brother David says the word 'great' has been misused a lot in tennis and I have to agree. If you win a Grand Slam singles title you are, in my books at least, a great player. Chrissie won 18 of them. What does that make her? There was a greatness in her from an early age and I was privileged to witness it up close and personal. She possessed a champion's DNA.

I once asked Chrissie what her driving force was in a career littered with victories and titles. I thought it might be that her inspiration came from those moments of hands-in-the-air euphoria as match point was won. Extraordinarily, she revealed it was quite the opposite. She hated shaking hands with someone, knowing they had beaten her. The fear of defeat was more powerful than the joy of victory. She alluded to this in Tony

Trabert's *Sports Legends* documentary about her, suggesting negative motivations and almost unhealthy thoughts made great champions.

There was a combination of mental toughness on court – her attitude was possibly beyond compare – and an insecurity off it that required me to constantly reassure her. Once the match started, Chrissie thought she was not going to lose. Her unshakeable belief on the big points set her apart: it is what splits the great from the good. But, amazingly, she would have real complexes before matches and worry about certain opponents, which was staggering to hear from such a champion. I would say: 'You've got to consider what's going on over the other side of the net. Trust me, she's crapping in her pants at the prospect of facing you. She's giving you a four-game start before you even walk on court.'

There was one huge occasion where Chrissie went into the match too confident: too sure of herself. It backfired massively … and I felt the full force.

Having lost in the previous two Wimbledon finals to Martina Navratilova – the first not helped by yours truly, of course – Chrissie came from behind to beat her in a pulsating 1980 semi-final. It ended a run of four straight defeats to Martina, who was developing some kind of air of invincibility on the Wimbledon grass. Chrissie hadn't believed she could win that match. I had spent a lot of time working with her, trying to change that mind-set, but she had felt she had no shot at victory. You can imagine, then, she was beyond thrilled when she defeated her great rival. In her mind, this was one of the career-defining moments for her: a game changer. Chrissie thought she had already won the final, that the title was hers.

It was a rainy, fragmented end to the fortnight – there was even an interruption to the final itself, early in the second set – so Chrissie didn't have much of a break between the semis and the final. Her opponent-in-waiting was Australia's Evonne Goolagong Cawley. While she was doubtless tucked up in bed, our phone was ringing off the hook after the semi-final. It seemed every man and his daughter wanted to chat to Chrissie that evening. She was still so ecstatic about her win over Martina she was only too happy to oblige. I was concerned and said: 'Look, it's a fantastic result but we haven't got much time here before the final.' She responded with a 'don't worry, it'll be fine' kind of line.

When Chrissie woke on the morning of the final, there was something different about her. The competitive edge had been blunted. I could see it as clear as day.

Chrissie had beaten Evonne in the 1976 Wimbledon final, coming from two-love down in the third to win 8-6. It was one of her best grass-court performances. And if her mind was in top gear, as it was most matches, she had Evonne's number. Not at Wimbledon 1980 she didn't: 30 unforced errors later, Chrissie had lost in straight sets.

I knew how hard she had worked and just how devastating a loss this would be for my wife. I also thought: 'Shit, now I'm gonna be in big trouble.' Chrissie didn't speak to me for the rest of the night. It was miserable. She didn't speak to me for almost the entire flight back to Miami. It was horrendous.

Close to landing, I tried to break the ice. I was thinking what would I do in this situation: you've just blown a big match, a match you should really have won and feel terrible. Why, John Lloyd would take a beach holiday, of course.

'Listen, should we go on holiday for a couple of weeks when we get back?' I suggested.

'Are you kidding?' Chrissie snapped back. At least she was talking to me again.

'Well, no I'm not kidding actually.'

'No. This is what we're doing.'

It proved to be the farthest thing from a holiday. We got home, gathered our tennis gear and went straight to the practice courts. In Fort Lauderdale in July it is hot and humid. But there we were, within two hours of landing back in the States, running around like maniacs in 90-degree heat. Chrissie was taking all her anger out on the balls. They were being punished – and me, too, I suspect.

'I don't ever want to lose to her again,' Chrissie said. This was her way of making that aim a reality.

My reaction was simply: 'Wow.' I was full of admiration for her in that moment. I was witnessing so intimately what the greats will do to separate themselves from mere mortals like me. This was the last time she would have her preparation for a final veer off track like it did after that semi success over Martina.

True to her usual form, Chrissie went to the next Grand Slam tournament and won it, avenging her previous year's final defeat by American Tracy Austin in the semis, before taking the US Open crown with a comeback victory over Czech Hana Mandlikova. Chrissie would also return to Wimbledon with a new purpose the following year – and win that, too. That's the champion's DNA I mentioned. 'John, you need to get some of this shit coursing through you,' I would tell myself. But there was no chance for me. I would still have taken that two-week holiday and bugger the red-hot practice courts.

Chrissie was once a set, 3-5 and 15-40 down to Virginia Wade in the Wightman Cup at the Royal Albert Hall. Just as I was bracing myself to be ignored for a week, Chrissie pulled it round and went on to win. 'That was a bit close there for a while,' I said afterwards. 'No disrespect,' she answered, 'I just knew I was going to come back today.' It wasn't said in a cocky way. Virginia was a fine player and Chrissie respected that. It was just fact. On my ex-wife's day, it went her way.

Chrissie won three Wimbledon titles but should have won more. She lost in seven finals, five times to Martina. Her overall Grand Slam record is stunning and includes a record seven French Open titles. To go 125 consecutive matches on clay without defeat from 1973 to 1976 is astonishing, while she also 'double-bageled' – that's to say thrashed them love and love – more opponents than any other player in history.

That's all the more remarkable when you analyse Chrissie's game, and I in no way wish to disrespect her with this breakdown because she was an amazing player. Her two-handed backhand was one of the great tennis strokes of all time and her forehand was good, especially on drop shots. Her serve was accurate but only adequate. Her speed around the court was average at best. She read the game well and was often a step ahead of her opponents, so that made her look faster than she was. Chrissie was not renowned for her volleying. I think the net scared her. When we played mixed doubles and I would serve-volley, I would look around for her and she was retreating to the baseline, paranoid about getting hit by the ball. She wasn't the tallest either.

When you look at Martina Navratilova, one of the greatest athletes to play the game, and all her weapons, you wonder how Chrissie managed to beat her so many times. When I was coaching Chrissie, I tried to encourage her to come to the net more, especially playing Martina: to shorten the points, to approach the net on Martina's backhand, to cut down the need for defending. Practising with a male pro like me sharpened Chrissie's game and she was in good shape. But there was nothing I could teach her in terms of mentality. Strength of mind is a crucial requirement in top-level sport. On the court, my then wife had it in spades.

There was all this talk about Chrissie and Martina being the best of friends off the court and how that translated to a friendly rivalry on court. I never bought into that. I am not saying they disliked each other, simply that they were the best of enemies during matches. It was pretty brutal, actually. That was illustrated in an exhibition tour in the US.

The world's top male players were used to the exhibition circuit. I had played on the undercard of some of them. Jimmy Connors or Bjorn Borg would beat the likes of me in the 'semis' and meet in the 'final'. They would play the first set for real. Whoever won that would lose the second set on purpose, then the deciding third set would be played out seriously. Thousands of people were paying good cash to see this, so they gave them their money's worth. Fellow pros could see how the second set was being 'thrown', with a double fault here and missing shots by a couple of inches there, but it was never glaringly obvious to the punters.

Chrissie and Martina signed up for a lucrative women's exhibition at the height of their powers and, as with the men, everyone wanted to see them face off. There were thousands of fans in the arena on opening night. Chrissie won the first set so quickly that some of the fans were still parking their cars and buying their popcorn. I had not discussed the protocol of the men's exhibitions with my wife. I thought she would know how it worked. I sat there believing Martina would rally to take the second set and then it was back to the real business in the third set. Chrissie shot out to a second-set lead.

'She's gonna have to tank it the rest of this set,' I'm thinking.

Wrong. There was no letting up. There was no tanking. Chrissie demolished Martina. It was an exhibition all right: of ruthlessness.

In the locker room, I asked Chrissie: 'What the hell were you doing? People have just paid for an exhibition.'

'Well, what did you expect me to do?'

'Lose the second set and win the third.'

Chrissie came out with an absolute gem, declaring: 'No, you can't let your guard down.'

'Let your guard down? Let your guard down? Do you honestly think Martina's going to learn something from you in an exhibition match that she doesn't already know?'

We moved on to the next city for the second exhibition. Martina was pissed off about the previous loss and crushed Chrissie in about five minutes, short-changing the paying public once again. They couldn't allow the other to get one up on them. Was their rivalry really so intense they would risk screwing up a great business opportunity like this? In a word: yes.

When Chrissie and I were first together, I would fly to see her play then fly off somewhere to take part in a tournament of my own. The men's and women's games were so different with regard to fitness and power. Chrissie was number one in the world on the women's side. But I would practise with her one week and rock up at a men's event the next week a step slower. Actually, make that two steps slower. I wasn't carrying weight but I was losing cardio fitness.

I carried on this way because I was in love. I wanted to be with Chrissie. I wanted to help her, too. She liked me at tournaments, she needed me at tournaments. The companionship was important to her. I was losing early in my events and flying straight back to be with Chrissie. My ranking started to drop, but I didn't care. 'I'll get it back at some stage,' I told myself.

If you are lazily inclined, as I am, it doesn't help when you have a reason in front of you that allows you to be idle. Not that Chrissie ever encouraged that in me. That was all me. She wanted me by her side, I readily agreed. If my career was suffering, so what?

What I should have done was stop playing for a while, then later make a plan for both our careers. We were just too young at 24 to know any better. The odds are not good when two people in the same profession are constantly at different events. Tennis is, by its nature, a selfish sport. There are certain things you have to do to prepare to be at your best when you go on court. You have to be focused, almost self-absorbed. Sharing our experiences of the game in our downtime was the only plus point. But there wasn't too much positive stuff for me to share. It was a struggle for me. I kept giving in to the situation rather than trying to correct it.

This was my life. This was my responsibility. No one could change things for me. Instead, I just went with the flow. Then what happened was, deep down, I started losing respect for myself. I was not giving 100 per cent to my profession, a profession I was practically born to do.

Chrissie obviously has her own take on our relationship, but our feelings on this particular matter are not dissimilar. She is quoted in an interview as saying: 'I was hardly young, yet I was too immature for marriage. Because tennis requires that you be totally self-involved, I never learned to be there for another person.' She went on to say her divorce from me was the beginning of her growing up and her 'emergence from some kind of emotional deadness'.

Such thoughts, feelings and pressures built and, much as we tried to hold it together, there was a certain inevitability about our split. We both came from religious families, so the word 'divorce' was not in our vocabulary. Therefore, we separated. We got back together. We separated again. Truth was, we had been leading separate lives anyway.

Neither of us made the move to end what should not have started in the first place. The marriage had happened ten years too early for us. If Chrissie and I had got together a full decade later, we might have had a shot.

Chrissie made an interesting comment to *Sports Illustrated* magazine that I managed to rediscover in working on this book. She stated: 'I know I'm no angel. I'm not as goody-two-shoes as people think. I'm a normal woman. I've dated a lot of guys, I've had a few drinks. I've told dirty jokes, I've cursed, I've been rude to my parents. There's nothing in my life, no skeletons in my closet that people should be so shocked about.'

Chrissie and I separated in 1983. Our joint statement at the time read: 'There's still very much a chance that we'll get back together. At the present time, we need time to be by ourselves.'

Unsurprisingly, the press, in particular the British tabloids, didn't give us that time to ourselves. Photographers dogged our lives and Chrissie remarked: 'The scandal sheets have gone berserk. I feel like reminding them that half the couples in America get separated.'

We genuinely believed we would reconcile – and we did. But our relationship was never the same after the split, for either of us. We became ever more distant. Chrissie used that phrase 'I know I'm no angel' in the *Sports Illustrated* piece, but by this point in our relationship, neither of us were exactly angels. It takes two to tango. Honestly, the marriage would not have lasted anyway. Divorce was a word that we – and our families – would have to accept. It finally came in 1987.

After Chrissie and I were divorced, some bloke in the *Daily Telegraph* newspaper wrote an article about men who had married wealthy women and taken advantage of them. He targeted me, comparing me to Peter Holm, who was portrayed as a money-grabber in his divorce from, and settlement with, actress Joan Collins in 1988. I was the Peter Holm of tennis, it was claimed.

The so-called journalist suggested I had taken all Chrissie's money. Number one: that's none of his business. Number two: no one knows but Chrissie, me and our lawyer. And yes, that is lawyer in the singular. We used the same one, in spite of friends saying to me at the time: 'Are you nuts?'

Chris and I had no prenuptial agreement. If I had wanted to, I could have employed my own lawyer and gone to town. The fact we used the same legal representation is proof, if ever any were needed, that I did not do that. That is not me. Many others, like this *Daily Telegraph* guy, made bad and incorrect assumptions. I left the marriage with nothing close to what I could have legally challenged for. Nothing close.

You can't go up against this kind of reporting most of the time. There will always be critics, irresponsible journalists and now, with the advent of social media, the vile trolls. Sometimes, in fact most of the time, I take stuff like this on the chin and move on. But there was something so unprofessional about the person writing this nonsense that I felt compelled to reply.

I sent a letter to the editor's page at *The Telegraph* and it was printed. In it, I pointed out this hack had not contacted me or even made an attempt to corroborate his story, throwing out figures as fact when they were utter fiction. I reached number 21 in the world in tennis, twice over. Is that great? Probably not, but in reality, ask almost any person in any profession and they would believe reaching such a level – becoming the 21st best on the planet – in their job is an achievement. I made good money. This was not some kind of career failure that would require me to marry into wealth. And yet that's the picture that had been painted. I was disgusted. I had to put the record straight.

Within a year of our divorce, Chrissie was married again to American downhill skier Andy Mill, who she met through Martina Navratilova. They were divorced after 18 years and she later married Australian golfer Greg Norman. That, too, ended in divorce a short time afterwards. I also married quite quickly after splitting up with Chrissie, spending 29 years with Deborah until we went our separate ways.

I still see Chrissie, mainly at Grand Slam tournaments like Wimbledon and the US Open, and we have a friendly relationship. We talk about the old times on occasion and always ask how our respective families are doing. Just regular conversations, really. We have appeared together on the BBC Wimbledon panel, interviewed by our friend Sue Barker, and Chrissie has never been afraid to bring up the topic of our marriage even then. We can still have a laugh about it.

Ironically, we have ended up living about 25 minutes away from each other. Chrissie has a successful tennis academy in Boca Raton, Florida and I'm in West Palm Beach. You might call us neighbours with a special history.

A RABBIT CALLED WENDY

THERE HAVE been some famous rabbits through the years: Beatrix Potter's Peter Rabbit, Bambi's mate Thumper, Bright Eyes from *Watership Down* ... even the Energizer Bunny. I was privileged to partner the most famous rabbit that tennis has ever seen. Her name is Wendy Turnbull and together we won Wimbledon twice.

There was a time when most players took part in all forms of competition: singles, doubles and mixed. I was no different. My doubles ranking was a false one. I peaked in the 30s, but I was better than that.

I put having fun in doubles above anything else. I preferred to play with my friends or, as often happened, my brothers David and Tony. Some doubles teams didn't socialise with each other off the court and were painfully serious on it. They entered into a business arrangement that worked for them, but that wasn't my style. The financial incentives weren't great and certainly didn't outweigh my desire for pure enjoyment on the doubles court.

With Wendy, a down-to-earth Australian with a great personality and supreme talent, I found a mixed doubles partner who could combine both aspects.

Wendy was nicknamed 'Rabbit' because of her speed around the court. No one else was as fleet of foot. She was a class act, certainly a pay grade higher than me, and was a consummate professional. But she had a great sense of humour, so we could have a laugh along the way. I liked to make her chuckle on court with a few choice stories or by pointing out certain oddballs in the crowd.

Wendy had a great deal to smile about, having won four Grand Slam women's doubles titles, including Wimbledon in 1978. She also reached three Grand Slam singles finals and secured world ranking career highs of three in singles and five in doubles, all before I teamed up with her.

The only other time I had played with a female player of her calibre was with my former wife Chris Evert and, even then, it was never in a tournament. That's probably just as well or we might have swung for each other at times – and Chrissie had quite the double-handed backhand.

Chrissie and I were invited to play in some lucrative exhibition events, like the time we took on Tracy Austin and her brother John in Tokyo and were paid an exorbitant amount of money. Then there was what was called the Love Doubles at Battersea Park in the May of 1980, when we defeated Bjorn Borg and his fiancée Mariana Simionescu in front of a royal and celebrity-laced audience. Princess Anne and her then husband Captain Mark Phillips were in attendance that night and we were introduced to them before the match. It was a bizarre set-up, in a red-and-white striped big top, with many guests arriving in evening dress. As the winning couple, we picked up £41,000.

Chrissie was a great singles champion but not the most instinctive doubles player. Her return of serve was so good that she was an asset in that regard. She won the Wimbledon women's doubles when partnering Martina Navratilova in 1976 and they won the French Open, too. Martina was embarking on a run that would see her win 31 major women's doubles titles. She was so much better than anyone else in doubles that if you were teamed with Martina, unless you were a zombie, you were going to be right up there in perennial title contention.

Doubles is about getting to the net, taking ownership of it. But with Chrissie, her natural instinct was to retreat to the baseline. She would find herself in no man's land, allowing opponents to volley at her feet. I would get pissed off with her. 'No, the enemy is this way. You've got to come up.' She, in turn, would get angry with me.

It is just as well we didn't ever play a competitive match together. God knows what could have happened. My advice is never play mixed doubles with your wife or husband unless you get a kick out of arguments or the cold, silent treatment.

Chrissie and I had known Wendy for years and it was my ex-wife who first suggested we might make a good mixed doubles pairing. It ended up being a great combination. We hit it off straight away and won the 1982 French Open title, beating Brazilian pair Claudia Monteiro and Cassio Motta in straight sets in the final. Wendy had won this event alongside Bob Hewitt three years earlier, but it was my first Grand Slam title and a moment to savour.

We had to wait an age to get out on court as we followed the men's final, in which Swedish teenager Mats Wilander beat experienced Argentine Guillermo Vilas in one of the most tedious finals ever played. There were four sets – one was won 6-1 by Vilas, one was won 6-0 by Wilander – and yet they somehow contrived to stay on court for four hours and 43 minutes. That's because some of their rallies were more than 60 shots long. We got our match finished before it went dark, at least.

Our partnership was instinctive. I saw up close why Wendy was called 'the Rabbit' because she was unbelievably quick in covering the ground. She read the game well, covered all the angles and could also take care of herself at the net. She was never one to be intimidated by a male opponent, even if he was all brute force. This was never more the case than in the 1983 Wimbledon final against the brilliant Billie Jean King and Steve Denton, a top 12 singles player from Texas who served bullets and was all power, no finesse.

Wendy and I had reached the Wimbledon final the previous year and lost. That was my fault.

Because of rain delays that year, we had to play the final on a smaller show court and not Centre Court. That was disappointment number one. It was one set all against Anne Smith and Kevin Curren, and we had reached a critical point in the decider, when I was presented with a volley that could have pretty much sealed the deal.

This was disappointment number two because, rather than fire the ball straight at Anne Smith just a few feet away from me, which was my natural instinct, I played Mr Nice Guy and volleyed the ball at her feet. She made contact with her racket and the ball looped over my head for a volley-lob winner. That helped turn the tide. They won the set 7-5 and with it the Wimbledon title. I should have been more ruthless when I had the chance. I would not make that mistake again.

Wendy and I were seeded two for the 1983 Championships, only behind King and Denton. We came from a set down in the semi-finals to defeat fourth seeds Fred Stolle and Pam Shriver and were combining better than we ever had. Now we had a chance to go one better than the previous year and I had an opportunity to make amends for my error of judgement. This time, the final would take place on Centre Court.

Wimbledon crowds were not used to seeing British players in finals, so there was an added air of tension and expectancy. There was also a fair bit of animosity aimed at Denton, who was booming down ferocious serves at Wendy as well as me. I think some in the crowd viewed it as bullying. But Steve was a great guy and there was no malice in anything he did that day. It's simply that he had just one pace: there was no second or third gear, only overdrive with him. Wendy could take care of herself, too. But the crowd were just so desperate for us to win they were not about to disguise their bias.

I had to channel that support in a positive way. Too often in singles, I had let the pressure that comes with wanting to please a home crowd throw me. Having a partner to share the burden of expectation certainly helped me.

If Billie Jean won, she would extend her overall record of Wimbledon titles to 21 – and there was no question, she was playing like a woman intent on making history. They won the first set on a tie-break, we fought back to take the second set – also on a tie-break. All of us were playing at the top of our games. It was a fantastic match to be a part of and would be decided by a solitary crucial break in the decider.

Billie Jean was serving at 5-6 down and it was 30-all. Wendy and I were two points away from the title. The nerves kicked in big time, meaning what came naturally could easily be trampled on by emotion. Your legs can turn to lead in those moments. I said to Wendy: 'Rab, move your feet.' She repeated: 'Move my feet, move my feet, move my feet.'

Wendy moved her feet alright, stepping into her return of serve and hitting a winner. We had championship point.

I remember looking up to my parents in the players' box and thinking to myself: 'Don't mess up now, John. Make this return … just somehow make this return.'

Billie Jean served to my backhand. It wasn't a great return. I didn't connect with the ball the way I wanted to. Denton moved to cover a shot down the line, but I had gone cross-court. Billie Jean moved to hit the looping ball, then decided to leave it. Everything seemed to go in slow motion. I was certain I had put the ball long, clearly Billie Jean thought so too. But, astonishingly, it dropped on the line. The crowd erupted. We had won Wimbledon.

Receiving the trophy in the Royal Box was a career highlight: an amazing feeling bettered only when I saw the look of pride on the faces of my parents. Hopefully, this was just a little bit of payback for all they had given up to get me to this triumphant point.

Wendy and I won the title again the following year, beating Denton and another American Kathy Jordan 6-3, 6-3 in the final. We were top seeds and had dropped just one set en route to the final. We were at the peak of our mixed doubles powers.

Sweet as that victory was, there was no comparison with the first Wimbledon title. Bjorn Borg always said the first title is the best and he was not wrong. Not that I am at all putting my mixed doubles success on a par with his singles glory, but a Wimbledon title is a Wimbledon title and that was a massive moment for me. Much as I don't want to downgrade my second Wimbledon victory, there was no beating that maiden victory. I find it hard to believe if players ever say otherwise. How can the first one not be the most special, when you are in unknown territory, so full of nervousness and emotion: when you have broken through the title barrier all your career has been geared towards?

To share the success with Wendy made it all the more special. We were ever firmer friends. She didn't even mind going on holiday with me. Wendy, Chrissie, Ana Laird – Chrissie's best friend – and I took a memorable trip to the exclusive Hamilton Island, some 550 miles north of the Australian city of Brisbane. The Beatles' George Harrison once had a place there. It was truly magnificent: the only island in the Great Barrier Reef with its own commercial airport, with stunning beaches, splendid accommodation and dolphin-inhabited waters.

One adventurous day, we went parasailing – that most exhilarating of pastimes, where you get attached to a speed boat and are sent sailing into the air strapped to a canopy that resembles a parachute. Chrissie was way up in the air and, from my viewpoint on the boat, it looked like she was having a whale of a time. She was waving in my direction. I was waving back. Chrissie waved again … then again. 'Yes, I can see you,' I thought. 'Enough with the waving now.'

When she was lowered down, Chrissie was cursing me. She had been waving furiously to get my attention because she was suffering motion sickness and wanted to come back down. She was sick for a few days after that and, of course, it was my bloody fault. She had conveniently forgotten that not only did I not own binoculars to enable me to spot her distress when she was hundreds of feet in the air, but my mind-reading powers were also non-existent.

Chrissie was, unsurprisingly, a non-starter for the snorkelling trip on a glass-bottomed boat, through which we could see breathtaking coral reefs and a rainbow assortment of fish and tropical life. I could also see a shark.

'That was a shark … did you see that … a shark? It's a bloody shark!' I thought my reaction was quite measured.

Our guide replied: 'No, no, it definitely wasn't a shark.'

'It bloody was, I'm telling you!'

We were meant to climb out of the boat and go snorkelling, up to a range of about 50 yards away. That had suddenly lost its appeal. Don't ask me why, but I was brave enough to get in the water, albeit that I stayed tight to the boat and let the other lunatics swim out further, thinking: 'The shark will have them before it gets near me.' Thankfully, no limbs were lost and we returned safely to the island.

The next day, a couple from a neighbouring condo went on a similar excursion and were snorkelling about 40 yards from the same boat when the shark appeared, swimming between the vessel and the suddenly terrified holidaymakers. I had not been imagining things. There was, indeed, a larger-than-life shark in the area. If that had been me in the water, knowing what I did from the movie *Jaws*, I would have soiled the azure blue waters and fellow guests in an instant.

The captain of the boat got everyone back on board without serious incident, and said there had been no need to panic because there were so many fish around the shark would have no need to eat a human.

That smelled of bull to me because what self-respecting shark would eat a few tiddlers when a big juicy Englishman was being served up on a platter?

A comic of a pilot thought it might be fun to scare me even more when Wendy and I were on a helicopter ride on the same trip. He asked us if we remembered the opening sequence to the television show *Magnum P.I.* 'Yes,' I replied in all innocence. 'I loved that show.' Then it dawned on me, the opening sequence involved a helicopter practically nosediving into the water before pulling up again. The pilot did just that to the pair of us, to the point we were screaming like a victim in a slasher flick.

It was never quite that hair-raising when we were together on court, although our first-round defeat at Wimbledon in 1987 had its fair share of turbulence. We were up against Italy's Raffaella Reggi and Spain's Sergio Casal on a packed outside court. The Italian contingent in the crowd was strong, boisterous and loud.

Back home in the States, I had been working with fitness trainer Greg Isaacs. He was a tough, no-nonsense South African who knew how to put the fear of God in people. I had seen it first-hand in a bar next door to a gym I used in Los Angeles. Parking was an issue, so I did a deal with the bar owner to use one of his spaces. On just the second time I had parked there, I returned from my workout to no car. I thought it had been stolen. Greg thought otherwise: 'No, it'll be those f*****s next door. They've had it towed.' His instinct was all the evidence he needed.

Greg didn't like anyone reneging on a deal. He marched from the bright sunshine into the dark and dingy bar to confront the suspects: a big mongrel of a dude behind the bar and his chunky mate in front of it. 'Oh no,' I thought, 'I don't like the look of this.'

Greg, with muscles sprouting from places I didn't know muscles could exist, slammed his fist on the bar and exclaimed: 'Which one of you two mother f*****s had my mate's car towed?'

The two bruisers immediately recoiled, soon confessing all and explaining it was a misunderstanding. Greg had a way of making people listen and comply.

In 1989, the year I coached Sweden's Catarina Lindqvist to the Wimbledon women's singles semi-finals, Greg showed her he was not to be trifled with. We put a 10lb weight around her waist to illustrate what excess poundage can do to slow you down. We wanted her to get into such great shape that she could honestly look across the net and believe whatever opponent she came up against was no fitter than her. She could not carry any excess weight. That had to be a given if she was to fulfil her potential.

We went out for dinner. Catarina placed her order, after which Greg said: 'Forget that. She'll have chicken without the skin, green beans and broccoli … no sauce, no potatoes.' She lost 12 pounds that next month. All the players we trained did as Greg insisted.

Now you have a picture of Greg Isaacs as we get back to Wendy and me taking on the Italian-Spanish duo at Wimbledon. Not that it felt like a home match for me. The unruly Italian supporters were making it feel like a Davis Cup tie in Rome. Four of them in particular were cheering our every mistake, including double faults, in a testing match that was to go the distance. I was imploring the umpire to get them under control, knowing that if we lost, this could be our last match at Wimbledon. These heckling taunts were not memories I wanted to carry with me into retirement.

I spotted Greg climbing from his chair. My eyes followed him as he moved to where this rowdy group of young Italian men were sitting near the umpire's chair. There was no space on their bench, but Greg squashed himself in between them anyway. Tennis etiquette was not his bag.

I saw him turn to the men on his right and utter something, then he did likewise to the men to his left. Greg stayed put. We did not hear another disrespectful peep out of the Italian fanatics for the rest of the match. It did not change the outcome – Wendy and I lost the decider 7-5 – but silencing the idiots made the experience more bearable.

After the match, I asked Greg what he had said to shut them up. 'Oh, nothing much,' he explained. 'I just told them that one more word out of them and I'd take them outside and f*** them over.' Wimbledon has rarely seen such classy behaviour.

As it transpired, that wasn't the last Wimbledon outing for Turnbull & Lloyd. We lost in the first round the following year to my Davis Cup team-mate Steve Shaw, who I coached for a short while, and my previously mentioned former charge Catarina. Now there's gratitude for you. Then in 1989 we were beaten in the second round by American third seeds Betsy Nagelsen and Rick Leach. That was our last Wimbledon. Both Wendy and I retired that year.

We are still great friends. Wendy lives not too far from me in Florida at the beautiful Woodfield Country Club, which is also home to German golfer Bernhard Langer and former French tennis player Sebastien Grosjean. I think I'm right in saying Woodfield did more business in tennis lessons than any other club in America in 2017. I like the Woodfield connection between Wendy and me. That was the name of my street growing up.

We play golf together. Wendy had her first hole in one there not too long ago, after which I said: 'Welcome to the club.'

I had mine in Raleigh, South Carolina – witnessed by 1977 Wimbledon champion Virginia Wade, no less.

Another former Australian player Janine Thompson posted a message on Facebook about her knee replacement surgery. I wrote that it would be worth the initial pain because the benefits are huge. I have had both my knees done and, as I pointed out to Janine, now play at least two hours a day.

Janine wrote back: 'Is it just hit and giggle tennis or more competitive than that?' I replied: 'It's proper tennis. There are some exhibitions, but it's good competitive tennis.'

At that juncture, Wendy – who has also had knee replacement surgery – joined in the exchange, writing: 'The difference with John nowadays is that he says "yours" a lot.'

WEDDING HIGHS AND WOES

'DO YOU want to watch our wedding video?' is normally a question that has guests running for the hills and the mice throwing themselves on traps in every corner of the house. But the tuneful excerpt I chose to show visitors from the taping of my second marriage is one that had them asking for a rewind and repeat viewings. Wedding nerves never sounded so melodic.

Deborah Taylor-Bellman, my bride-to-be, would call herself spiritual if not religious. I'm not religious at all, unlike some of my family. I did not want to offend them, but didn't want a priest to conduct the ceremony. I had already endured the big Catholic wedding first twirl around the marital floor. Time for something entirely different.

Deb came up with the idea of a Buddhist monk: someone who could carry out a non-religious ceremony, but with enough of the spiritual about him to satisfy family. We drove down, in between Los Angeles and Palm Springs, to meet a man with a deep voice and a quiet presence, who resembled a Buddhist Peter Sellers. He explained how the ceremony he conducted would unfold.

'Look, can you make sure you don't mention anything that's out there,' I said.

'What do you mean by that?'

'Anything, you know … too different.'

'Different?'

'My family already think I'm way out there just living in California. LA especially has a certain reputation in England. Now I'm getting married on a hilltop by a Buddhist monk. There's potential here for people to think I've lost my mind.'

The big day arrived and the setting at the Bel-Air Beach Club could not have been more magnificent: high above LA, overlooking the ocean in 80-degree weather, with a gorgeous sunset due on the horizon. The monk arrived to be greeted by a gang of press photographers. It suddenly dawned on him this could be a bigger deal than he had imagined and his nerves kicked in.

The best way to calm his nerves, he thought, was this. He stepped up to the microphone and in his dulcet tones said: 'Before we get to the marriage ceremony, can we bow our heads and meditate.' Not pray, but meditate. My parents, sister and younger brother were at the front of the congregation – if that's what you call a Buddhist gathering – and I felt their eyes burning into me. What kind of Californian hippy had I turned into? Dad closed his eyes and didn't wake for the rest of the ceremony.

Kathy Smith, a well-known fitness trainer in the States, very much in the Jane Fonda mode, and her husband Steve Grace, who worked for American television network NBC, kindly offered to shoot our wedding video as their present to Deb and me. Steve's involvement meant it would all be done on a professional footing, so we were fitted with microphone packs, ready for the pre-wedding interviews.

Before we appeared in front of the monk, questions were being fired at me from the other side of the camera in my waiting room at the Bel-Air Beach Club as I stood resplendent in my suit, tie and cummerbund: 'Are you nervous? Have you remembered the ring? Have you read through your vows?' Deb was similarly quizzed as she was getting ready in a neighbouring room, capturing the pre-wedding moments for posterity.

On the balcony, we had a young all-female string quartet playing beautiful, calming music as guests were being seated. I was far from calm, though. I needed the toilet.

When I entered the bathroom, I saw a reporter from the British tabloid *The Sun* having a pee. I recognised him from previous encounters. He was clearly taken aback to see me, zipped up quickly and scarpered. How the hell had he got into this exclusive club? More to the point, why was my wedding of such interest back in the UK? What was his angle? His photographer was hiding in a bush outside.

Deb emerged from her room looking beautiful. Soon we had moved beyond the meditation phase and the ceremony was underway. The Buddhist monk wasn't half bad, actually. At least, I don't think my family believed me to be possessed of demonic darkness.

When my friend Steve went into work to edit the wedding video, he could see the camera had picked up some glorious shots of the ocean, the blue sky, the colourful guests, the string quartet. At one point, there was a close-up of one of the musicians in full flow. She had just stopped playing her instrument and was smiling. Suddenly, a sound erupted from the screen like she had just farted. She carried on smiling serenely. Then there was another farting noise ... and another ... and another. It was like Mount Vesuvius had erupted. And yet on her face, not a flicker.

The guys from NBC gathered round to watch the string musician deliver her powerful wind performance and were laughing uproariously. That was until one of the edit team pointed out: 'There are two channels of sound on this recording. That's not the camera microphone picking up her noise ... it's coming from another mic. It's coming from one of the personal mics.'

That personal mic had been attached to me. When I had visited the bathroom to expel my 'nerves', I still had my microphone attached to my suit. And it was still switched on. I had let rip with about ten cannonballs and every one of them had been recorded. This was the sound that was mistakenly overlaying the pictures of this lovely, fragrant and ever so innocent female musician.

There was even a snippet of me telling my brother Tony, as he entered the toilet after me: 'I wouldn't go in there if I was you.'

Much to Deb's annoyance, I delighted in showing this impromptu musical rendition to visitors with the words: 'Now this is one wedding video you have to see ...'

Back in Britain the following day, *The Sun* must have felt like they had come up trumps as their story read: 'Lloyd gets married in hippy wedding'.

Deborah didn't do anything to dispel the hippy myth when she took me along to yoga. She was always keen on introducing me to the 'new'. She was into yoga, I was trying to get in better shape and there seemed no harm in trying something different. Strangely enough, the release of wind featured here as well. What can I say? Flatulence makes me laugh. It's my inner Benny Hill.

The class we attended in LA was run by Indian Bikram Choudhury, who became famous worldwide for 'Bikram Yoga' and his massively popular hot yoga studios. Hot yoga is performed in sweltering rooms employing 26 of Bikram's trademark poses and is designed to promote healthy, peaceful living.

His devoted clients included Hollywood stars like Shirley MacLaine, Candice Bergen, Martin Sheen and Juliet Prowse and the Los Angeles Lakers basketball legend Kareem Abdul-Jabbar. Actress Raquel Welch was an early celebrity follower. She liked his yoga poses so much she put them in her own *Total Beauty and Fitness* video in the 80s and was sued in a $1million-plus damages law suit. Bikram told me that paid for his house in Beverly Hills.

Bikram was obnoxious most of the time: he would insult pretty much everyone during his classes. He called me Sheffield Steel. That's how stiff my body was. But I laughed along with his taunts. To be fair to him, he told me it didn't matter if I couldn't bend myself double or stick my leg over my head: I would still feel the benefits of yoga. He was right and it later became one of my training tools.

Yoga reminded me of tennis in some ways. Fail to concentrate fully on a yoga pose and you will fall out of it. Tennis is unforgiving in a similar vein. If your balance and footwork are incorrect, your technique goes off and you miss shots. It didn't surprise me to see Andy Murray taking up Bikram's hot yoga in London for all its inherent advantages.

At the time I was attending classes, I was working with a few female players and introduced them to the studio. Their concentration on court could be a problem, so I asked Bikram to make sure they stayed focused in class. That was easier said than done. There were seriously fit blokes wearing nothing but shorts getting into sweaty poses all around them. Bikram had to bark orders at the girls to snap them back into putting all their focus on him.

One of the poses involved lying back, raising your legs and pulling your knees into your chest. It was the wind-relieving pose. I soon found out why. Believe me, I could have ripped the roof off if I'd wanted to. But I was in a packed room and thought better of it. So did many others. A few would just go for it.

In the corner of the room, there were unrelenting farting noises during this part of the workout. Every day, the same corner. Every day, the same noises. I couldn't help but laugh, which led to a ticking-off from Deb.

Then I made the discovery. Yvette Mimieux, a beautiful, demure and classy actress in her 50s, star of the 1960 cult classic *The Time Machine*, was the phantom farter.

'It's her, Deb, I'm telling you. Yvette is letting 'em rip.' My ex-wife was having none of it. But I knew. When the tennis girls came in, they were equally amused by the sounds of wind-relieving pose time. They took no convincing it was in no small part down to Yvette.

Bikram is in his 70s now and, the last I heard, had gone on the run in India after facing sexual assault and discrimination charges in the United States. Oh, how the mighty fall.

As an aerobics instructor, Deborah was used to holding classes of her own, with no such scandalous behaviour afoot. We were introduced in 1986 by a mutual friend at a time when we were both looking for the same thing: namely, to find a lifelong partner and start a family. Unlike me, Deb had not been married before.

We didn't plan to have children quite so early in our relationship. But life doesn't always follow the blueprint. In fact, Deb was pregnant when we married in that breathtaking clifftop ceremony the year after we met. Our son was on the way. It was very speedily to be the family life for us.

I always thought the Lloyd family Christian names – Ann, David, John and Anthony – were a sign of unimaginative parents. Deb and I chose Aiden as the name for our first born, after the actor Aidan Quinn – albeit with a different spelling. We used to look at the credits at the end of movies to come up with ideas. People thought we were a bit weird, as there weren't too many Aidans around at that time, with an 'a' or an 'e'. Just a few years later it became the most popular boy's name in America. We liked to think we got in ahead of the trend. Sticking with the acting theme, we named our daughter Hayley after British actress Hayley Mills. That was more my choice, I suppose. I was in love with Hayley Mills when I was 12.

When Deb gave birth to Aiden, I was still travelling a lot on the senior tennis tour. That was also the case when Hayley arrived. With me away so much, Deb became the main disciplinarian. She was strict but fair and always the most loving of mothers. Her mum had not been the maternal type, to put it mildly. Deb therefore felt compelled to do her research into 'good parenting'. She didn't need books, though. She had an instinctive way of caring and nurturing and did one hell of a job raising our children.

When I came back from my travels, I wanted to break the routine she and the kids had established. I wanted to make up for lost time, I suppose, with a large amount of 'Let's do this … Let's do that.' That led to arguments. Even though I knew Deb was right, it was hard for me to accept being a husband and father negotiating his way back into his family's daily lifestyle. They travelled with me when they could, but that was not always possible. Long spells apart were never easy, never good. This would come full circle as our marriage neared the 30th anniversary mark.

We had a great life in an affluent LA neighbourhood, Pacific Palisades. We had wonderful children, lots of great friends and many memorable journeys together. But when the children were grown up, the truth is that – as happens with many couples after so many years together – we began to drift.

I had just resigned as British Davis Cup tennis captain when I received an offer from George Norcross, a friend who was a successful businessman and prominent figure in the Democratic Party in New Jersey. I hadn't even started thinking about the next chapter in my career when he said he had a role for me in his new realty company in Palm Beach, Florida. 'Does that mean I have to know the difference between different kitchen worktops and that kind of stuff?' I asked him. 'I can tell you now, I don't.'

'No, your job is to be a rainmaker,' said George. 'Play tennis and golf with would-be clients and bring them to the company. We've got other partners who can take care of the finer details of the houses we're selling.'

The offer appealed to me. The problem was, it was a six-month contract that took me away from my LA home to the other side of the country. It was an offer I couldn't resist, even though I knew Deb hated Florida and would not relocate. She was reluctant even to visit. I got that. Her life, her friends were in California. But I had to make the most of this opportunity.

There was a test I needed to pass to become a realtor – or estate agent as we call it in the UK – even if I wasn't exactly doing the selling or legally binding bits. With my learning difficulties of old, I knew I was in trouble. I hired a tutor to help me with the mathematics section, then realised it was an act of futility. I was better off guessing the multiple-choice questions on maths, given that it was only ten per cent of the overall total. I wasn't much better with the rest of the examination, though. I sat the test something like 15 times. I thought that had to be some kind of record, until I discovered a little old lady had failed it 39 times. The people at the test centre in Pasadena got to know me. 'How do you think you've done today, Mr Lloyd?'

'I've butchered it again, I'm afraid.' There was an indicator that pointed up or down to show you whether or not you had passed the test. 'Let's hope that's not the case,' said one of the examiners. Suddenly, for the first time, the indicator pointed upwards to show I had passed. It felt like I had won Wimbledon. I could get to work.

Within a couple of years, I had fallen in love with Florida. I had lived in Fort Lauderdale for a while when married to Chris Evert and couldn't stand it. The constant rain in the summer, the heat and humidity and the flat expanse of the state bothered me. I was a Californian guy. Now, having spent quality time in and around Palm Beach, I was a convert. Los Angeles started to unnerve me. The traffic jams gave me road rage. I had become used to the quiet life in Florida and I liked it.

When the company I was working for went under, I was offered a job at Sotheby's in Palm Beach – but with no up-front salary this time. Deb thought that was the time I should move back full-time to LA, but that would have meant starting at ground level in the property business in one of the most competitive markets in America. I had built up a clientele in Florida and no one else was fulfilling the kind of niche role I had in Palm Beach. I was beyond striving to make enough money to live in an expensive part of California, to fund a certain kind of lifestyle. I wanted an easier time in this phase of my life, not a harder one. When it came down to the crunch, my life was going to be in Florida and Deb's was not. This wasn't the one and only reason for our split, but it certainly contributed to it in a major way.

We tried couples counselling, but the spark had gone. What we had was fading. Divorce was inevitable. Thankfully, we kept it as amicable as possible. There was nothing explosive: none of the 'you did this to me, I did that to you' blame game. The children were grown up and could understand why our divorce had to be.

Of course, I didn't like the fact that my second marriage was ending, although after 29 years together I refused to consider it a complete failure. It wasn't. It is not like we were the worst of enemies at the end, either. It was simply that I believed no one should stay in a marriage if it's not working. Life is too short for that.

FATHERHOOD

A letter from the John Lloyd of today to his former self as he is about to become a father for the first time.

Dear John,

You had a great role model for fatherhood. In many ways, Dad's a hard act to follow. With a new baby son on the way, you can put some of the decent values he taught you into practice.

Though you can never question how much Dad adored his children, he was never outwardly affectionate. We can't even remember him kissing Mum in public. But you have been around enough Latino tennis players and their families to know there is a different way. You have looked on that with the knowledge you want to have that same kind of open relationship with your children. Hugs and kisses between parents and their kids are wonderful and nothing to be embarrassed about. Teach them that. Show them that.

Your children will make you proud and bring you so much love and joy. But there will be worry, there's no escaping that. You're a father. It comes with the job.

In fact, fatherhood will bring you the most harrowing challenge of your life. When that time comes, all I can say is be strong. Do the best you can. Don't blame yourself. Trust you will find a way through it.
John

THE FEAR on his face as we left him in that place is something I will never forget. What had I done wrong? Had I failed him? That look can torment me to this day, if I allow it in.

Parents are supposed to protect their children. It is some innate thing that comes bursting out of you once you have a child: that overwhelming need to keep them safe. It starts from the very moment you hold them in your arms and know life will never be the same again. I saw this tiny, helpless being, so delicate and fragile, and thought: 'Whatever you do, don't drop him.'

Little did I know then, when Aiden was swaddled to my chest, that this was the time when protecting him was as simple as it ever would be.

My daughter Hayley arrived within two years. As they grew, they became as close as two siblings could be. Along with my then wife Deborah, we did everything together. It was no different when we were faced with the darkest time any of us have known.

Aiden was a late arrival. The disconcerting sight of me taking on basketball superstar Michael Jordan in Kenny Rogers's television special hadn't stirred heavily pregnant Deborah into labour and she was soon past her due date. I decided to take her to the movies to see the scary spider film *Arachnophobia*, hoping a few jumps at the right time might get things rolling. It didn't work. Aiden was clearly in no hurry to see the world.

When delivery day finally arrived, it all became rather tense. Deb was in labour for a long time. The pain she experienced I could never contend with in a million years. I was full of admiration for her. She was somewhat less admiring of me when I had to keep leaving the room for fear of fainting. 'Who's giving birth here,' she snapped, 'me or you?'

There were complications in the delivery room and Deb had to have a C-section. The doctor said to me: 'If you think you might faint, perhaps you can stand in the corner and pass out over there.' Basically, it was a reminder there were more important things at play than my weak knees. I did as I was told and didn't add to the drama.

When Aiden was born, I saw this blue head with pointy hair and – aside from questioning whether he might need putting back to warm up a bit more – was completely amazed. What a life changer.

Deb came from a dysfunctional family. She had a terribly rough upbringing. Her mother and father both had problems with alcohol and would think nothing of leaving their children at home when they visited bars. There was no money for clothes and Deb had to survive Colorado's bitterly cold winters with bits of paper shoved in holes in her shoes. It is testament to her that she turned out the way she did because the easier option might have been to go off the rails herself, clinging on to the excuse: 'It's because of what happened to poor old me growing up.'

So, Deb had no good example of parenthood to follow but turned out to be a wonderful mother in spite of that. She read numerous parenting books and did all manner of research, while I was away playing on the senior tennis tour. Some things with children are done off the cuff, of course, but there's so much that can be learned ahead of time and Deb had all that covered.

Aiden had colic as a baby, so his screaming when we tried to put him down led to many sleepless nights, especially for Deb because I was still travelling almost half the year at that time.

In contrast, we hardly got a peep out of Hayley. She had the cutest face, with plump cheeks, like she was a hamster storing food for later. She sat quietly and simply observed everything going on around her. Maybe it was a tranquillity she found from her mother's enforced confinement for the last three months of her pregnancy. Had Deb not rested, we would have likely lost Hayley. This precious little girl with blonde hair and blue eyes would remain quite shy, but when she wanted to say something she made herself heard. This curiously loud voice would emerge from her tiny frame. There was confidence in there, amid the shyness: an inner belief that matured in adulthood to allow her to ace every interview she ever had in the supremely competitive entertainment industry. Hayley has ended up working for Netflix, going from strength to strength there in her own inimitable style.

When we travelled across the Atlantic, keeping the children entertained on 11-hour flights was another part of our parental education. Aiden was fond of walking up and down the aisles, stealing shoes and hitting people on the head to wake them up. As you can imagine, that made us enormously popular: as did Hayley's propensity for projectile vomiting. She had motion sickness and I could almost see it brewing up inside her as she became pale and clammy.

One time on a flight, when I spotted the warning signs, I tried to hand her off to Deb across the aisle, but I got: 'Oh no you don't. You take care of it.' Suddenly, Hayley turned into the child from *The Exorcist* as vomit spewed forth, covering this poor guy at the side of me and ruining his shiny new briefcase. I held up my hand as a shield, as if that was going to be any use in the face of such colourful up-chucking. 'I'm so sorry,' I said, 'I'll pay for any damage.' My sickly scented fellow passenger was understanding to a fault, saying: 'Don't worry. I've got kids. I know how it is.'

That was a life lesson I have always remembered. If boisterous children – even puking children – are sitting near me on flights now, my patience is born of my experience as a dad. Been there, done that, bought the t-shirt.

Deb was a great disciplinarian: firm but fair. Without her, I might have been more of a pushover. In restaurants, if one of the children misbehaved, she would give them just one warning. If they did it again, we were up and off and out. I could be in the middle of the most delicious meal ever. It didn't matter. The bill was paid and we would leave our plates of food. Aiden and Hayley soon learned the choice was impeccable behaviour or hunger.

We were lucky, though. They were generally good kids. Better than good. And boy did I hate having to leave them when I was heading off on tour. They would cry and scream: 'Daddy, please don't go!' Talk about tugging at my heartstrings. It never got any easier.

When I was a young player, first travelling abroad for tournaments, I was terribly homesick. There were even times I didn't mind losing early if it meant quickly getting back to

Heathrow and the bliss of home. My father was calm about it, simply pointing out: 'Sorry, son, but you've picked the wrong business if you're going to get homesick. It's up to you, but if this is the case maybe you should give up tennis.' I had to get over it and I did. I had to shut my mind to thoughts of home.

And it was that same kind of mentality I had to employ when I left Deb and the children at home. When I was on the senior tour, I was expected to be a certain person, not only on the court but in the corporate world off it. I was entertaining people. I couldn't be this moping guy, missing his kids. I longed to see them, but I had to cut out those thoughts as soon as the front door closed behind me.

When I started working at Wimbledon for American network HBO, the family could at least come with me. We learned the hard way that taking a house in the village was not the best idea. I was broadcasting until midnight some days, while Deb was again stuck at home, with all the usual domestic chores, and with the London sights hardly on the doorstep. Deb didn't exactly fall in love with England, largely because fond memories weren't being created. It had to be the hotel life for us after that and two of my favourite words in all the world: 'Room service'.

We didn't see much of my parents during Wimbledon, but they loved coming over to visit us in the States and my kids adored them. It took Mum and Dad a while to adjust to Aiden and Hayley running up to them and showering them with hugs and kisses. That was not their way. But I told my children to never, ever be embarrassed to show affection to your loved ones – and my parents soon remedied their reserved ways. In fact, they learned to appreciate just how friendly a welcome they received across the board in America. An initial three-week stay would grow, over the years, to fantastic three-month holidays. Mum invariably spoiled the kids with sweets and treats ... the role of every irresponsible but doting grandparent. All the Lloyd generations together: those were special times.

As were the times the kids could come along and see me play, when the senior tour rolled into my home city. It gave me such a kick to show them what Dad did for a living and having them courtside was one of the great pleasures of this phase of my career. Not that Hayley always saw it that way.

Just a couple of miles up the road from our house, I was taking on John McEnroe in the quarter-finals at the Riviera Club in Brentwood. I was playing well and was on top of him, much to Mac's annoyance. When he flipped his lid in frustration, the umpire received the full McEnroe tirade. Aiden and Hayley, who were sitting just yards away, didn't hear swearing at home. Suddenly, they were receiving quite the colourful education. Jimmy Connors felt the need to employ referees on the Champions Tour after this outburst. That's how verbally outrageous it was. I looked over to the children. Aiden was in shock. Hayley's eyes were as wide as saucers.

After the match, she said: 'I don't like that bad man, Daddy.' Whenever I was on the road, she would ask me on the phone: 'Is that bad man going to be playing?' I told Mac how he might just have given my darling daughter a few mental scars, so he made a fuss of her, showed his less offensive side and was no longer 'Mac the Mouthy Monster', the creature of teeny-tot nightmares.

Hayley, like innocent infants everywhere, found it difficult to disguise her true feelings. Out of the mouths of babes, and all that. One Christmas, I managed to scoop her up and whisk her off just in time to avoid her telling another bad man just what she thought of him … one OJ Simpson.

I became obsessed with the OJ trial, but then the murders had been committed within a couple of miles of my family home. It was too close for comfort. In searching for my inner Perry Mason, Aiden and Hayley would see me glued to the television coverage, at times almost ready to kick the screen, as I exclaimed: 'Are you kidding me? Whose gonna fall for this rubbish? He did it … of course he did it.' The children were too young to understand exactly what was going on, but they understood Daddy was not at all happy with this naughty man on TV.

When the verdict came, I was playing Argentine Grand Slam champion Guillermo Vilas in a Champions Tour match in front of about 2,000 spectators at Hilton Head, South Carolina. Having watched so much of the trial, this was not where I wanted to be for the epic conclusion. It was one set all when there were unmistakable rumblings in the crowd. We stopped playing and I shouted: 'What's the verdict?' Hundreds hollered back: 'Not guilty!' I was devastated Simpson had got off. My focus had gone and I lost the match.

Later that year, during the festive season, I was with sweet little Hayley in the Fred Segal store on Santa Monica Boulevard when we turned to see the infamous OJ standing just five feet away from us. Hayley's big blue eyes were suddenly on stalks. Her jaw dropped. All that was missing was her tongue rolling from her mouth in the style of a Tom and Jerry cartoon. She was staring at OJ Simpson and he was staring right back. She was working it out. 'This is that man off the TV that Daddy used to get angry about.' She turned to me, turned back to the villain in our midst, and started to pronounce: 'You're a very bad …' I had to move fast to sweep her away before we heard Hayley's full verdict, one that could have led to a Christmas aisle showdown between Daddy and the bad man. Not long after that, I was playing golf at a public course in LA when Simpson – now something of a pariah at private clubs – was in the group playing immediately behind me. The smart-arsed guy I was playing with chimed up: 'I wonder if he slices the ball.'

Aiden and Hayley's schooldays were a million miles away from mine back in Southend, both in terms of quality and enjoyment. They started out in Santa Monica at Pluralistic School One, where the headteacher believed: 'It's not how smart a child is, it's how a child is smart.' The school thought outside the box and liked their pupils to do the same. Music icon Bruce Springsteen, who was searching for the best school for his children, liked the concept enough to spend a day testing the interaction there. It was Hayley's birthday and he wholeheartedly joined in the rendition of 'Happy Birthday to You'.

Hayley enjoyed writing stories. At PS1, she was allowed to create to her heart's content without constantly being picked up on things like spelling. That would be addressed at a later date. Her creativity had free rein. There were team sports but no winners or losers. Children learned to enjoy sport first, find the competitive spirit later. I had my doubts, coming from such a conventional set-up in England. But Aiden and Hayley loved it there and, remembering how much I hated my school life, I knew this progressive school had to be on to something to make youngsters feel this way about education. When my two moved on to high school, they were every bit as clever as the kids who had come through a more traditional route.

Their high school was Brentwood in Los Angeles, a private school renowned as the place where many Hollywood celebrities send their children. Deb and I were more concerned with finding the place where Hayley could blossom. Like me, she had a certain learning disability. In the public system, as I found to my cost all those years earlier, she might have been lost. Brentwood was a supremely supportive and nurturing place for her. By sending Hayley there, we were giving her a chance to shine.

We had to keep an eye on Aiden and Hayley, though. There were children at that school who had everything they ever wanted and more. Spoiled rotten, in other words. We didn't want that rubbing off on our kids in a negative way or for the material side of things to get out of hand. Thankfully, both surrounded themselves with good friends. But a run-of-the-mill experience, it most certainly was not.

Arnold Schwarzenegger and Maria Shriver's daughter came over to work on a project with Hayley. Arnie was Governor of California, so when Maria dropped her off there was a secret service guy with them. That was just bonkers when the kids were simply getting together to do a bit of homework. When we went to parties at the Schwarzenegger residence, we had to go through security checks. That was bizarre, too, but such was life at Brentwood.

Both Aiden and Hayley thrived on their opportunities, including their time on the tennis team alongside the children of actresses Sally Field and Cybill Shepherd. Former American player Brian Teacher and I helped out with Hayley's team: a former Australian Open champion and finalist uniting to give the school's tennis coach some support. We had an absolute blast.

Every year at the school's fundraiser, I would donate a two-hour tennis lesson and lunch at the Beverly Hills Country Club as my contribution. It usually went for about $3,000-4,000. I knew it was no average school function when Seal or members of Fleetwood Mac agreed to perform for the parents.

One year, the day after the fundraiser, I got a call from singer-songwriter Burt Bacharach. His voice was distinctive and unmistakable. I had met him a couple of times at tennis events, but we had never exchanged numbers so I thought it was a bit odd he had called me out of the blue. It was on the pretence of sounding me out about Brentwood. He was asking the wrong person. Deb was the one at the heart of what was going on there. I was on the road all the time. There had to be a catch to this conversation.

Sure enough, Burt got to the crux of the matter. He mentioned his wife had been outbid on my auction prize at the fundraiser, but that she very much enjoyed tennis and would like to play sometime. I'm thinking: 'You've got millions. Bid an extra 500 bucks and she'd have her wish.' He said maybe we could play at the club that coming weekend. I said: 'No, I actually don't do that kind of thing. I'm way too busy.' Burt was not impressed and hung up the phone.

Deb told me to deal with this kind of request differently in the future, to say: 'I'll happily play tennis with your wife if you don't mind coming over to sing at a cocktail party I'm having for a few friends next week.' There's no way he would do that for nothing. It's that delusional gene some celebrities possess: 'My time and skill comes at a price, but yours isn't really that valuable.'

Hayley valued her tennis education, but, after several years on the team and playing a few tournaments, decided it was no longer for her. When she told Deb, Hayley burst into tears, asking: 'Will Dad be devastated?' This is typical of my daughter. She's so adorable, so eager to please, she is always putting the feelings of others before her own. I have seen tennis parents that apply pressure on their kids verging on the diabolical. Although I had always wanted my children to enjoy tennis, I couldn't have cared less if they chose not to take it further. I told Hayley: 'I'm proud of you. Play tennis, tiddlywinks or nothing at all – it doesn't matter to me. It's your life. Just as long as you are happy.' She cried some more.

Aiden loved his team sports at Brentwood, be it American football, basketball or tennis doubles. He liked being part of a team and his infectious positive attitude meant team-mates wanted him around. One year he was given the Director's Award, voted for by all his schoolmates, and another year won an honour voted for by the faculty. That's how popular he was with his peers and his teachers. People have always been drawn to Aiden because of his spirit and his manner. He's a great listener and always one to offer smart advice. I've used him as my sounding board many a time in his adult life. He would have made a fine psychologist and, deep down, I believe he might like to have taken that career path.

We have certainly played amateur psychologist to each other through the years when talking about our beloved Wolverhampton Wanderers. Once upon a time, I'd watch Wolves on television early in the morning in the States with only our dog Flossy for company. But with Aiden I finally had another person with whom to share my football highs and lows: who got my passion for the game. We still discuss Wolves almost every day and I love how he refers to the club as 'we', as only true fans do.

Both he and Hayley have the gift, which not everyone possesses, of being able to talk to anyone of any age at any level and relate to them. I saw it when they worked as interns at Wimbledon during the Championships, I see it now they are adults with successful careers. Hayley had to grow into this more than her brother, emerging from her shyness to shine.

At high school, the older Aiden and Hayley became – certainly from 14 upwards – the more temptation was in their path. They would be invited to parties where parents were less strict than us and turned a blind eye to their children drinking alcohol. That's their family's choice, their house rules. But if we heard there might be drink on offer, we stopped our children from attending. We would get all the usual: 'It's not fair. All our friends are going.' Our reply: 'Tough. You are staying put.' Aiden would come to me, knowing I was the softer of his two parents and might cave in, but I explained: 'Mum and me are both on board with this.' To say we were unpopular in those moments is a gross understatement.

Deb had been intent on sharing her childhood troubles with them. She told them how it was entirely possible they might have the same addictive gene that afflicted her parents and that meant she was going to be very strict on them when it came to alcohol and other temptations likely to be laid before them. We had already seen signs Aiden might have a compulsive side to his nature. 'This is my job until you are adults,' she said. Until Aiden and Hayley graduated, this was the Lloyd family law and we upheld it as well as we knew how.

University life beckoned for both children. First Aiden cast his net. If he had got his way, he would have landed a big fish of a college many miles from home. He had told us he intended to go to a school as far away as possible from us, his parents. He was only half-joking. Hayley, on the other hand, had inherited my homesickness. Summer camps were a nightmare for her. Even sleepovers could be testing. She was a real homebody and I loved that about her. Hayley insisted she would only go to college in California. Daddy's girl wouldn't be far away and that was music to my ears.

Then, wouldn't you just know it, the exact opposite happened. Aiden ended up studying business at the University of Southern California – or USC for short – just a 25-minute drive from our family home. Hayley signed up for film school at Syracuse in the most northerly part of New York, clean across the other side of America. That place is cold compared to LA. Snow is a given. But Hayley never was very good in heat and humidity. Syracuse and its climate actually suited her. The homesickness? Not even a hint of it.

Again, she thrived. She had to find another way to tackle that learning disability she had overcome in the past. Rather wonderfully, Syracuse paid older students there to help her, making sure she didn't fall behind. She typically fought her way through. What a contrast to me and my learning problems, which I got out of by playing the fool at school. It was a stupid thing to do to pin everything on tennis when there was no real money in the game back then. I got lucky. Not Hayley. She took on the challenge and won through in a way I never could.

In his college days, Aiden was just down the road from us. University life seemed to agree with him, too. When we visited him, all appeared to be rosy. He looked fine. He acted normally. But Deb and me weren't aware of the full picture. Aiden made sure of that.

It evidently all began for Aiden in the process of trying to join a college fraternity – where rituals, often involving alcohol, form part of the initiation ceremony. His adult freedom brought access to the very temptations Deb had warned him about during his high-school years. Beyond the frat house drinking, there was drug-taking. Aiden acquired a taste for marijuana and his addictive nature took care of the rest. The bottom line was, he was doing a lot of that stuff and it was potent. We were oblivious.

He told his sister Hayley about his drug use before we had even an inkling. They were unbelievably close and he wanted to share this problem with her. But he told her that under no circumstances could she tell Deb and me. That was so unfair on Hayley but, of course, when Aiden was doing drugs the word 'fair' wasn't in his dictionary. Having to keep this secret was devastating for Hayley. Aside from the fear for his health, she also knew how much it was costing us to send him to college and he was abusing the privilege by skipping classes to get off his head on weed. He was bluffing a perfect college existence each time we saw him.

That could only go on so long, though. There was a change in him. Finally, Aiden admitted to us that he had a drug problem.

I think it blindsided him how quickly the problem escalated. He's an intelligent guy. I honestly think he didn't believe it would get hold of him in that way.

I am not a saint, but I have never taken drugs. I have never wanted to. But people that have tell me the kind of marijuana out there now is stronger than in days gone by: that if you have an addictive personality, this stuff will land you in trouble. Aiden was in big trouble. He was doing it so much during the day, his brain was basically fried.

He was failing to turn up for this, not showing up for that. His memory was shot. He was in bad shape ... really bad shape. The realisation was only now hitting us square in the face.

Aiden wasn't in denial. He knew he had a problem and he wanted to stop. We explored the possibility of getting him into rehab and he was on board for that. Hayley's relationship with her brother had been badly compromised. She had been aware of his drug use for some time and was distraught at having kept this secret from Deb and me, feeling she had let us down. But now was the time to come together as a family and try to fix this.

To see this fantastic kid abusing himself with a substance to the point he didn't know what day it was had a punishing effect on all of us. This was going to be rough for us, especially Aiden. That stuff stays in your system a long time, it wouldn't be easy to kick.

Deb did her research and sought out recommendations. We booked Aiden into a renowned rehab place in LA called Promises. There's a similar facility in Malibu. Both deal with mental health and addiction treatment. It was like another planet to me. Deb had been around addiction in her childhood, but this kind of thing had never impacted on my life before. All I knew for certain was that my son was in trouble.

The caring staff at Promises outlined what they would do to treat Aiden, without dancing around any of the issues. They were blunt. They spelled out that it was going to be extremely tough. Aiden was nervous. This was a frightening prospect but he was brave enough to know it was essential to stopping his addiction.

It was explained to us that during this first phase of treatment 'You are not going to be here. He's going to be in our hands.' We could visit, but only when they said so. In that moment, it sounded ridiculous. Your first instinct as a parent is to think: 'No. Aiden needs us now more than ever. We have to be with him.'

This is what they called a 'safe period' for us. The Aiden entering rehab wasn't the Aiden we knew. He was agitated, he was angry. At times, he was a little scary. This young adult standing before us, barely out of his teenage years, was our son; was Hayley's brother. And yet, in personality, he wasn't. It was the strangest feeling.

'This three-month period is your safe period,' we were assured. 'You know he's getting the best care, the proper treatment and you are not in harm's way.' Much as it jarred with me initially, I soon realised they were right.

The day came to admit Aiden to Promises. At that point, it was categorically the worst day of my life. Deb had experienced some rough days in her upbringing, but I know this was simply the worst day ever for her and Hayley, too. We stood together as a family in the face of our fears. We knew we had to do this, but it was agony.

We filled out forms and carried out the formalities. Other men and women in there were peering at us, almost with knowing looks of empathy and appreciation. They had all been through this fearful process, too.

We were made aware Aiden was to share a room with a 40-year-old man coming down off heroin. A heroin addict? Our son's room-mate? Aiden still seemed like a kid to me. Where had this come from: my child in this situation? This was our shocking reality.

Then it came to saying goodbye. I remember looking at Aiden and seeing fear etched on his face. That's when the overwhelming questions hit me: what had we done wrong? Weren't we meant to protect our kids? Is this my fault?

We had a long walk to the car park, Deb, Hayley and me. We were emotional to the point of hysterical. I reiterate, it was the worst day of my life. But only to that point. I didn't think anything could feel worse. I was wrong.

The only option in the immediate aftermath of Aiden's admission seemed to be lots of crying and to spend all day thinking about what he was going through. That was going to help precisely no one. If we couldn't be there to protect him, maybe we could be proactive and find a way to protect ourselves through this terrifying process.

We visited a support centre that offered help and counselling to families of addicts. During our first time there, we sat in a room of maybe 30 people with a mediator controlling proceedings. He would invite family members to stand up and share their stories. I was uncomfortable from the outset, looking round for the exit door and thinking: 'There's no way I can do this.' I was mortified at the prospect of letting myself reveal the most private side of me in front of a bunch of strangers.

One parent stood up and told how his son was on heroin and had almost died. The next woman said her husband was an alcoholic who regularly abused her. Famous faces shared experiences that illustrated this kind of suffering can affect anyone from any walk of life.

Other parents told how they had to pack their son's bags and kick him out of the house, admitting: 'As far as we know, he's still living on the streets.'

'There's not a chance in hell I'm ever going to do that,' I thought. 'How utterly heartless.'

Then the attention turned to us. Deb spoke first and, like all those that had gone before, broke down in tears. I did the same thing when it was my time to speak. Our emotional state wasn't helped by the mediator telling us that rehab and treatment programmes don't always work: that in the first six weeks after treatment, a loved one coming out of rehab is 70 per cent likely to reoffend. They were brutally honest in that regard; this was no time for sugar-coating. We needed to hear this if we were to find a way out of the abyss.

We learnt so much in this remarkable place. It became our therapy sanctuary. The most important message for me was when the mediator said that what Aiden was enduring 'is not your fault'. They enforced this to all of us and it became a kind of mantra: 'Do not blame yourself. This is not your fault.' When all I wanted to do was blame myself, this was crucial to me trying to eradicate those thoughts. They would never let up on this, declaring: 'If a loved one overdoses and dies, it is not your fault. If you have to throw them out on the streets, it is not your fault. Do not blame yourself.'

Deb was stronger than me throughout all this – a lot stronger. I eventually got there, but only when the support centre taught me that this need I had to protect and help my son could more likely make me an enabler. You feel like you can help, when what you are actually doing is the opposite and making things worse. That was a tough lesson for me to learn.

After a while, I started to look forward to these meetings because it became a place of strength. We were all in it together. We could share and learn together. Alcohol and drug addictions don't discriminate and they affect more people than I ever thought, across all areas of society. I wasn't abnormal or alone.

Some of us would go for pizza after meetings, often just to chat about normal life. But even then, stories would emerge that would stop you in your tracks. Some parents talked candidly about how their drug-addicted children were dying before their eyes. One couple revealed their son had been watching their house until they left, then tried to barge in on his 14-year-old brother, banging and screaming to let him in. We learned that it doesn't matter who you are, if substance abuse takes over it is the most terrible, horrifying ordeal.

We visited Aiden when we were given permission. Even early on, I could see he looked healthier. He made friends in there and we got to know a lot of the other addicts being treated alongside him. It became a kind of family. Most importantly, Aiden was receiving the help he needed.

The next phase of treatment involved Aiden staying in the equivalent of a halfway house, where he could be monitored but had more freedom. This would be the precursor to him returning to the family home.

As that time got closer, the experts at Promises advised us that the best way to proceed when Aiden returned home was to have him sign a contract. Basically, it would comprise a list of house rules – curfews, drug testing, that kind of thing. They insisted we would have to be tough. If Aiden broke his contract, we would have to pack his bags and kick him out. 'If you don't,' we were told, 'you will be enabling him and his addiction.'

I was still haunted by this. I had been made fully aware that if you keep giving in to addicts, they will keep taking from you. It doesn't matter how much they love you or you love them. They can't help themselves. They are addicts first, your children second. And yet I was still fighting this all the way.

It caused problems between Deb and me. The last thing we needed was to be torn apart by this. Again, I had learned from our group sessions that if you don't stick together, addicts find the weaker of the two and put pressure on that person to give them what they want or need, be it money or a bending of the rules. I had to boldly buy into this or we were all in trouble.

Aiden returned home to live with us. He looked better, but he was different. This still wasn't the son we once knew. We told him we wanted him to sign a contract of house rules and he got angry, really angry. His demeanour was threatening, his language was abusive and I felt things were going to turn physical. For the first time, I looked at my son and was almost scared of him. I realised there was still this shit coming out of his system and we still had work to do. He chose not to fight. He did sign the contract.

This is where the knowledge we had collected at the support centre was invaluable. They said we had to take ourselves out of the equation as much as possible. So, when Aiden was angry about the contract, verbally attacking us, we knew what to say to help defuse the situation. It was words to the effect of: 'This is all new to us. Do you think we know what to do? Do you think these ideas are ours? No, it's what the experts have told us to do – experts who have been dealing with this for years. If you have a problem, take it up with them.' This took a lot of pressure off us.

Small pieces of this would sink in for Aiden. But it wasn't automatic, not with his system still fighting his demons. He did start to figure it out, though, and there were signs of improvement and progress along the way. But we were walking an uncertain path, often one sprinkled with eggshells. We decided a few days away in Palm Springs might help, especially as my parents were in town.

We hadn't told them about Aiden's addiction. They just wouldn't have understood. Dad was teetotal and anti cigarettes after his father, a 60-a-day man, died from lung cancer. Dad found my brother David smoking once and gave him a good hiding. It was best we kept Aiden's trouble away from them, although while we were there it was tricky because he wasn't behaving well. He was agitated. He was secretive. The signs were not good.

When we got home, Deb said to me: 'You're going to have to test him.'

'What do you mean?'

'Listen, you know something's going on as well as I do. You've got to drug test him.'

We rang a counsellor at Promises for advice. He said we needed to buy a drug-testing kit from the store and, when Aiden returned home, do the following: 'Meet him outside. Tell him what you want him to do. Make sure he doesn't go upstairs on his own as some addicts have a stock of someone else's urine. Watch him urinate, then wait a couple of minutes for the test result.'

I said: 'I'm not going to do that. I just can't.'

'Well, you wanted to know. That's what you have to do if you want to test him.'

Only after another heated argument with Deb did I eventually relent and agree to test my son.

Aiden was due back home about 3pm. I was counting down the minutes, dreading what was to come. Seconds felt like hours. It was agony. If he failed this test, I would be forced to tell him to leave the house. I could barely comprehend it: 'Here's your suitcase – now go.' Forget what had gone before, this now ranked as the worst day of my life.

Three o'clock came. Against all my fatherly instincts, I had to do this. I headed him off in the driveway.

'What's up, Pops?'

'Well … to be honest, we are a bit worried. You've been agitated lately and …'

He looked me straight in the eye and said: 'You need to test me, don't you?' I nodded.

'I understand,' he said. 'I'm gonna pass … but I understand.'

I had heard so much and seen even more about the traits of addicts that even now I didn't know if he was telling me the truth. Could he, would he, even now, try to talk me out of it on the walk to the bathroom?

Thankfully, Aiden was as good as his word. We went upstairs to the bathroom. I watched him take the store-bought drugs test. Then we waited.

What was it with time that day? The seconds again ticked away so desperately slowly. Until … eventually … finally … we had our reading.

It was negative. Aiden had passed the test.

The worst day of my life had turned into the greatest day of my life. I can't effectively put into words what this meant to me and my family. We were not out of the woods. Of course we weren't. But on that momentous day I knew my son was not being turned out onto the streets. It was a win, win, win.

From then onwards, it got progressively better. Aiden was tested regularly and never failed one. He would return home at the time he promised. He did not have even one strike against his name.

The day would arrive when he was able to return to university – and this is where my newfound admiration for my son took hold. Though abuse of marijuana had been Aiden's issue, we discovered that his addictive nature was such he could just as easily turn to drink. He was back in an environment where alcohol and drugs were readily available to him, where his friends were partying hard, and yet he never once fell off the wagon.

I remember being in the car with him and his friends in the early days of his recovery. He took a call from another student from his college, who was having similar problems and was seeking advice. I was driving, Aiden was in the back with his pals. I don't think he was aware I was listening in when he said: 'Here's the deal. Marijuana makes me stupid – and I don't want to be stupid anymore. It's that simple. I have no interest in it anymore. My advice is don't do it. If you need anything, call me.'

Aiden wasn't saying this for my benefit. It was from the heart and I knew right then this was a fight he was going to win. But, as they teach you in the support group, you are never cured. Once an addict, always an addict. It's about making the right choices and Aiden continues to do that. He's a great spokesperson, in fact, for the rehab system he came through and is only too happy to share his story if it can help someone in need, which is why he agreed to me writing about it here.

Aiden went on to work for huge companies like Google and Airbnb. The fact he has enjoyed success in the business world is testament to his strength when, once again, there can be temptations at every turn at corporate functions.

I hear people talk about making certain drugs legal: that 'a bit of marijuana can't hurt'. That might be the case if you don't have an addictive character. But if you do, marijuana is dangerous. It can take control of you. I have seen it with my own eyes. I have seen it turn a bright, popular and likeable young adult into an altogether different being.

Aiden has been clean for more than a decade. It's a tremendous feat. He took on an immense challenge and, with landmines all around him, came through it. I couldn't be more in awe.

But then that goes for both my children. They refused to let the dark times destroy them. Aiden's relationship with Hayley repaired itself and they are now back to being as close as a brother and sister could ever wish to be. It gives me immense pleasure to know their special bond is eternal. They will always be there for each other. My respect for them is boundless. My love for them is endless.

There's huge pride, too, of course, in that both have gone on to enjoy successful careers. Each is on track financially, so much so that I always tell them they will have plenty of money to put me in a luxurious retirement home down the road, where I can be waited on hand and foot. They say: 'Absolutely, Dad. We think you're almost ready now.' (I think they're saying it in jest.)

Hayley's wedding last year was a joyful day, but not quite as she had once imagined. That's because she had a Zoom wedding day, marrying Dan in front of a handful of in-person guests, while over 100 more tuned in online. This was some much-needed light relief as we emerged from the Covid pandemic. Mind you, there were tears as well. I couldn't get through my speech dry-eyed. But then I'm someone who shed tears watching the *Friends* reunion, so there was never any hope for me on my daughter's wedding day.

Now Hayley and Dan have given me the joy of a first grandchild: a beautiful baby boy.

Deb is the go-to person for babysitting, though, not me. I can spoil him, do tons of fun things with him. I can introduce him to the greatest sports in the world: tennis and football. And I mean proper football. That's the one with the round ball, played with feet and not, as Americans like to think, the one with an oval ball that's thrown and carried. We will hopefully have another Wolverhampton Wanderers fan in the family, joining Aiden and me. But when it comes to changing nappies? No. I'm no nearer being an expert diaper-changer than I was decades ago with my own kids. The poor lad is likely to end up with a nappy on his head if it's left to me. Deb and Hayley will fully understand. It was ever the way.

Hayley will be a wonderful mum. Of that, I have no doubt. And Aiden will make a great dad when he starts a family with his lovely wife Sheyda, who he married in the spring of this year.

Actor Mike Myers summed it up best when he said: 'Anyone who tells you fatherhood is the greatest thing that can happen to you, they are understating it.'

Dear Aiden and Hayley,

Parents are quite selfish if you think about it. We choose to bring you into the world. You have no say in it at all. Then you are stuck with us. I hope you haven't found it too taxing being stuck with me because I have loved being a dad to you.

You have been the pride of my life.

All My Love,

Pops

CELEBRITY

A letter from the John Lloyd of today to his former self, offering advice on the fame game.

Dear John,

Celebrity is a strange thing. It doesn't matter how much you try to grow accustomed to the attention, it never feels anything but weird. Actress Lauren Bacall once said 'stardom isn't a profession; it's an accident'. That's worth remembering, as is the fact that you chose this career path. You knew what it might bring. Don't start complaining about it now.

It's best not to waste time trying to get a handle on fame. You won't work it out. Instead, just go with the flow. Keep your head down when the going gets tough. Make the most of the opportunities when celebrity opens a new door for you.

The good news is, you will have a taste of fame on your own in Britain before it goes to a whole new level when you marry globally renowned Chris Evert. This early experience will help you more than you can ever imagine.

You will find perks and pitfalls along the celebrity way. You will meet and work with some remarkable people, none more famous and beloved than Princess Diana. Your orbit will suddenly include movie stars like Dustin Hoffman, sporting icons like Michael Jordan and private cinema viewings with A-listers at the mansion of country music legend Kenny Rogers. Enjoy these moments because, unfortunately, there will be times when fame will lead to uncomfortable intrusion in your private life.

John

PRINCESS DIANA electrified any room she entered. I had the honour and pleasure of meeting her several times and absolutely adored her. But the way my two ex-wives acted in front of Diana might be the reason I have never been recognised in the Queen's Honours' List. See what you think.

The first time I met the Princess was alongside my first wife Chris Evert, not long after Diana had married Prince Charles. Diana was still extremely shy at that stage, but no one in the world commanded more attention. I coached Chrissie and she had just played and won on Centre Court at Wimbledon, watched by Diana – who offered an invitation to both of us to meet her. We were delighted to accept and waited at the foot of the steps from the Royal Box.

Americans love the royal family but don't necessarily understand the traditions and protocol attached to meeting them. People from the States are very open and more likely to be on the front foot than take a backward step. 'Hey, Diana, how ya doin'?' might come spewing out, whereas we Brits would be more like:

'Better not talk until I'm spoken to, must remember to bow or curtsey, doff my cap, make sure there's no spinach in my teeth.' Worry, worry, worry, in other words.

Diana walked down the stairs accompanied by one of her security guards, with Chrissie standing just in front of me. Before I had a chance to take stock of the regal situation, Chrissie dived in with: 'Thanks for coming out to watch today.' I'm already bowing behind my wife, thinking: 'Oh my God, she should have waited until she was asked a question or something.'

Diana said: 'It was my pleasure. It's nice to see you play.'

Chrissie responded with: 'What about your husband. How come Charles isn't here?'

I was having another OMG moment.

'Well, he doesn't really like tennis that much,' the Princess explained.

Chrissie said: 'Tell him that's not a very good excuse and that I expect him to be here the next time I play.'

'Oh no! What did you say that for?' was my next OMG thought, before Diana was led away with me having said nothing very much at all.

Some years later, Diana was officially opening one of my brother David's tennis and leisure clubs in Raynes Park, London. The Princess watched us play an exhibition match after which there was a cocktail party where Diana would meet as many of the patrons as she could. I was now married to another American, Deborah, who was so nervous about the prospect of meeting royalty that she researched the correct etiquette for being introduced to a princess.

Diana was on the other side of the room from where we were standing. Deb, who was dressed beautifully in anticipation of this seismic moment, was twitchy with nerves. About 40 minutes went by and Deb grew increasingly frustrated and nervous, thinking our turn to meet the Princess might never come. In the end, I think she believed that might be the better option. Anxious Deb was ready with her excuses: 'She'll be tired, maybe we should just go and leave her to it. Come on, let's go.'

Deb was facing away from where Diana stood, but I could see the Princess. 'It'll be fine,' I said. 'Just wait.' No sooner had I uttered those words than Diana was there at my side. She had covered the floor far quicker than I expected. I didn't have the chance to warn Deb she was heading our way, let alone tell her she had arrived.

Deb turned sharply and saw the Princess right in front of her. 'Oh, hellooo!' Deb announced in a forceful American welcome, blurting out the first thing that came into her head. It wouldn't have surprised me had Diana's minder pounced at this point. Deb then tried to curtsey – or was it a bow? It ended up a hybrid of the two, causing her to almost topple over. So much for the etiquette research. 'That's the OBE recommendation gone again,' I thought.

Princess Diana used to have tennis lessons at a now defunct place called the Vanderbilt Racquet Club, where I also had the honour of meeting her a couple of times. There were fewer tennis facilities in those days. My brother's clubs were just emerging, but until they appeared in and around London you had Queen's Club, the All England Club and draughty places like the Vanderbilt in a chilly hangar by Shepherd's Bush. Each encounter there was enough to warm the heart. Diana was nothing short of a delight. She was taken from the world tragically early and, though I joke about the OBE thing, I couldn't be more serious when I say

One of the few singles matches at Wimbledon where I actually played well. On court no 1, I managed a win against the number 4 seed Roscoe Tanner.

My loss to Vitas Gerulaitis in the 1977 Australian Open finals. Shorts definitely short in those days.

Myself, brother Dave, Mark Cox and Buster Mottram before the Davis Cup Final in 1978 against the USA.

Relaxing with the great Bjorn Borg.

What was billed as The Love Doubles, where Chris Evert and myself took on Bjorn Borg and Mariana Simionescu at Battersea Park in 1980.

Partnering with Wendy Turnbull for our first Wimbledon mixed doubles title in 1983.

Being interviewed by Richard Williams at Wimbledon for a video he was making. Still haven't seen it.

Commentating on a Wimbledon final with Andrew Castle and Jimmy Connors.

Family time in the 90s with Deborah, Aiden and Hayley.

My parents Dennis and Doris, with Aiden, Hayley and Flossy.

With my beautiful girlfriend Svetlana Carroll.

My lovely daughter Hayley.

The Lloyd clan, Dennis, Doris, Anne, Dave and Tony.

With Aiden and Hayley at my favourite tournament, Indian Wells, California.

Me and Aiden at Hayley's wedding.

My lovely daughter, now Mrs Pine.

Love chilling out with Aiden.

Princess Diana possessed something special ... the ability to light up a room with her presence alone.

Fame impacts in various ways. Diana was the most famous person on the planet and her death came amid a paparazzi frenzy. Others become famous for one thing, then notorious for another. American comedian Bill Cosby is a prime example. His American sitcom was huge and when I went to watch him in his stand-up show he was hilarious. More recently, he was embroiled in a scandal, where he was jailed for aggravated indecent assault but later cleared of all charges on appeal. I used to play lots of celebrity tennis events with him and he was a half-decent player, but he was as arrogant as all hell. He was so opinionated, insisting I was coaching my then wife Chrissie all wrong. He said I had the worst game plan for Chrissie to beat Martina Navratilova and told me what I should be coaching her to do. Here was a jumped-up comedian with delusions of tennis grandeur. What an idiot.

It's so funny what celebrity can do to a person. Okay, he could hit a few tennis balls out of the centre of his racket. But Cosby suddenly believed his own hype to the point he truly believed he knew the best way for Chris Evert to defeat Martina Navratilova. Now that's a classic ego trip. Cosby, however, was not the only one.

Dustin Hoffman, an Oscar-winning actor blessed with enormous talent in that tiny frame of his, used to play tennis with me and had some misguided views on women's tennis. He was 100 per cent convinced he could beat Steffi Graf, the amazing German talent with 22 Grand Slam singles titles to her stellar name. Dustin was an average tennis player at best and I would tell him: 'You wouldn't get a single game off Steffi. There's no way.' He wouldn't have it. In his head, he would beat her every day and twice on Sundays. Truly mind-boggling what a fame-fuelled ego can do to a person.

Fame for Elton John seemingly had a devastating effect on his eyesight. I have been privileged to see him in concert and know him to be a top bloke. Sir Elton is known for his trademark glasses, of course. The ones he wore on court were somewhat less outlandish than his 70s collection – and I'm not altogether sure he had the right sort of prescription lenses in them. That's because when I played him on a scorching hot day at the Beverly Hills Country Club in LA, Elton would see balls that were clearly out as in and vice versa. Once or twice I could accept, but eight or nine times? That's just plain cheating. Then I thought, 'A nice guy like Elton, he surely wouldn't do that to me.' Therefore, I had to conclude it was a problem with his specs.

Celebrity was playing tricks on him again, most likely. Get your own way often enough and you think that's the way it will always be, whatever the endeavour. The reality is that Elton couldn't win a game off me in a thousand years if I didn't want him to – bad calls or not. He should perhaps look (if he can see that far) to Sir Cliff Richard, who loves his tennis but accepts his limitations. He's a great guy, Cliff, but has absolutely no tennis talent whatsoever. If he could find the strings of the racket, he would be dangerous. But he plays the game for the pure enjoyment he gets from it, not the misguided belief he can seriously challenge the professionals.

What some of the celebrities I played against didn't realise was that I could put them in hospital with just one shot to the forehead. They would never want to play tennis again if I hadn't let up on them. But you see, that's what it's all about. When pros play amateurs, we go easy on them. We call it customer tennis. When they play you in half-cocked mode like that, they start believing they can win games against you. It's the most extraordinary thing.

The late country music great Kenny Rogers hired Kelly Junkerman, a full-time tennis pro, to hone his tennis skills at his magnificent mansions and also took him on tour. One of my best mates, movie producer Ron Samuels, and I used to play doubles regularly with Kenny and Kelly. We always made it close and competitive, in the ballpark of 7-5, 7-5. Kenny became so enamoured with the game and read so much into these 'competitive' matches that he thought he was good enough to play in a professional event.

Famous American comedian Alan King ran a big tournament at Caesars Palace in Las Vegas – the Alan King Classic. It was the primo event on tour as far as the players were concerned thanks to the excellent prize money, the quality of the free food and wine and the star-studded fancy dress party. Kenny Rogers asked King for a wild-card entry into the qualifying event for the doubles tournament. My pal Ron said to Kenny: 'What the hell? Are you in a coma?'

'No, no. We play well against you and John,' said Kenny.

'That's because I'm not a pro and John's being nice.'

Kenny and Kelly took their wild-card place, spent what must have felt like five minutes on court and didn't win a single game; 6-0, 6-0: celebrity delusion had struck again.

I would never have wished that for Kenny. He was a great guy and was always so generous of spirit to me. Playing regularly at Kenny's mansion in Beverly Hills was always a joy. Once we got to know each other well, I was fortunate enough to be included on his exclusive movie list. As a film fanatic, this was heaven for me. Twice a week, Kenny's secretary would send out invitations to about 100 of his closest friends to attend seven o'clock viewings of films that had yet to hit the cinema.

Driving up to the mansion, there was a petrol pump – you know, just in case you wanted to fill your car up on the way to the door. Extraordinary. I would pull up to a cinema theatre, built separate from the main house, where huge reclining lounge chairs, buckets of popcorn, M&M's by the sackload and countless fizzy drinks awaited the guests. No sooner had I taken my seat than celebrities like Lionel Richie would show up. 'Hello!' indeed. Next to arrive: Dolly Parton. It was surreal. I love movies, I love popcorn and I love watching films in peace. With the added fun of celebrity spotting, I couldn't have asked for more.

Kenny Rogers would play tennis at least a couple of hours a day, sometimes heading straight off court to his private jet, before flying off to a concert. He would land as the warm-up acts were on stage, arrive at the venue in perfect time for his performance, fly back and be home before midnight 100 grand richer. Kelly Junkerman was his loyal tennis buddy for decades, eventually producing and appearing in movies himself – and having a hand in creating the *Kenny Rogers'Classic Weekend* TV show.

Kenny had such power in the music industry at the time, in the late 80s, that his concept for a celebrity entertainment/sports special was picked up by American network television and filmed at his Beaver Dam Farm near Athens, Georgia. There were music performances by Kenny and such stars as Gladys Knight, combined with tennis, basketball, golf and fishing competitions: admittedly a strange combination. Kenny's place was so vast –

it had a lake, nine golf holes, tennis and basketball courts, the lot – he could stage everything there. It was the most amazing place I had ever seen, complete with indoor Jacuzzi for Arabian stallions and a heated driveway in a southern state where ice is hardly an issue.

There were four teams, each containing an actor/singer, a tennis player, a golfer and a basketball player. The entertainers were Kenny, Woody Harrelson, Kris Kristofferson and James Caan, who starred in my favourite movies of all time, *The Godfather I & II.* The incredible Michael Jordan led the basketball quartet, joined by Larry Bird, Dominique Wilkins and Isaiah Thomas. The golfers were Raymond Floyd, Hubert Green, Payne Stewart and Lanny Wadkins. I was in a tennis foursome completed by John McEnroe, 1985 Wimbledon finalist Kevin Curren and 1986 French Open finalist Mikael Pernfors.

My ex-wife Deb was about seven months pregnant at the time and, for a small woman, she was big: like she had swallowed four basketballs. Kenny was kind enough to invite us to stay in his house, along with a few of the other 'contestants' – the basketball players included. Deb was nauseous, trying to eat a few morsels at breakfast, when the NBA stars came down and started demolishing every bit of food in sight. They were harpooning six pancakes at once and devouring the stack; the lazy Susan had that much rotation it resembled a roulette wheel. The sight of four Fred Flintstones scoffing so much food made Deb increasingly sick, while the maid serving us was kept on her toes for a good hour. We had never seen such a volume consumed.

The bottomless pits of men were good to go for the first event of the day: basketball. I had never played in my life. We Brits grow up with football, of course, so booting rather than bouncing a ball was my thing. The first game was against Michael Jordan's team. He was heading to the height of his powers with the Chicago Bulls, on his way to a decade of NBA domination. Twice I got the ball, twice I bounced it with two hands. My captain, Dominique Wilkins of the Atlanta Hawks, said: 'That's a foul you fool. You're only meant to bounce it with one hand at a time.' You could almost see him thinking: 'Great. Thanks for giving me this idiot.'

Wilkins instructed me to do one thing: guard golfer Raymond Floyd. 'What does that mean?' I asked.

'Don't let him have the ball,' he replied indignantly.

'Oh, mark him. Got ya.' Now Wilkins had it confirmed I was about as useful to his basketball team as a chocolate teapot.

'Okay, he's got a bit of a gut ... I can manage to mark Floyd out of the game,' I thought. The problem was, we all had to have a shot at the basket at some point. Jordan and Wilkins were nailing everything for the Red Team. Kenny Rogers, on my White Team, faked MJ – at least, I think that's what they call it – and sank a fantastic shot to get the crowd right into it. This indoor arena was in Kenny's mansion, remember. Meantime, I'm hanging around Floyd like I've got a rash I'm keen for him to catch.

Wilkins then tells me I have to shoot and my heart sinks. Jordan is about five feet away from me when I receive the ball. Rather than try to stop me, he lets me have the space to take a shot. He wants me to take a shot. He wants me to humiliate myself. 'No f***ing way, man,' he says as I take aim. I threw the basketball without fear of failure, thinking 'I'll show him.' It flew about 100 miles an hour, smacked the backboard, clattered the rim and shot into the crowd. Cue the laughter from the audience and my opponents. Dare I say it, even from my team-mates. MJ, the greatest player of all time, chimed up: 'I told you. No f***ing way, man.'

Tennis was next. Brilliant. I could instantly redeem myself, although I had to learn one lesson very quickly. Don't try to lob the NBA players. Not only are they giants but they can leap ridiculously high and slam dunk tennis balls almost as well as basketballs. We had a serving competition for the professional players, with $10,000 going to the winner. I won it, much to McEnroe's annoyance. He said: 'I'll give you another ten grand if you don't tell anyone you beat me.' I did and, therefore, he didn't.

Golf came next and, as with basketball, I was a novice. Though I would eventually play more golf the older I got, at this point I was raw and rubbish. A penny for Dominique Wilkins's thoughts as he discovered this. Hubert Green was the pro golfer on our team. He looked at me play and simply said: 'Oh, shit!'

The golf was an alternate shot competition with each of the four team members taking it in turns to hit the ball. We were warming up on the practice range, when these numbskull spectators started encroaching. They lined up either side of where we were hitting, creating a sort of 'fan funnel' you might see at professional events. Did this lot have a death wish or something? They were just feet away and had no comprehension quite how bad I was. Wilkins wasn't much better.

Now, I didn't know much about golf other than a) I was very poor at it, and b) I knew a wedge was a good choice of club to get some elevation. I might not get the ball far with a wedge, but I could maybe get it high enough not to put someone in hospital. Then I spotted Wilkins with a driver in his hand. He clearly didn't give a crap. This towering man suddenly belted the ball with all his might. Smack! It hit one poor woman in the leg and she fell tenpin-style. Medics were called. Our team finished last in golf.

The final event was fishing. Yes, fishing. Not the most televisual of sports, this one. I had never been angling in my life. Did I mention that, outside of tennis, I was a completely worthless member of this team? No wonder Kenny didn't ask me back the following year. For now, though, he was gracious enough to say: 'Don't worry about a thing, John. This is my lake. I know where the fish are. You're coming with me.'

So, I was on Kenny's boat thinking, 'We will have this one sewn up in no time.' The camera crew came with us, believing they would get the most action thanks to our host's inside knowledge. An hour later, all I had caught were a few weeds. Over the other side of the lake, Jordan had an armful of fish. We came last in fishing, too. What a weekend, though. It's one I will never forget: made possible by the King of Country Kenny Rogers.

Another celebrity sporting competition I had more success at was the John F. Kennedy Pro-Celebrity tennis event at Forest Hills, New York, which preceded the US Open there each year in the 70s. Ethel Kennedy and Ted Kennedy were the hosts and it was a big deal, shown on national television in the US. The players loved it because we were treated unbelievably well and were intrigued to be surrounded by stars from other walks of life, such as Jacqueline Kennedy Onassis, Elton John, Charlton Heston, Bill Cosby and Burt Bacharach. Muhammad Ali used to come along to watch. Actor Gene Wilder, Willie Wonka himself, was one of my favourite partners. He was just one of the most charming men I have ever met. Olympic champion decathlete Bruce Jenner was the opposite. I sometimes wonder if he's less egotistical now he is she: since Bruce became Caitlyn.

I was about 22 and – as my profession dictated – spending lots of time on the road. I met this lovely girl that year (let's call her 'Melissa') and took her to a tournament in Hawaii. We had some fun times together. We got along well and she was beautiful. But only later did I find out that she had a thing for wealthy men and had dated quite a few of them. I wasn't wealthy by any means, but she was all over me like a cheap coat. Perhaps she thought all tennis pros earned big bucks.

We were chatting away in the hotel room one day when she revealed she had been in an on-off relationship with Senator Ted Kennedy. I had met him the year before at the JFK event. One morning, the telephone rang and I picked it up. I recognised the voice instantly. It was Ted Kennedy asking to speak to Melissa. I put her on.

'What was that about?' I asked.

'Oh, he was just wondering how I was. He's good like that.'

Our brief relationship had come to an end by the time I played in the next JFK event the following year, again staged at Forest Hills. If there was one celebrity you didn't want to be paired with in the doubles it was Oleg Cassini. Guess who drew the short straw this particular year?

Cassini was an American fashion icon, the grandson of a Russian-Italian Count and designer for Jackie Kennedy when she was First Lady. The 'Jackie Look' immortalised him in the design world, but he was also lauded in Hollywood, creating costumes for stars like Audrey Hepburn, Marilyn Monroe, Veronica Lake, Rita Hayworth, Joan Crawford and Natalie Wood. He had relationships with many of the actresses he designed for –

marrying Gene Tierney in the 1940s and becoming engaged to Grace Kelly in the 50s. When Kelly later married Prince Rainier of Monaco, Cassini was quoted as saying: 'Grace told me she would rather be a princess than a countess.' Apparently, he was more accustomed to getting his own way.

All the pros that had played alongside Cassini at the JFK event in Queen's said he was the biggest arsehole on court; that you couldn't have any fun with him; that he took it all too seriously. His favourite saying was: 'Better than most – second to none.' He was so proud that he had won the Forest Hills event in 1976. Yet it was all meant to be a fun, sometimes downright comedic, charity knockabout.

Cassini approached me on the morning of the event and said: 'I know all the celebrities we are up against. We've got the best team. We're going to win this.' The victorious professional was to receive a jet ski, which was worth a lot of money. I decided if I had to play alongside someone so intense, I might as well try to come away with something at the end of it.

We were up first against Donald Rumsfeld, who was US Secretary of Defense under President Gerald Ford and who later returned to that role under President George W. Bush. Whatever your politics, I have to say Rumsfeld was a lovely guy, but he couldn't play tennis. He held the racket like it was a frying pan.

Cassini was in his 60s, but this was a former Italian Davis Cup junior. He could play. After just a couple of games, he crossed in front of me and swatted the ball at Rumsfeld, hitting his arm … hard. He meant business and I was mortified. It got worse in the quarter-finals when we faced Clark 'Superman' Graebner, a former Wimbledon semi-finalist and US Davis Cup winner, and his celebrity partner Cheryl Tiegs, the supermodel who adorned so many covers of the *Sports Illustrated* swimsuit issue. I had played a tournament with her the year before and she was lovely. But, as with Rumsfeld, her level of tennis wasn't great so we would have to go easy on her. Or so I thought.

We were live on national television. Cassini told me: 'I know you know Cheryl and that she's pretty and nice, but we've got to win this thing.'

'We couldn't lose this match if I turned around and played backwards,' I snapped back. 'Impossible. Let's go easy.'

We were four-love ahead in a first-to-five contest when Cassini again crossed in front of me at the net and smacked the ball into Cheryl's stomach. She was winded and on the ground. The crowd started booing. I had been paired with a right ruthless Count. I was holding my hands up, mouthing: 'It's not me.' They didn't want to recognise that fact. My playing partner was an ultra-competitive ass, therefore I was tarred with the same brush.

We ended up in the final against Senator Ted Kennedy and Mexico's Raul Ramirez, world number four in singles in 1976 and one of the best doubles players that ever lived. Ted, like Cassini, was a win-at-all-costs kind of guy, but he was nowhere near as good as Count Oleg. Our opponents' tactics? Ted and his gut would hang a foot from the net, racket up, looking for rain, swatting anything in his arc. Raul would run around like a jack-rabbit on acid. Apart from having to serve, Ted was doing pretty much nothing, in the firm belief Raul alone could clinch the family prize. It was difficult to hit the ball Ted's way because, the way the senator was standing, there was every chance of hitting him, on the head most likely. I was tempted, but we were already the most hated duo in Queen's after the Cheryl Tiegs stomach scandal so I resisted. Ramirez kept hitting the ball to

Cassini, who – great as he thought he was – couldn't live with one of the world's best, and inevitable defeat followed. Actor and comedian Buddy Hackett, voice of Scuttle in *The Little Mermaid*, saw what had played out and said to me: 'You are such a gentleman, John.'

'Don't say that, Buddy. You don't know how close I was to smacking Ted. If he hadn't been a senator, I swear I'd be the proud owner of a new jet ski right now.'

That night at the post-event dinner, Senator Kennedy was greeting guests in the receiving line. As I shook his hand, he leaned in and whispered: 'She's a nice lady, isn't she?'

Even though I was no longer with Melissa, he was aware of our history and not afraid to acknowledge I almost certainly knew about his relationship with her.

'She is indeed, Senator. She is indeed.'

It was when I was married to Chris Evert that the impact of fame was at its peak for me. We were on the cover of *People Magazine* in the States: the so-called golden couple. Reporters and photographers always wanted a piece of us. We had a house in Kingston, England and much of the time press were hanging around the place. They couldn't come right up to the house, but they could get close enough to take photos of us inside the property to the point we had to pull the blinds to protect our privacy.

When we were going through one of our separations, reporters followed me from LA to a tournament in Memphis. They were even bold enough to sit on the same plane as me. The first night in town, there was a knock at my hotel room door. I thought it was room service. It was – just not the kind I had ordered. Three attractive women stood at the door and asked if I wanted some company. I knew instantly it was a set-up. If I had invited them in, the press would have had their story.

We had photographers hiding out near the Catholic church where Chrissie and I got married and it wasn't much better at my second wedding at the private and exclusive Bel-Air Beach Club in California, with *The Sun* journalist and his photographer in attendance.

I look back on it now and think, 'Boy, if there'd been mobile phones and internet in my day, it could have been so much worse.' One click of a phone camera nowadays and anyone can run to the papers to sell a story on a big name. We had it relatively easy compared to the stars of today. That's why so many players settle down early, I'm sure. If you find someone you like and trust, they are keepers.

Michael J. Fox, who found worldwide fame in the *Back to the Future* movies, did an interview with *Esquire* magazine back in 2007 in which he said: 'No matter how much fame you have, it's not something that belongs to you. If I'm famous, that doesn't belong to me – that belongs to you. If you can't remember who I am, I'm no longer famous.'

It's a profound statement that rings ever more true, the older I get and the less famous I become.

Dear Fame,

I knew you were going to be part of my life. Maybe not when I was 12 and dreaming of a tennis career. But as I grew older, I realised that if I was successful in my chosen profession, it was destined to be part and parcel of the deal. That was fine by me.

I was only too happy to welcome you with open arms when you brought me the good things in life: the glamorous parties, the fancy restaurants, the front-row seats, the first-class travel.

But I wanted to run a mile from you when you invaded my privacy in the darker times: when I would have given anything for peace and anonymity.

I realise your game is a mixture of good and bad. When I hear celebrities complain about you, I don't have much sympathy. There should be private moments, when eating out with your family at restaurants for example. But there's no point fighting it if your private space is invaded by the public. If you are a celebrity and don't like the intrusion, pick another line of work. Otherwise, get on with it. Fame: that's what you showed me.

John

TV DAYS

A letter from the John Lloyd of today to his former self as he embarks on a broadcasting career and learns how to share a confined space with a certain John McEnroe.

Dear John,

This is a new venture for you, something you never planned or expected to do. Try to ease into it. Don't be too hard on yourself if you have a few 'deer in the headlights' moments or trouble working out television talkback. In normal life, you don't have someone talking – often swearing – in your ear when you're trying to string a coherent sentence together. Give it time, you will get used to it.

American channel HBO has given you this chance. They want you to sign an exclusive contract – but they only do two weeks of tennis a year, at Wimbledon. You might gain a variety of experiences if you are free to do more broadcasting for other networks as well. But the HBO deal is a good one, including first-class flights, luxury hotels. Sign it and get on with it. You'll learn plenty, trust me. And the BBC will come calling one day. That's when your TV education can develop.

One of the biggest pieces of advice I can give you is be careful how much fluid you take on when you're doing a long commentary stint. It can get painful and lead to you exposing yourself in situations you could never imagine. Also, look and listen and learn from the great pros around you. They'll be rooting for you.

One day, you will be broadcasting alongside a genius of the courts John McEnroe. That's right: the one who lets rip with angry rants on court will be trusted behind a microphone in a commentary booth. He will deliver his own kind of genius in that role, too. When you're sitting alongside him in commentary, you might struggle to get a word in edgeways. Don't fight it, just go with it. Let him have his head, let him have his way. Sip a cup of tea, enjoy his insights and remember you're not being paid by the word.

Break a leg,

John

CAN I pee in my pants and get away with it? After all, I have got dark-blue trousers on. Will anyone notice other than me? The smell could be an issue. A yellow puddle on the floor might be a dead giveaway. If I don't go now, I'm going to pass out and I'll piss my pants anyway. I point to my nether regions. The pain etched on my face tells the television floor manager I'm in dire need of a toilet. She laughs. It's not funny.

It was men's quarter-final day at Wimbledon 1993. It was my first year as a commentator with American television network HBO. I had felt the need to urinate from the end of the second set. Pete Sampras had won them both for the loss of just four games against his great American rival Andre Agassi. Sampras was cruising. It would be over in no time and I could make a beeline for the bathroom. Wrong. Agassi hit back to win the next two sets 6-3, 6-3 and force a fifth-set decider. My bladder was not impressed.

There was construction taking place at the All England Club that year so the HBO set-up was in some weird area, at least a couple of hundred yards from the nearest toilet. We presented and commentated from the same small studio. I was alongside HBO stalwart Jim Lampley, renowned for his work on numerous Olympic Games and big-time boxing. Supportive as he had been, Jim didn't advise me on my intake of fluids. There were no commercials on HBO. Once a match started and we were on air, we were captive. Like an idiot, I was happily drinking away. We were in week two of the fortnight and I had not been caught short so far, so gulping down water didn't strike me as an issue. We had a few of the HBO crew to keep us company: a cameraman, a statistician, a researcher and a floor manager. They could come and go more easily. But they couldn't pee for me.

I was so inexperienced TV-wise, I didn't know how to use the cough mic properly: a tool of the broadcasting trade that allows you to temporarily cut your microphone while you clear your throat or communicate with the director in the production truck. The floor manager, realising the urgency of the situation, did my communicating for me. 'John needs to get to the restroom – and fast, judging by the look on his face.' The director came through on my earpiece: 'You're gonna have to hold it in buddy. I don't want to leave Jim on his own during such a big match. You'll have to suck it up … be a pro.' This was about the time Agassi won the third set. He then nudged ahead in the fourth set. *Sampras, you idiot! Don't you know I'm fit to burst?*

I was now shaking. I couldn't think of anything else but relieving myself. Jim was asking me questions but I didn't have a clue what he was talking about or what was coming out of my mouth. I was more concerned with what was about to come out of my penis. By this time, the stats woman was in on the story. Like the floor manager, she was finding it all terribly amusing. She offered me an empty Evian water bottle. I thought: 'I may have a small one but I can't get it into that.' Sweat was coming off me. It was torture.

Enter stage left, my hero: another member of the production staff. He unclipped my mic, handed me a metal bucket and pointed to the corner of the room. The cameras were, thankfully, facing the other way. I placed the bucket as far away as was reasonably possible, thinking the further away it was the less noise I would make. I unzipped, took aim and whoosh! I had no control. It was like Niagara Falls down there. Everyone was looking at me as I was gushing away. The noise had to have been picked up on Jim's microphone, like some distant puzzling rainfall on what was a gloriously sunny day. Ping, ping, ping. The last few drops rang out. I felt so good.

I took my seat, plugged back in and was finally ready to absorb the fifth set of Sampras-Agassi. Jim asked me a question and as I started to answer, I noticed the bucket was now underneath him. He pulled out his old man and pissed in the pail. He even commentated midstream. Now that was just showing off. At the HBO wrap party a few days later, we were each presented with commemorative buckets. Needless to say, I only took small sips of water during commentary stints thereafter, preferring dehydration to bladder inflation.

The HBO gig taught me a lot. The channel is a powerhouse in the US and first televised Wimbledon in the mid-70s. Wimbledon was covered at a loss, but the prestige could only have helped the network take firmer root and build subscriptions. Legendary Arthur Ashe had sadly passed away in February 1993. He had been Jim Lampley's co-commentator on HBO. Replacing him wouldn't be easy, but HBO Sports executive producer Ross Greenburg – winner of more than 50 Emmys and later to become president of HBO Sports – had two other American stars in mind: Jimmy Connors and Vitas Gerulaitis. Both were pals of mine and we were having dinner one night, talking about our summer plans. I knew I was going to be in London around Wimbledon time and asked Jimmy if he planned to be there. Jimmy said he had been approached by HBO but had already done some TV work for NBC in the States and wasn't keen on doing more. Vitas revealed he had been sounded out by HBO, too, but thought he might go down the CBS route in America instead. About a month later, Ross Greenburg called me to chat about Wimbledon. We had been introduced to each other some months before, as my then wife Deborah and Ross had a mutual friend.

Ross said: 'I'm considering you for Wimbledon. But I'm gonna put my cards on the table. My first two choices are Jimmy Connors and Vitas Gerulaitis.' Immediately, I thought: 'Good luck with that.' I knew what he apparently didn't. Sure enough, soon after, I heard from Ross again. 'There's been a change of plan,' he said. 'I'd like you to do a screen test.'

It involved me sitting alongside experienced anchor Jim Lampley in a mock-up of the Wimbledon studio, while we presented and commentated on an old Andre Agassi match. To say I was nervous as I entered the studio is putting it mildly.

Jim's a great pro, but it struck me he didn't know much about tennis. He was asking me some odd questions. HBO encouraged a lot of talking and not too many pregnant pauses during commentary, so I was doing my best to sound coherent and vaguely interesting. I was wearing an earpiece for the first time, allowing the director and producer to give me instructions. One of them chirps up: 'During the next changeover, John, we're going over to Court 13 for an update. Don't say anything for that minute or so.'

'Okay,' I replied.

'No, no, don't say "okay" when I'm giving you an instruction.'

'Gotcha,' I said.

'No, not "gotcha" either! If this was for real, you'd have just said "okay" and "gotcha" on air. You'd have been talking over Jim and confusing a million viewers.'

'Oh, shit, yeah,' I cluelessly blurted out.

'No! No! F***! Just put your thumbs up to show you've heard me or something like that.'

Wave a white flag in surrender might have been the 'something like that' he had in mind. I clearly had no idea what I was doing. I was sweating through my shirt, like Albert Brooks in the film *Broadcast News*.

Jim was very kind, saying that being English would make me a great fit for Wimbledon and that we would make a good team. I was terrible, a stuttering deer in the headlights, so it did cross my mind he might be full of shit. Mine had to be the worst commentary in the history of tennis broadcasting. I was useless. I left the studio thinking: 'I'm never doing that again'.

Two weeks before Wimbledon, Ross Greenburg rang me and said: 'Good news, John. You're on the team.' I imagined they had tried and failed to persuade everyone else in the human world, leaving them no option but me.

I signed this ridiculous deal in which they paid me so much money for just two weeks' work. It was an exclusive contract. Not that any other networks were knocking down my door to commentate for them, trust me. But I got paid enough that I didn't have to bother about anything else. HBO flew me first class and we stayed in magnificent hotels.

As Wimbledon dawned, Ross told me: 'I'm going to be very honest with you, John. You are now a professional broadcaster.' Surely he wasn't full of shit, too? A professional broadcaster? Me? He continued: 'These players you're going to be commentating on, they are not your friends anymore. If you soft-soap it when there's something we need your opinion on or someone's being an asshole, it's not going to work. You can't be making excuses for people. If you do, you'll be out of this job very quickly.' At least I knew where I stood.

HBO, an uncensored network, actively encouraged me to be straight-talking: to be positively blunt. The producers didn't even mind if I swore on air. Nothing bad, of course, and nothing gratuitous. But the odd 'shitty backhand' was allowed.

When we went live for the first time, the language I heard in my earpiece was even more choice. The colourful talk from the director contained such eloquent phrases as: 'For f***'s sake, Bill … what the f***! Are you trying to make me lose my job, you f***ing asshole!' I thought everyone in the production truck talked like this until I worked for the BBC. There was an HBO swear box for the foul-mouthed. It was always full of cash. Off air, there was less lurid language. It was an amazing group, actually.

If I had handed myself a report card for the first week of my broadcasting career, I would have given the effort three out of ten. Maybe I'd have given myself more had Arthur Ashe's widow Jeanne not entered the studio, taken one look at me and run off in floods of tears. Was I really that bad?

Soon after, Jeanne wrote to me explaining she walked into the HBO studio almost expecting to see Arthur sitting there alongside Jim. The realisation he had gone hit her anew and she burst into tears. She wrote: 'Arthur always liked you. He would be happy you have taken his place. He would be proud of you.' It was the most beautiful, reassuring letter.

There was a fair bit of winging it, on my part. HBO had a second studio near the old No.1 Court, where we commentated on the action from a single monitor. Grand Slam collector Martina Navratilova and I would rotate between the two studio positions. The Court One gig allowed time for tea and biscuits, even the odd doughnut. My co-commentator Barry MacKay, an ex-American player with a big presence and wonderful commentary style, liked his British biscuits. Production would throw to us on occasion for updates and cut up another court on our monitor, likely between two obscure players whose names ended in 'ova'. Most times, we wouldn't have a clue who we were commentating on or how the match had progressed. Cue the bullshit. Barry had stock phrases. He normally opened with one of them. 'There's a packed house on Court 13, Jim.' There wasn't. 'It's been a barnstorming match.' They might have actually been playing like drains. Then he would throw me a curve ball: 'John, what's the story so far?' How the hell did I know?

'Well, Barry, Supernova was dominating at first with her forehand, but Upandova came powering back with some deep groundstrokes. We're at one-all in the third set and it could honestly go either way.' What insight. Of course it could go either way, you idiot. Barry would hand back to the main studio with a confident: 'That's the story of the match, Jim,' and we'd get back to scoffing doughnuts.

In later years with HBO, I was commentating on a match involving Wimbledon champion Boris Becker and the warning words of the boss Ross Greenburg came to prominence. Boris and I weren't what you would call close mates, but we were friendly enough for me to ask him if I could use his condo in Palm Springs for some of my guests. They were coming over for my second wedding in Los Angeles. He happily obliged. I often practised with Boris, and my coach at the time, Bob Brett, went on to work with him. We had good history.

During this particular Wimbledon commentary, Boris was struggling. He took a bathroom break. Word came to us at HBO that Becker's coach had gone with him and given him instruction in the locker room. Illegal coaching, in effect. Jim Lampley fed me the line and asked me what should happen. I said Boris should be thrown out of the tournament. I knew he wouldn't be happy, but – as Ross had pointed out – I was now a broadcaster. I had to call it as I saw it. If someone, friend or otherwise, has done something bad on court and you don't call it, you are not being legitimate. That's why I believe former players shouldn't enter the broadcasting world until they have been off the circuit for five years. Are you going to criticise recent colleagues and friends, bad-mouth them in front of millions of viewers, if they've choked or behaved badly? Not likely. That's difficult even years down the line which is why John McEnroe in tennis and Johnny Miller in golf proved to be pure commentary gold. Outspoken, frank, sometimes controversial, but always saying it as they saw it. That's rare and to be applauded.

HBO's Wimbledon coverage came to an end in 1999 and I switched to commentating and doing punditry work for the BBC. The difference between the two broadcasters was like night and day. I had to learn not to talk all the time, but to let the pictures breathe. My tennis mentor John Barrett was a huge influence, a fantastic broadcaster. I watched closely how he worked, how he paused and when he chose to deliver a telling line. Dan Maskell, the BBC's voice of tennis for so long, was the king of understatement. His commentary lines included: 'Oh, I say!' and: 'What a peach of a shot!' Dan was a household name, a Wimbledon institution. But he rarely talked about the actual match on which he was commentating. He advised me: 'Keep it simple. You've got to realise, dear boy, that 75 per cent of the audience watching are housewives and they don't even know how to score a tie-breaker. If you start talking about pronating your wrist, they won't know what the heck you're talking about and just go and do more washing-up.' Talk about a different time. Dan would not get away with that kind of remark in today's BBC.

Commentary was conservative. There were things I wanted to say, but felt rocking the Wimbledon boat was not the BBC way. In an exact opposite to HBO, I felt censored. Then along came a man named John McEnroe.

Mac was a maverick. He would say whatever the hell he wanted and you could take it or leave it. That wasn't his problem. There were undoubtedly a few 'holy shit'-type reactions at first from the less liberal lobby. But he made compelling viewing. In many ways, he changed tennis broadcasting on the BBC.

Dave Gordon and later Paul Davies, two of BBC Sport's Wimbledon hierarchy, were the men I recall welcoming this kind of change. There was a limit. They didn't want us swearing on air like HBO, of course, but they wanted us to have an opinion. They also backed their commentators, which was just as well because I publicly criticised the Lawn Tennis Association more than once. The LTA came after me, through our editorial chief Dave. I told my then wife Deborah that if I was made to apologise or back off on my criticism of the organisation, I would quit. But Dave supported me. Paul was the same.

I loved listening to the dulcet tones of some of the older commentators, but they said little of substance. People increasingly wanted to be told how it is in the real tennis world.

No one does it better than Johnny Mac. With him on the BBC team, combining his duties with considerable work for American television, we soon started doing 'three-balls' in the commentary box. Before that, it had been a two-person thing, but now it would be Mac and me, plus a commentator like John Barrett. Immediately, I was intrigued by working alongside Mac and found myself doing more listening than talking. His comedic touch was priceless, his fearlessness so refreshing. Just like in his playing days, he sees the game a couple of seconds quicker than the average mortal, then he paints a picture all his own. I have often found myself looking over at him after he's delivered a gem and thinking: 'He's absolutely spot on. Why didn't I think of that?'

As generous a co-commentator as he can be, Mac can also be a bit of a bully in the box – or even in a punditry situation.

He's John McEnroe, I'm not, and he uses that. Sue Barker was presenting from the side of Centre Court one time, with Mac and me as guests. We each gave our views on the upcoming match and threw in a few facts. Mac got one of his facts wrong and I knew it. Sue said: 'Well, we've got a difference of opinion with the two Johns. Who should we believe?' Mac declared: 'The one with three Wimbledon singles titles.' What am I supposed to say to that? He's done me like a kipper – and he knows it. I had nowhere to go.

When I have commentated with him down the years, I have largely kept quiet. I don't have a very big ego and don't care how many words I can squeeze into commentary. If Mac's got more interesting things to say than I have (and he usually has more interesting things to say than anyone), just let him go. I would have a cup of tea and enjoy listening to him with the rest of the country. He's a genius in the commentary booth, as he was as a player.

My former BBC boss Paul Davies was once directing a match with us both in the box and asked was I still alive: I had spoken that little. Fifteen words in three hours, maybe. Some would call it wonderfully understated commentary.

The silence was occasionally born of nervousness about saying the wrong thing when alongside the great man. If you're tired or having an off day and happen to make a verbal mistake, some co-commentators will cut you some slack. Not McEnroe. He tells you you're wrong and why and that's the end of the story. The key, then, was always to get a quick and obvious word in, like: 'That's a big serve by Sampras.' No shit Sherlock, but at least he couldn't argue with that.

Mac, you won't be surprised to hear, doesn't like to listen to the director when commentating. The headphones might be on, but the talkback is turned off. Mac, taking direction? He thinks not.

That meant he couldn't hear the director crying out: 'What did he just say? Correct him … correct him!' on the day of the famously rain-interrupted Wimbledon semi-final between Tim Henman and Goran Ivanisevic in 2001. Mac was talking to Sue in her presentation studio from our commentary position on Centre Court during one of the many annoying rain breaks. He was staring straight down the lens, I was at his side. What happened next went something like this (at least, this is how I remember it).

McEnroe: 'What needs to happen now, Sue, is for the guys supporting Henman to put down their beers and get back in here and make some noise for him to get him through this thing … for his female fans to put their fannies on their seats and cheer him all the way to the final.'

Director: 'What did he just say? Did he just say fannies? He can't say that.'

I heard it alright, but wasn't sure how to react. Mac, minus director's sound into his headphones, could only hear Sue and not the shocked reaction. There's no one more professional. Sue's unbelievable. But even she was a bit flummoxed by the mention of fannies, probably knowing we were live on air in the homes of some 12 million people.

Director: 'Someone needs to say something. Someone needs to correct him. He can't get away with fannies.'

That was my cue to chime in with: 'That means something else in the States, Sue. He means their bottoms.'

McEnroe, oblivious to the director's insistence we cover up for his faux pas, thought he would add his own clarification.

'Yeah, I'm talking about asses, Sue … asses!'

Henman would eventually lose that semi-final. All the British fannies on all the Wimbledon seats couldn't prevent Goran's date with historic title destiny.

On other occasions, Mac has become bored with his own commentary match, flicked the monitor to a screen full of latest scores and given away details of matches the editors were holding back for later. 'Hey, we should be on this match,' he would say. 'Wow, it's gone five-all in the fifth.' Editorial plans be damned.

Fair play to him, though. Johnny Mac can make even the dullest matches sound interesting, whereas I tend to nod off. Seriously. In fact, I'm full of admiration for the way he can be as insightful and entertaining at the end of a long day of commentary as he was at the start of play. Talking up maybe 12 sets of tennis in a day across various networks takes a hell of a lot of enthusiasm. Even when he's seeing so many similar points played out before his eyes, he always finds something captivating to say. He shows no fatigue and is razor-sharp at the end of a marathon session, ready for an appearance on the highlights show if required. I'm in awe of that. Does he get well paid for it? Of course he does. But he deserves it. The man has taken sports commentary to a whole new level.

I have been very lucky in my broadcasting career to be surrounded by other top-class professionals. One of the true greats of the commentating world is Barry Davies and I have always loved working alongside him. He is the ultimate professional with a marvellous turn of phrase. Some lead commentators like the sound of their own voice too much, but Barry is all about the viewer. He wants to welcome them in and make the spectacle as good as he can for the audience. Barry is never one for mailing it in, either. He always puts the work in. At Wimbledon, his enthusiasm shone through if it was a Roger Federer classic on Centre Court or an obscure mixed doubles match out on Court 17. I also liked that he didn't take himself too seriously. When I was commentating on a match on Centre Court one time, there was a shot of Barry in the Royal Box. I said on air: 'How the hell did he get in there?' Barry loved that.

At Wimbledon 2017, Barry was due to join me on a mixed doubles commentary but was held up on another court. When the producer spoke into my headphones, I explained I was on my own. 'You'll have to take care of the match until Barry arrives then, John.' I was not comfortable outside my role as an analyst – what American TV calls 'the colour' – but had no option. I looked up and saw two Chinese players on one side of the court. I had notes prepared for two South Americans. 'This can't be right. Where are the South Americans?' I said. 'It is right, John,' explained the producer. 'The Chinese pair have replaced them. They're lucky losers.' When one couple drops out last-minute, this kind of switch can happen. I did not have the first clue who they were or how I should pronounce their names. Thankfully, a substitute was sent to cover for Barry and I could breathe again.

If I had been left on my own, I could always have tapped into my memory banks for how I dealt with another Chinese pair I had never heard of at the 2004 Athens Olympics. I was working with former Grand Slam champion Tracy Austin – who I adore – for the BBC. We were the only two tennis commentators that year and worked ourselves into near exhaustion. Matches were finishing in the early hours of the morning, then we were straight back out there just a few hours later. By the time we got to the Chinese duo, I could barely get my mouth around their names.

I was going to embarrass myself and disrespect them with my pronunciation, so I told Tracy: 'I'm done. I'm sorry ... I just can't do it anymore. I'm not going to say their names for the entire match.' I referred to them by height: 'The taller one is holding this team together.' I referred to them by nationality: 'The Chinese pair ... duo ... couple ... team.' I referred to them by world ranking: 'The 50th-ranked player messed that up.' Not once did I mention their names. It was so obvious, it was all Tracy could do not to crack up with laughter. We were both sleep-deprived and verging on hysteria.

I actually took a nap in the box during the 2008 Olympics, when tennis commentary for the Beijing games was done out of a booth in Shepherd's Bush. My flight from LA to London was delayed and by the time I joined up with co-commentator Chris Bradnam, I had not slept for 23 hours. I could never sleep on planes, so why I found it so easy nodding off on live television is beyond me. Chris was a star and carried on solo, his commentary doubtless punctuated by the odd snort and snore from me.

On one occasion at Wimbledon, during a match involving one of the more tedious players on tour, Nikolay Davydenko of Russia, I warned my co-commentator Mark Petchey that I desperately needed 40 winks or might just keel over in the box. 'Petch, seriously, I feel I'm driving a car late at night and am about to veer off the road with tiredness.' He generously covered for me but, thousands of miles away in America, my nap was not going unnoticed. I would rather have a root canal than watch Davydenko, but for some reason his match was picked up on cable TV in the States and my wife Deborah and one of her friends were watching. When Deb's friend hadn't heard me speak for about 20 minutes, she said: 'What's happened to John? Has he left the booth, do you think?'

'No,' said Deb, 'he's fallen asleep.'

'What? On the air?'

'Exactly.'

When I rang Deb later that day, she asked me if I had enjoyed my sleep during the commentary. 'How could she know that?' I thought. 'Only Petch and me were privy to that piece of information.'

'Have you got a spy camera on me or something?'

'No. You just went quiet for 20 minutes. I know you. It had to involve sleep.'

I'm full of admiration for my play-by-play colleagues – and not just because they bail me out from time to time. Whereas I can be spontaneous and talk about what's going on in a match like I would if I was talking to a friend on the couch, they have to be far more erudite: setting the scene, building the excitement in the right places and capturing the conclusion. They make it look and sound so easy and I promise you it isn't.

That is even more difficult to do on the presenting front and yet Sue Barker has done it better than anyone else. On the day of the Queen's Club final a few years ago, I was due to join Sue on court ahead of the match. En route, I was receiving calls in the car asking me where I was. I was thinking: 'I've been doing this 100 years and have never been late. Why the sudden panic?' Only when I was ambling over to the court did I see Sue waving frantically. My watch had stopped. I was an hour late. I hurriedly moved alongside her, sweat dripping off my brow, barely able to remember who was in the final and yet Sue did not skip a beat. In fact, I think the only time I have seen her a bit flustered was in the aforementioned story when McEnroe said the word 'fannies' to her live on air.

Sue was always a determined and confident woman. She was a player to be reckoned with – a French Open champion no less. But to reach the top in her second profession is nothing short of amazing. She had the benefit at the start – as did our colleague Andrew Castle – of working for Sky when there were only about 50 people watching. That was a good place to learn and make mistakes, rather than be thrown in at the deep end with the BBC. Once Sue joined the corporation, she was quite extraordinary. I know the reputation she has with American broadcasters: they absolutely love her and admire the way she never uses Autocue. If she had wanted to, Sue could have named her price in the States. Not that she hasn't done well for herself in the UK, of course. She has just never chosen to commercialise herself. She was happy presenting Wimbledon and *Question of Sport* and combined that with a contented home life.

Sue is the best Wimbledon presenter there has been, without question. There are other excellent presenters around like Clare Balding and John Inverdale, but the difference is that Sue has been there and done it in professional tennis and then gone on to present the sport at the highest level, too. Sue Barker is one hell of a tough act to follow.

Dear HBO,

You took a chance on me, even after that horrendous screen test, and kick-started a phase of my tennis career I had never imagined ... that of a pundit and commentator. For seeing some potential behind that sweaty brow and fixed stare, when others would have run a mile, I thank you. Little did I know then that you were setting me on the road to commentating on a multitude of Grand Slam finals, Davis Cup ties and the Olympic Games – as well as witnessing the broadcasting brilliance of John McEnroe up close and personal. Oh yes – and thanks for the bucket.

Yours in the commentary box,

John

JIMMY CONNORS AND THE STAR WARS CONNECTION

IT WAS a murder that shocked the community. Mark had pulled up in his car, wound down his window and greeted his brother Edward in his usual warm way, ready to take him to a family Hanukkah celebration. Edward produced a kitchen knife and stabbed Mark in the chest. He died later in hospital. He was just 43.

Mark's eight-year-old son witnessed the stabbing from inside the car. This devastated young boy would go on to play Han Solo.

Mark was such a kind person, who gave up his time freely to coach my son Aiden's soccer team; a side that also included a super-skilled youngster by the name of Theo Spielberg, son of esteemed director Steven and actress Kate Capshaw, who had a house in my Pacific Palisades neighbourhood. Steven and Kate would attend games and see their boy run rings around the others. He was a goal machine.

Mark, as coach of kids aged eight and nine, was more like a beekeeper than a soccer tactician. As children do at that age, they see the ball and swarm after it. Theo would emerge from the swarm, speed the length of the pitch and invariably score.

But Mark made sure every youngster was involved. He was one of the good guys.

That also showed in his insistence that his brother always visit his house for family celebrations, even though Edward was in a facility being treated for schizophrenia. Including him was important to Mark. He never wanted Edward, who reportedly had a problem with the mind-altering drug LSD earlier in his life, to feel he had been abandoned.

On the day of the Hanukkah celebration, Edward was given his medication and awaited Mark's arrival. Unbeknownst to staff at the home, Edward had picked up a kitchen knife and hidden it.

Mark approached in his car, with his son sitting in the back seat. Mark's window down, he smiled and welcomed his brother. The attack was unprovoked and tragic. Mark somehow managed to put the car in gear and drive away, doubtless fearing his son was also in jeopardy. But it was too late to save himself and he later died from his injuries in hospital.

The Pacific Palisades community was in shock. To compound the misery, it was discovered that Mark had financial difficulties and left wife Sari and their son facing a worrying future. The people in the area wanted to help.

Steve Bellamy ran the local tennis centre about a mile from our family home and was a friend of mine. We came upon the notion of an exhibition match to raise money for a college fund for Mark's son.

There were grass banks by the court, where several hundred people could gather to watch. Local restaurants would provide free food on top of the hill. Comedy actor Martin Short and renowned American voiceover artist Joe Cipriano agreed to co-umpire. I would take to one half of the exhibition court. All we needed now was someone to take me on; someone to bring in more spectators; someone to keep the donations flowing. I rang Jimmy Connors. His immediate response was: 'Tell me where and when and I'll be there.'

About 500 locals came out to watch us, crammed on to the grass bank. There was banter and laughs aplenty as Martin and Joe, who were both on mics, debated the merits of Jimmy's backhand. Martin quipped: 'A lot of people admire the double-handed backhand. Me, personally, I think it's cheating ... a sign he's too weak to hold the racket with one hand.' Jimmy sent a ball fizzing passed Martin's head in response.

It was an amazing event that raised around $40,000 for the college fund. Jimmy invited Mark's son on to the court to join in the fun. Our hearts went out to him. We all knew what a difference this could make to the kid's future.

This kid is Alden Ehrenreich, who so superbly portrays Han Solo in the Star Wars prequel *Solo: A Star Wars Story.*

Alden studied acting in New York, but received his biggest break when Spielberg saw him performing on a bar mitzvah video, alongside the director's daughter. That Pacific Palisades community connection had worked again. Television jobs followed, then roles in such films as Francis Ford Coppola's *Tetro*, Woody Allen's *Blue Jasmine* and the Coen brothers' *Hail, Caesar!* I sent Jimmy emails to inform him of Alden's growing success. After all, he had been there at the very start.

Now Alden has made it big on a global stage. His father Mark would be so proud.

Jimmy's involvement that day meant the world to me. Maybe he saw something of himself in Alden. Jimmy was also just eight years old, playing on the public courts in East St Louis, when he saw his mother and two grandparents viciously beaten by local thugs. His mother Gloria had more than 100 stitches to her mouth. Those images never left Jimmy.

We get asked to take part in so many charity events, it is impossible to say 'yes' to everything. Certain charities will pay for stars to show up, knowing the charity will more than recoup that money from increased ticket sales or donations. Without a star name, events can fall flat. But I couldn't offer Jimmy anything that day and I have never liked asking players to do something for free. Time is the most valuable thing there is and to ask colleagues to give up their free time to help someone they don't know and have never met, when these kinds of requests are coming in on an almost daily basis, is awkward. Jimmy made it easy for me. This is the measure of the man.

Any of you hoping there might have been some underlying tension between us because Jimmy was engaged to Chris Evert just a few years before I married her will be disappointed. Not that it stopped the press from building up the love rivalry ahead of our first-round match at the 1981 US Open, when I was already married to Chrissie.

When the draw came out, I was mortified. I was in that phase of my career where loss followed loss and was on the brink of dropping to a lowly ranking that would have resigned me to qualifying for tournaments. I was carrying an injury, wasn't in great shape generally and – terrible as this now sounds – was just turning up at events and going through the motions. I hoped I might draw an average player on an outside court, maybe get lucky and sneak a win. If not, it was no big deal. My mind wasn't in the game at the time.

Instead, I had to face one of the world's best on the biggest New York show court in front of thousands of spectators and a television audience of millions. With hindsight, I should have pulled out. Jimmy's not the sort of player you want to face if you are not 100 per cent fit because he is relentless. Every point was like gold to him. He was a points miser, hoarding everything he had and refusing to give anything away.

And so, I found myself embroiled in the worst match of my life, being humbled by a legend. He won the first 14 games. That's 6-0, 6-0, 2-0, in case you need the humiliating scenario ramming home even further. I don't believe Jimmy wanted to beat me more because of what happened with Chris. He doesn't think that way. I was just another opponent to be torn down limb by limb. It was a will to win at all costs nurtured by his upbringing in a tough neighbourhood in St Louis.

When I commentate on players having an absolute nightmare on a huge stadium court, I feel for them because I have been there. It is one of the loneliest places you can imagine. Millions are witnessing your humiliation. You are getting your arse kicked. In my case, the crowd were booing me because they didn't think I was putting the effort in. I won just two games in a miserable defeat.

The press had a field day, of course, asking why on earth I was still playing if this is all I could muster. In general, they were right. I was just punching the clock. It was pathetic. But it wasn't the case that day. It was more that I froze in the onslaught and didn't know what to do to respond.

I am often asked at corporate events who was the best of the big three I faced in my era: Borg, Connors or McEnroe. In terms of how my style matched up against theirs, Jimmy was the toughest opponent for me. That's not to say he was the best ever or the most naturally gifted player, more that he had my number in a way the other two did not. I played Jimmy five times and didn't win a set. I finally broke that duck on the senior tour and had him at one set all when he retired hurt. Even though he fell over and almost broke his leg, do I still claim that as my first win over Connors? Damn right I do. To paraphrase our mutual friend Vitas Gerulaitis, no one beats John Lloyd six times in a row.

It was after my US Open debacle, funnily enough, that Jimmy and I got to know each other better, starting around the time of the French Open the following year. He was going through a difficult time in his marriage to Patti. They were separated, the press guys were hounding him and he was looking for a safe haven. He found it in Chrissie and me. We had dinner a few times and he just kind of hung out with us. I don't know how it really happened, now I think about it. It sounds a bit weird, actually – the husband, the wife and her ex – but that's how it was. We bonded then and became firm friends.

Jimmy is the toughest competitor I have ever seen. If I wanted someone to play for my life, it would be Connors every time. All great champions have a hunger for victory, but Jimmy's desire was greatest. He would go through any pain barrier to win any match.

In his autobiography *The Outsider*, one can get an understanding of how his passion was fuelled by rage. When he needed something to push him to another level in matches, he would remember the attack on his family when he was just eight and play with an anger few of us can understand.

It wasn't pure rage that won Jimmy eight Grand Slam singles titles, a stunning 109 tournaments and kept him at World No.1 for 268 weeks, but it certainly didn't hurt. Nor did his ceaseless drive to find a crucial edge on his opponents, even if it meant training at three in the morning.

We were both involved in the US Pro Indoor tournament at the Spectrum in Philadelphia, where Jimmy made a record five final appearances in succession. There were no practice facilities on-site other than the main court. If you turned up around breakfast time, you might get on court for a hit but would have to share the court with three others. Once play was underway for the day, it went on until after midnight because there were both singles and doubles competitions to get through.

Jimmy and I were having dinner when he said: 'I've got an idea.' He had a look that suggested he meant business. 'We'll get them to turn the lights on and have a practice, just you and me. How does 3am sound?'

'Well, not too enticing if I'm honest. Where does sleep come into this?'

'We sleep, we play, we sleep some more. Simple.'

That's exactly what we did. Jimmy declared: 'Now we've got an advantage. None of those other saps will have practised like that.'

'Yeah, but I've lost two hours sleep and feel rubbish.'

'Don't worry about that. You'll be fine.'

Jimmy went on winning. I lost in the next round. Therein lies the difference. I saw the impromptu practice as a negative, he saw it as a positive. It gave him the mental edge. That one hour of practice was huge in his eyes. That's all that mattered if it made a telling difference to him on court.

The best example in Jimmy's career of this mental strength and tireless will came at the 1991 US Open, when he staggeringly reached the semi-finals at the age of 39.

Jimmy entered the tournament ranked 174 in the world. The previous year, he had played just three matches because of a wrist injury and surgery and lost all three. He was a wild-card entry into the US Open: a ticket for one last go on his favourite ride. Everyone expected he would step off that ride after the opening round.

And so it appeared when he was two sets and three-love down to Patrick McEnroe. An old master was tamely bowing out on the stage he once owned.

This was a painful watch for me. Jimmy had asked me to join him for the duration of that tournament as his hitting partner. I was playing over-35s events back then, alongside the likes of Stan Smith and Bob Lutz, and was in good shape. I thought the New York trip would be fun but short-lived.

Then came the most astonishing comeback. Jimmy won the last three sets 6-4, 6-2, 6-4 in a match that lasted more than four hours. He polished off his next two opponents in no time and in the last 16 faced American Aaron Krickstein, ranked in the world's top ten. It was the Labor Day holiday in the States and Jimmy's 39th birthday.

Krickstein won the first set, Jimmy won the second on a tie-break but – as he later revealed in his memoir – he was so exhausted at that point he had to 'tank' the third set to get his second wind.

Wow, did he ever. He won the fourth to set up a decider. I was courtside watching this in absolute awe.

Krickstein led 5-2 in the final set only for Jimmy to pull out some astonishing shots and flip it around again. The crowd was going berserk as this US national treasure won the tie-breaker and the match. Jimmy's famous fist-pumping celebration adorned the front cover of *Sports Illustrated* with the title 'The People's Choice'.

It was a celebration we all witnessed again when he chased down a seemingly endless number of smashes from Dutchman Paul Haarhuis in the quarter-finals, almost clambering into the stands to get the ball back, before winning that match, too. No one got a crowd going like Jimmy did. New York was raucous anyway. Now he took them to new decibel levels. Though he lost in the semis to Jim Courier and Stefan Edberg won the title, this was Jimmy Connors's US Open. I was privileged to share it with him.

I also saw what it took out of him. It was truly mind-boggling. He went into the locker room after one match, crashed on the bed and put out his arms. In went IVs to replace lost fluids. He would have to glug down more liquid in the limo on the way back into Manhattan, so much so that we had to take toilet breaks every 15 minutes. If I made him laugh on the journeys he would start cramping up across his stomach, saying: 'No, stop ... no laughing allowed.' His body was done match after match and he kept forcing it to go just that one round more. It was quite extraordinary.

Two of the greatest weeks in all of tennis history and I was so honoured to be a part of it: to see this true great go through this incredible experience. If I hadn't seen it with my own two eyes, I might never have believed it. Jimmy was already a big name in sport, of course he was. But after that performance at the US Open, he was a megastar who transcended sport. I partnered him at a doubles event in Indianapolis the following year, in what turned into something of a farewell tour for Jimmy, and saw how much affection there was for him. It was overwhelming.

Some fans loved him so much they would lock themselves in the bathroom, sobbing and refusing to come out, if he lost a big match. Actually, there is one person in particular that I'm reminded of and she just happens to be the sister of popular British comedian and actor Johnny Vegas.

Catharine was visiting Wimbledon with Johnny and their mum. Johnny is known for his comical rants and was only too happy to share his thoughts on the high-brow nature of the event – him being a working-class lad from Thatto Heath in St Helens – in a funny BBC interview. Once Johnny had held court with a rowdy crowd just below the players' lawn, he and his family walked down the long corridor of the Broadcast Centre. Catharine had already revealed to a BBC producer that she adored Jimmy, explaining her need to lock herself away when he lost. Who should be standing in the corridor as they approached the BBC production office but the man himself. It was his first year on the BBC commentary team and we were stood chatting. What were the odds?

I was asked to make a formal introduction: 'Jimmy Connors meet your number one fan Catharine. Catharine meet your favourite player Jimmy Connors.' Good ol' Jimmy, he went straight in with a kiss on her cheek to make her year, after which she announced: 'I won't wash that bit of my face ever again!'

Jimmy and I became ever-closer friends through the years, although in recent times we haven't seen each other as much as we used to. I liked his banter, I liked his humour and I liked practising with him. I only wish I had done it earlier in my career. One hour on court with Jimmy was like four hours with mere tennis mortals. Even now, after two hip replacements, he always has the most remarkable balance and just doesn't miss the ball. Some pros slam the first few balls into the fence until they find their rhythm and range. Not Jimmy. He's at it from the outset. If you aren't, he looks at you with a disdain that says: 'What the hell is that? Are you wasting my time or what?' He's in the right position for every ball and, though he can't quite glide around the court like he used to in his heyday, he is still unbelievably good.

When Jimmy started the Champions Tour in 1993, I would get to know how he ticked even more. There had been senior events for over-35s for a while, but for the concept to flourish it needed an injection of corporate money and star quality. Jimmy delivered on both, working with co-founder Steve Benton. He initially signed up players like Bjorn Borg, Guillermo Vilas, Roscoe Tanner, Jose-Luis Clerc and yours truly and a few years down the line John McEnroe and Andres Gomez joined the troupe.

The main proviso was we all had to be in shape. Being overweight would simply not cut it. Jimmy sat us down and explained what he expected of us and pointed out that for the tour to be taken seriously we could not have spectators watching us thinking: 'My local pro is better than this lot.' Jimmy had been playing on the regular ATP Tour into his 40s, so was not only fit but in the public's consciousness. For the rest of us, we had to re-engage with an audience and, though we had to be entertaining, we couldn't be laughing stocks. There were cocktail parties and golf events thrown into the corporate mix, while the tennis was of a high standard and bona fide quality. The formula worked like a dream.

When Mac joined us, he was defeated a few times when I honestly imagined he thought he would rock up and coast to a final showdown with one of the other big draws, like Jimmy or Bjorn. It wasn't long before Mac was doing yoga and getting himself in seriously good shape to compete and beat the rest of us. Along with his arrival in the commentary booth, this was kind of the second coming of John McEnroe.

While most of the players were off schmoozing on picturesque golf courses for hours on end, I – as a non-golfer – was taking tennis clinics. After a while I thought: 'Sod this for a lark. I'm missing out on all the fun here.' I took to the clubs.

One of the first times I played – or should that be hacked – was at California's stunning major championship golf venue Pebble Beach, of all places. I was in a foursome that included Alan Shepard, one of the original Mercury astronauts of the late 1950s and the first American launched into space in 1961. What a legend. He was commander of the Apollo 14 mission to the moon and, on that epic moonwalk, famously hit a couple of golf balls with a six iron attached to the tool he used to collect samples from the lunar surface. The lack of gravity ensured he hit the longest drive ever. Now he was playing with me, a rank amateur who could barely get the ball off the ground let alone launch it into orbit. Skimming balls across the ground when you are meant to be driving does not go down well at Pebble Beach, I discovered.

Thankfully, you don't have to gain any elevation when you are putting. As we neared the end of the round, Alan was still quiet – I suspect a bit stunned and not at all impressed by his partner's efforts. I lined up a 50ft putt. I could almost hear his brain whirring with: 'Here we go again. How will I have to bail him out this time?' I struck the ball sweetly and it astonishingly found the middle of the cup. Alan's silence was broken as he declared: 'That's the best f****** putt I've ever seen.' We got along famously after that.

At the Riviera Country Club, also in California, there are trees around the 12th hole, along with a punishing bunker. One is named Bogey's Tree in honour of Hollywood screen icon Humphrey Bogart, who was a member there and had a house adjoining the course where he lived with Lauren Bacall. Players he knew would often interrupt their round to join him for a quick tipple.

Jimmy is a tremendous golfer and had driven the ball well on this hole and so, for a change, had I. But his second shot found the bunker, while my ball sat happily on the green from where I watched Jimmy disappear into the trap as he prepared to escape the sand. Not even his head was visible from my viewpoint. Next thing, up flew the sand ... but no ball emerged. Up flew the sand ... still no ball. And so it continued. Once we had completed that hole, Jimmy marched off saying: 'Best f****** 10 I've ever had.' Funny how golf brings out the f-word in all of us. The next day I rang him and told him Riviera had a new name for the bunker to accompany the nearby Bogey's Tree: Connors' Catastrophe. I can neither confirm nor deny I might have heard the f-word again at that juncture.

From a few shots that got away to a couple of projects that escaped our net. One was a reality television show based on tennis, the other a coaching opportunity with Andre Agassi.

I was approached by a couple of guys in my neighbourhood with the TV idea. It involved putting talented male and female players – those who maybe hadn't quite made it on the tour or couldn't afford to pursue their passion beyond college – into shared accommodation. They would be put through their paces, play games and generally hang out while their interactions were filmed. The concept was pitched as sexy. When they asked me who I thought should act as the Donald Trump/Alan Sugar 'Apprentice' type, I suggested Jimmy. We enjoyed putting the format together and travelling the networks and studios to pitch it. We came so close on a couple of occasions, without ever securing a firm commitment. But we had fun trying.

When Andre Agassi's ranking was plummeting after undergoing wrist surgery in 1993, he wanted help to reverse the slide. A call was made to Jimmy Connors, much to my amazement.

Jimmy and Andre just didn't get along and had some well-publicised spats. Jimmy told me: 'You're not going to believe this but I've had a call from Agassi's agent. They want me to coach him.'

'I didn't think you guys liked each other.'

'We don't, but Agassi feels he needs help. Whether he likes me or not doesn't come into it if I can genuinely help him.'

Jimmy was interested, but only if he could include me in the package as Agassi's hitting partner. I was more than up for the idea.

A practice session was arranged at the prestigious Sherwood Country Club at Westlake Village in LA, the only place I know where roses are entwined in the fences around the tennis courts. Andre was on one side of the net, Jimmy and me were on the other.

We basically ran Andre around a bit in the stifling heat. He was hitting the ball just great. Jimmy asked me: 'What do you think?'

'It all depends whether or not his mind is in it.'

I had always got on well with Andre, so it seemed the most sensible move for me to go over and quiz him rather than Jimmy. Andre said all the right things: he wanted to reach number one in the world for the first time, he wanted to win more Grand Slam titles.

'And what are you willing to do to achieve those goals?'

'Whatever it takes.'

When I reported back to Jimmy, I told him: 'If you want to be a coach, you've just been handed a gift from the heavens because my grandmother could coach this guy back into the top ten. He's that good. As long as he does the work he says he will, this is a speeding bullet heading in only one direction.'

I wasn't involved in the financial discussions. Jimmy asked for a certain figure, but they couldn't agree terms. Instead, Agassi's camp suggested Jimmy work on a bonus basis. That could have brought more rewards than a straight contract and again it seemed like a win-win. But the negotiations stalled. Jimmy Connors would not be coaching Andre Agassi. A few weeks later, Brad Gilbert was announced as Agassi's coach. The following year Agassi became the first unseeded player to win the US Open and the year after that became World No.1 for the first time. The rest, as they say, is history.

That could have been Jimmy helping Andre to glory. Would he have delivered the same success? I suppose we will never know. But, I reiterate, I have the strongest feeling even my grandmother could have done it with a talent as sensational as Agassi's.

Jimmy Connors's legacy was never going to be cemented or liquidised by coaching, though. It is what he delivered on the court that singled him out for Hall of Fame greatness. Whether you loved him or loathed him, there was no ignoring him: this orchestrator of crowds, this pugnacious warrior, this straight-shooting champion.

Jimmy says his greatest victory was that every time he walked out to do his job, he gave it all he had and never left anything out there. That made him most proud, more so even than the major titles. How I wish I had just a semblance of that attitude. Hell, don't we all?

HURRAY FOR HOLLYWOOD

THE YEAR was 1979. The place was Wimbledon. I was in the quarter-finals of the men's singles championship. My opponent was a brash American. He was involved in a tempestuous romance with actress Ali MacGraw, who was watching on intently.

I was match point down and thinking: 'I'm as mad as hell and I'm not going to take this anymore!' But it was too late. He dived full-length to connect with the ball and it passed me in a flash. My Wimbledon dream was over. We shook hands. He would have to wait to fall into the arms of his lover because she was involved with another.

The director said 'Cut' and my movie debut – indeed my movie career – was over. But I had my £1,000 acting fee and I could at least claim to have gone further at Wimbledon than I ever had before. It was there on film for all posterity. There was no denying me.

The film was *Players*, an American drama starring not only MacGraw but Maximilian Schell, Steve Guttenberg and Dean Paul Martin as my quarter-final opponent and the hero of the piece. Tennis great Pancho Gonzales played himself – coach of the unlikely champion – and there were cameos from John McEnroe, Guillermo Vilas and Ilie Nastase. Like me, they doubtless said: 'Show me the money!' and signed up. I had hoped I might get to deliver a moving and meaningful line of dialogue. 'You don't understand! I could'a had class. I could'a been a contender. I could'a been somebody, instead of a bum, which is what I am.' But I didn't get my Brando moment. I didn't get to say anything at all. My Hollywood looks or my immediate availability led to me being cast. I will leave you to decide.

The film was known during the production as *Getting Off*, although there was no getting off on this absolute shocker of a story in which a bronzed and blond would-be tennis star has an affair with a jet-setting older woman. It was an epic failure, even though Dean Paul Martin was nominated for a Golden Globe for Best New Star of that year.

'Dino', as he was known, was the son of Dean Martin and had tried to make it on the tennis circuit. He was a friend of old: one of those guys who struggled to emerge from the shadow of his legendary father, trying 20 different things and never really quite making it in any of them. He married and divorced both actress Olivia Hussey and Olympic gold medal ice skater Dorothy Hamill.

A keen pilot, he became an officer in the California Air National Guard in 1981 but died just six years later when his Phantom jet fighter crashed in California's San Bernardino Mountains during a snowstorm. He was just 35.

Our *Players* scene was filmed the week after the Wimbledon tournament, out on Court 7. The moviemakers imported a crowd and tried to recreate a Centre Court feel. They failed. A woman shouted 'make-up!' as she approached me. I love the movies. This was my big moment. 'All right, Mr DeMille, I'm ready for my close-up.' She then splashed water in my face and down my white shirt. No make-up, just fake sweat. I was meant to be at the end of a five-set marathon match, so I had to be dripping, apparently.

We had just a couple of scenes to shoot, but it took a while. You have heard of actors fluffing their lines. Well, Dino was fluffing his shots. I kept 'dollying' the ball back so he could smack a glorious winner and continue his relentless march to Wimbledon glory. But he was so nervous, he missed time and again until, on the tenth take, he dived and connected and the 'match' was over.

The action in tennis films can be so contrived and often looks ridiculous. My sequence was no different. The film *Wimbledon* was even worse. Paul Bettany is a fine actor, but his tennis was distinctly Sunday-in-the-park fodder. His co-star Kirsten Dunst couldn't hit the skin off a rice pudding. If they couldn't convincingly capture match sequences, why put them in? Golf films can get away with it. Kevin Costner was said to have practised his swing for the movie *Tin Cup* for about three months. As long as that looked believable, it didn't matter where the ball went. The director could cut to it landing sweetly on the green, even if it had been sliced half a mile to the right. They could make Costner appear a genius with a club in his hands. It just ain't so with tennis.

A friend showed me the script of *Wimbledon* before it came out and I instantly declared it complete rubbish. Just like *Players*, they made the fatal mistake of trying to make a tennis version of boxing film *Rocky*: the underdog coming through from nowhere to win the Wimbledon title. It's so hackneyed, so dated. I can't believe the All England Club were so gung-ho about the project. They must have seen the terrible script, too. It was all so far-fetched. This kind of thing could never happen – surely? Then, along comes a British teenager by the name of Emma Raducanu. She wins the 2021 US Open from nowhere and is our sport's very own *Rocky* after all. Astonishing.

What tennis needs is a character-driven sports movie in the mode of the Costner classic *Bull Durham*. There doesn't have to be a hero, there doesn't have to be someone coming through to win Wimbledon. Simply capture life on the road, the struggles and the funny stories along the way, and leave the sporting action on the periphery. A film of this book, anyone?

Acting was never my forte. I wish it had been. I appeared in a couple of commercials when I was married to Chris Evert and soon realised I was no good. Put a camera on me as a tennis pundit or in commentary and I'm fine, but ask me to sell Lipton Ice Tea and I am useless. Cheers Chrissie, 'Here's another nice mess you've gotten me into.' I just about got away with it in the TV ads because Chris was the main star and I only had to smile and mutter a few words. Hopefully, no one will go digging around the archives for them. Please do not accept this as a challenge.

Acting talent might not run through my veins, but movies are in some way my lifeblood. I have always adored them, ever since my father took me to see British comedian Norman Wisdom hanging off the top of a speeding ambulance in all his black-and-white hilariousness. Dad used to laugh so loud we came close to being thrown out of the cinema on a few occasions. I inherited that from him. I'm often being 'ssshhh'd' in cinemas. Oh, for the memory of those Saturday double features. First, an Audie Murphy western like *Six Black Horses*, *The Texican* or *Bullet for a Badman*. Then, a classic adventure like *Lost World*, in which feuding lizards posed as battling dinosaurs. I'm still first in line for creature features – anything from *King Kong* to the *Jurassic Park* collection – because they take me straight back to those childhood days of escapism.

Movies also filled many an empty hour on the tennis tour, plugging sizeable gaps in tedious downtime. Girlfriends who didn't know anything about tennis would suggest going shopping for four hours, not realising that wasn't the best preparation for a match the next day. 'But it's only walking,' I would hear. If I wasn't in a relationship, I didn't want to go out hustling in nightclubs as some of the other players did. I was no saint, but that wasn't the way I went about things. Therefore, taking myself off to the cinema was my preferred option. In France, I would even sit through films without subtitles, not understanding a bloody word. 'Toto, I've a feeling we're not in Kansas anymore.' I always hoped a great action sequence would make up for my lack of understanding.

To this day, the most blissful thing is for me to catch a film that's been around for a few weeks on a quiet Tuesday afternoon and have the movie theatre all to myself, feet up, popcorn in hand.

Living in and around the Los Angeles area for a large part of my life meant I saw in person many of the stars I so admired on the big screen. One of them became a great friend and gave me an insight into movie making I never imagined possible.

Harold Ramis was a Hollywood triple threat: a gifted actor, writer and director. He was also an incredibly smart and likeable man. Stardom found Harold when he played Dr Egon Spengler in the 1984 smash hit *Ghostbusters* and its sequel – films he also co-wrote. He was one of the most sought-after comedy directors in the business, delivering *Caddyshack*, *Groundhog Day*, *National Lampoon's Vacation* and *Analyze This*.

His two sons went to the same Californian progressive infant school as my children – Pluralistic School One – and that's how my ex-wife Deborah and I came to befriend Harold and his wife Erica, who was the daughter of director Daniel Mann and actress Mary Kathleen Williams. A more grounded and less flashy Hollywood couple you could not wish to meet. Harold was one of those guys you would instantly fall in love with, who interacted in the same warm and wonderful way with all ages, from young kids to old folk. He was interested in what people had to say and joined in conversations with a consummate ease. It was the same when he joined me and my British Davis Cup team for dinner when he was filming in London. He thought hanging out with international players like that was fantastic: that he had been allowed into the inner sanctum.

Of course, he returned the favour and then some. In the mid-1990s, I spent time on the set of *Multiplicity*, a comedy/science fiction film in which Michael Keaton is cloned several times over. The film made less than half its budget back at the box office, although I have never understood why. It was funny and Keaton was superb. I was fascinated by the amount of time it would take to set up a scene. Sometimes it would be half an hour for a ten-second clip. I finally got why actors talked about spending more time in their trailers than on set. There was no wasted time with Harold, though. He knew what he wanted, he would get his scene and he would shout 'Cut!' He could put his actor's hat on and appreciate they didn't want to do 50 takes. It was a case of do it well – just once if possible – and move on.

I once again saw, just a few years later on the set of *Bedazzled*, the tremendous atmosphere Harold could create on set. Brendan Fraser and Liz Hurley were the stars. Both of them, as with Michael Keaton before them, could not have been more accommodating to an intruder like me. When Harold introduced me to Liz, she was about to shoot a scene and was wearing quite a revealing outfit. She knew who I was from my tennis days and gave me this alluring wide-eyed 'Hello John' that oozed star quality. There might have been a little flutter in my heart.

Harold directed the smash-hit American version of *The Office* for a spell. That allowed me a glimpse behind the scenes of a juggernaut success in television and to meet the supremely talented Steve Carell and John Krasinski. I was so privileged to watch them rehearse and record, producing a magical cast dynamic that was led by this fabulous director. They all quite clearly worshipped Harold and so evidently loved what they were doing. It was special to witness.

One peep behind the movie curtain I could have lived without was when Harold invited me to a screening of comedy sequel *Analyze That* in New York. This is not to be confused with a film premiere. No, this was the first time the film was to be seen by some of the cast, producers and money men. There were perhaps 25 people there in all.

The hilarious *Analyze This*, starring Robert De Niro and Billy Crystal, had been one of the big hits of 1999. The follow-up didn't match up. I was sitting close to Harold and felt this added pressure to laugh at all the 'right' times or risk insulting him and his actors (minus De Niro, who wasn't there). It was incredibly awkward. I found myself laughing in a more exaggerated fashion at scenes I didn't find funny. Then, when the lights went up, there was the inevitable debrief and more awkwardness for fear of saying the wrong thing about a mobster-psychiatrist premise stretched too thinly. It wasn't a fun place to be, nor a situation I would want to experience again.

Harold and Erica lived in the Los Angeles neighbourhood Brentwood, not far from where the infamous OJ Simpson lived. During and after his trial for the murder of his ex-wife Nicole Brown Simpson and Ron Goldman, there was a macabre desire to see where it all happened so people were coming to Brentwood from all over the greater LA area.

One night, Harold was looking after his infant sons while Erica went out for dinner with her girlfriends, including my then wife Deborah. Erica was such a loving and protective mother that to persuade her to do this kind of thing took some doing. Harold read a bedtime story to his boys and fell asleep alongside them. He woke with a start to see a gun pointed at his head.

Two burglars had broken into the house. The one with the gun demanded money. Astonishingly, Harold kept incredibly calm – even as his sons woke to see their father being threatened. Erica was a Buddhist and some of those teachings must have spilled over into her husband's demeanour. He was always a soul at peace. Harold explained: 'We don't keep money in the house. We're not those people who stash money in a safe. We have three watches – one's a Rolex. Take them – take anything. I've got about 300 bucks in my wallet. Here, take that.'

The phone rang. It was 9.30pm. 'It'll be my wife checking in on us,' said Harold. They told him to answer so as not to raise suspicion. Cleverly, Harold talked to his wife in a way he would not normally to arouse suspicion in another way. Erica picked up on it immediately. 'Harold, are you okay? What's going on?

Is there someone with you?' He replied: 'Yeah, yeah, exactly right ... now you have a great time with the girls.' Erica asked should she call the police. 'Yep, you better do that ... and as I say enjoy your time with the girls.' The burglars returned to rifling through the family's possessions until sirens could be heard and they bolted with the watches and the $300.

As the burglars headed back to East LA that night, they saw a police cordon and thought it was set up to trap them. It wasn't. They sped off, triggering the police to follow them and they were captured. Erica was so upset by the frightening episode that she decided she could not live in LA anymore. They moved to Chicago and we had lost our neighbours, although we still saw them when Harold was working in town.

The greatest tragedy was how it all ended for this brilliant man. He was working on a third *Ghostbusters* script when he took seriously ill in May 2010. He was admitted to hospital for the nasty intestinal condition diverticulitis. Erica spotted he was becoming somewhat swollen and puffy and it was discovered he had developed a serious infection. The complications from autoimmune inflammatory vasculitis affected his ability to walk and he had to use a wheelchair. Although he would get back to his feet, he suffered a relapse the following year.

When I spoke to Harold on the phone, this genius of a man was as lovely as ever – but his spark had gone. His condition worsened. He died at his Chicago home in 2014. He was 69.

We attended the private funeral in Chicago, where the adoration for Harold was tangible. His beloved collaborators Dan Aykroyd and Chevy Chase were there, but Bill Murray was not. Their careers had been so intertwined during the late 1970s and 80s. When I had asked Harold about the breakdown of their relationship – around the time of *Groundhog Day* in 1993 – he told me: 'Bill's a tough guy to be around. I didn't want that bad energy around me anymore. We never speak.' Just before Harold's passing, Bill Murray visited him and they talked for the first time in 21 years. Murray then paid glowing tribute to Harold at the Academy Awards.

There was a wonderful tribute also from US President Barack Obama, who released a statement stating: 'When we watched his movies – from *Animal House* and *Caddyshack* to *Ghostbusters* and *Groundhog Day* – we didn't just laugh until it hurt. We questioned authority. We identified with the outsider. We rooted for the underdog. And through it all, we never lost our faith in happy endings. Our thoughts and prayers are with Harold's wife, Erica, his children and grandchildren, and all those who loved him, who quote his work with abandon, and who hope that he received total consciousness.' That last line is in reference to the caddy in *Caddyshack*, who is told by the Dalai Lama that 'total consciousness' will be his when he dies, after the spiritual leader is helped in his round of golf by Murray's character. Typically, and wonderfully, Harold remained friends with the Dalai Lama.

Harold helped me appreciate that, for all its glitzy exterior and ego-driven underbelly, Hollywood is just as awash with good and decent human beings as self-important arseholes.

I was in a store in my neighbourhood, Pacific Palisades, with my young son Aiden when I spotted Oscar-winning actor Anthony Hopkins. He had a baseball cap on and was quietly going about his business. It wasn't long after *The Mask of Zorro* had been released in 1998 and Aiden was a big fan of that film. 'Aiden, look – there's Zorro,' I said, pointing to the esteemed man. 'Why don't you ask for his autograph?' No sooner had I said that than Anthony Hopkins moved towards the door. We had missed our window of opportunity. As he was about to leave the building, I thought: 'I never do this. But today, you know what, I will.' I chased after him.

'Excuse me, Mr Hopkins. I'm a fellow Brit, John Lloyd. That's my son, Aiden.' I pointed to where my son was standing, probably wondering what the heck Dad was up to and thinking: 'Please Dad, don't do your Hannibal Lecter impression!'

'I'm sure you've heard it a thousand times, but he's a big fan of your film *Zorro*. Could he please have your autograph?' Anthony Hopkins ushered him over and asked: 'What's your name again? Aiden? That's a very nice name. Here, let me sign something for you, Aiden. Now let me tell you, I live here. I'm in the village a lot. Any time you see me, please feel free to come over and we can have a lovely chat.' Aiden nodded his approval. Anthony Hopkins equals class act.

I could see how a place like Pacific Palisades would appeal to him. It was Santa Monica-lite: a sleepy village in many ways, where 'last orders' at most restaurants was 9pm and famous people could go about their business incognito. Well, unless excited dads like me doorstepped them, of course. That was a one-off, I promise you. Hand on heart, I never once approached David Hasselhoff or Pamela Anderson when they were filming that global television phenomenon *Baywatch* on my local beach – and trust me, there were times when I wanted to offer myself up as a drowning extra ready to be resuscitated by Ms Anderson. They largely filmed from December to February because the beach was less populated. The water in the summer isn't exactly warm, so in the winter it is bloody freezing. I would see the actors being lathered in gunk to keep the cold out, watch them complete the scene and then rush to be enveloped in a warm blanket. While I became blasé about the whole thing, friends who visited would find it all endlessly fascinating and I would be reminded that to have this on my doorstep was pretty cool.

Talking of which, one of the kings of cool is actor David Duchovny – star of television gold, *The X-Files*. Producer and manager Melanie Greene, an old friend of mine, asked me if I would play tennis with David, one of her clients, as part of his 40th birthday gifts from her. I gorge on *The X-Files*. It was an immediate 'yes'. I took him to Pepperdine University overlooking the Pacific Ocean, one of the most beautiful settings for a game of tennis imaginable. David's then wife Tea Leoni was there to film all the action. Once again, I have to say this massive star could not have been friendlier. He wasn't half bad at tennis either, most enthusiastic and a damn good athlete. Whenever I saw him at restaurants in the neighbourhood after that, we would always have a bit of a catch-up. When I was playing a senior tour event in Vancouver, Canada, they were filming *The X-Files* there and I got the chance to meet David's marvellous co-star Gillian Anderson and see them both in Mulder-Scully mode. I was so close to asking David to put me in a scene as an extra – just someone wandering by in the back of shot or something – but I bottled it. Regrets, I've had a few.

Most people would keel over with excitement at the chance of taking in just one of their favourite shows being made, which makes me sound boastful and greedy when I add powerhouse American soaps *Dallas* and *Dynasty* to *The Office* and *The X-Files*. Yes, I got to hang out on set with villainous JR himself, Mr Larry Hagman, and his TV wife Linda Gray, thanks to an invitation from Bud Grant, president of entertainment at the

American network CBS. Later came a chance to take a peek behind the scenes at ABC's answer to *Dallas* – massive shoulder pads and all – *Dynasty*. Joan Collins was a huge star in the States at the time the show was at its peak, but could not have been more welcoming and gracious. She was even kind enough to say she remembered me from my tennis days. Joan's co-star Heather Locklear was asked if I could hang around to see her next sequence being filmed. It was a bedroom scene, normally shot on closed sets. Heather said: 'Absolutely! No problem.' What seemed like 20 takes later, I was still there, seeing her in an amorous clinch. I've had worse days.

Down the years, both country music legend Kenny Rogers and billionaire businessman Jeff Greene have invited me to their houses for private screenings of new films. Jeff's wife Mei Sze set up a candy room in their home cinema on my request and there are now about 40 dispensers, including one for Liquorice Allsorts just for me. It's movie heaven. Jeff's guest list has included film director Oliver Stone, members of the Kennedy clan and heads of major companies. I have learned to let the intellectuals have their say first, once the house lights have gone up, before giving my opinion on an art-house movie. I work on the theory it is better to keep your mouth shut and let people think you are a fool than open your mouth and prove it.

I am much more a man of the people when it comes to films. Blockbusters have more of an appeal than the collection of Best Foreign Language Movie nominees, but I can appreciate and enjoy all genres. When people ask what would I like to have done if I had not played tennis as a profession, I say: 'Become a film critic.' I dabbled when I did movie reviews in the *Grand Slam Sports* magazine a number of years ago, awarding a number of rackets rather than stars to films. Sitting in a darkened room, guzzling popcorn, watching films for a living: what's not to like about that?

My viewing of all things British goes up about the time I am heading back to Britain to work at Wimbledon. There's still some surprise, after all these years living in the States, that I haven't got more of an American accent. I tell people that I work on eradicating the twang by watching British dramas. I'm serious. That's my homework before coming home.

Working in television gives me a small taste of the world of acting, or at least its superficial nature. It is all about how you look and sound, how popular you might be, and not always about the talent and skill you have for the job. In tennis, it doesn't matter if your face fits as long as you are good enough on the court. You can be butt ugly, a nasty piece of work and bore for the nation, but if your ranking is good enough you are in. I used to watch all those beautiful women and men serving me in restaurants in LA and know they were doing that job – paying their way in tips – so they could audition through the day with hundreds of others. All were after that one big break. How long do you carry that dream until you decide, 'Okay, this isn't for me'? It all seems too superficial: too cruel. But then I suppose life is like a box of chocolates. You never know what you're gonna get. Now where did I hear that?

MY IDOLS

UNFORTUNATELY, I had an extra spring in my step this most thrilling of afternoons in the shade of New Hampshire's White Mountains. I say unfortunately because, had it been any other humdrum kind of day, I would not have been taking the stairs down to the practice court two at a time, at speed.

This was careless in the extreme considering I was about to have a dream come true. By allowing my excitement to overtake my wits, I was about to jeopardise that dream. I was a giddy youngster, drunk on the mountain air and the anticipation of playing my hero.

Rod Laver was the greatest player ever to grace a tennis court: a genius. He had won two calendar Grand Slams – all four major titles in the same year – not once, but twice: a feat never likely to be repeated.

I had drawn Laver in the first round of the Volvo International at the new Mount Cranmore Tennis and Recreation Club at Bretton Woods, some 200 miles from Boston. It was an event that Hall of Fame tennis writer Bud Collins dubbed 'Wimbledon in the Woods'. It was a peculiar but enchanting venue, where spectators, probably only in their hundreds, gathered on sloping lawns that formed a kind of arena around the courts.

With a Volvo car and $50,000 in prize money, it wasn't only the breathtaking location that attracted the big names. From the outset, it was, as Laver himself quaintly put it, 'a little old country hit'.

Bretton Woods was known for its golf, climbing, fishing and skiing. Laver, who conducted a summer coaching clinic there each year, and his fellow Australian Roy Emerson led the project to put tennis on the map. They guided the hotel in its development of the clay-court tournament, which had begun as an exhibition event in 1970 but was now a tour fixture.

Laver was the headline attraction this particular year – and I was about to play him for the first time in my fledgling career.

The purse for losing in the first round was about $200, which was a vast sum of money to me at that time. Defeat seemed inevitable, but at least I would have the great honour of sharing a court with the best ever while banking some desperately needed cash.

It was three hours before our match when I came bounding down the stairs – resembling a freshly scrubbed Labrador puppy – from the fourth floor of the hotel lodge to hit the practice courts. All I actually succeeded in hitting was the floor, in pain. I lost my footing on one of the steps and badly turned my ankle. It was excruciating and, in no time, my ankle was inflating like a balloon.

My mind was racing, my heart was pounding. How could I mess up what was to be the biggest match of my life to this point, with a guaranteed substantial payday? It couldn't end here. It just couldn't. I cut one of my tennis shoes so I could fit my swollen foot and ankle into it, then hobbled on a mission to find Rod Laver.

'Excuse me, Mr Laver, I'm John Lloyd and I'm due to play you today.' Not only did I call him mister but I think I might have bowed as well. 'There's just one problem.' I showed him my ankle. 'The thing is, I could really do with the money so I'm desperate to play.' The great man replied: 'Don't worry, mate. Leave it to me.'

We took to the red clay, him looking as imperious as ever and me strapped up to within an inch of my life, and we somehow played the match. By 'don't worry' and 'leave it to me', Laver meant he would hit almost every ball within a 3ft radius of me so I didn't have to run around like a maniac and cause my ankle further damage.

Laver would win in straight sets – just as he would have done if I had possessed two good ankles – but at least he gave the public a few rallies to enjoy and allowed me to pick up my pay cheque. Did I mention it was desperately needed? Tennis experts would have clocked he was going easy on me, but the average punter would not have picked up on the exhibition nature of our contest. He was convincing.

I shook his hand and said the most earnest 'Thank you very, very much.' He replied with a typically laid-back Aussie 'No worries, mate' and our business was done. When you think your heroes can't soar to new heights, trust me they can. Imagine any player in the modern era being that kind and accommodating. Not a prayer. You wouldn't even dare to ask for such help and kindness. But that was the mark of the man that is Rod Laver.

Many years later, when he was playing in the Grand Masters tour and I was playing in over-35s events, a combined senior competition was staged in Florida where another dream was almost scuppered, this time by illness.

I happened to draw Laver as my doubles partner: one of the biggest thrills of my career. The day before we teamed up, I was feeling decidedly rough. I couldn't breathe properly. It was worrying.

I was taken to the local hospital where the doctor diagnosed me with walking pneumonia. They put me on some kind of apparatus to help me with my breathing and booked me a bed for the night.

Match day arrived and I told the doctor I had a tennis event to play that afternoon, one I simply could not miss. He advised: 'You really shouldn't do that. You are not well enough to exert yourself.'

I asked: 'Am I contagious?'

'Well, no.'

'Then unless I drop dead, I'm playing.'

They pumped me full of antibiotics and off I went to partner my idol in a competitive match for the one and only time in my life. After the momentous occasion, I went back to hospital and really did feel like I was dying for the next three days. But it was worth all that suffering to play alongside Rod.

Fortunately, I managed to work with him on numerous tennis clinics and developed an even greater understanding of just how amazing a character he is. His knowledge of the game is extraordinary and he has to be the most modest champion I have ever encountered. I would put Roger Federer right up there at the pinnacle of the mountain of all-time greats, but Laver would be right alongside him.

Actually, for me, even a few inches above him. The word legend can be overused in sport, but not where Rod Laver is concerned.

The earliest example of meeting and playing some of the game's most exulted luminaries – players I had adored from a distance when wandering the grounds of Wimbledon with my father – came when I was a teenager at my old mentor John Barrett's BP training camp. Two or three times a year, a top name was employed to help British youngsters who had been invited to take part in the scheme, Australian greats like Ken Rosewall and Margaret Court among them. I was in awe.

Court was tall and powerful, a serve-volleyer extraordinaire and a phenomenon in the women's game. Rosewall oozed class and had us in his thrall. I got to feel the heaviness of their shots: the depth and precision was an education, too. They could not have been more engaging, more enthusiastic.

The same was true of another brilliant Aussie, Lew Hoad, Wimbledon champion in 1956 and 1957. When I was 16, my good friend Peter Risdon sponsored me to train for six weeks at Lew Hoad's Campo de Tenis in Fuengirola, near Malaga in Spain, which he set up with his wife Jenny in 1972.

Lew was an incredible player. Some of his peers, like Pancho Gonzales, told me they considered him to be the best ever; that a racket became a wand when he flicked his wrist. But he was dogged by a crippling back problem and hindered by a certain nonchalance that was both his charm and his curse. In 1956, Hoad arrived at the US Open needing to win the title to complete the Grand Slam. He already held the Australian Open, French Open and Wimbledon crowns. But he claimed he was oblivious to the term 'Grand Slam' or its significance.

An American magazine had Lew on the cover, with the words 'Grand Slammer from Down Under'. He said he saw it and 'didn't know what the bloody hell they were on about'. His great mate Rosewall beat him in the US Open final, so Lew got no better acquainted with the term, as it turned out.

My first workout at Hoad's training camp involved a volleying drill. I stood alone on one side of the net; Lew and larger-than-life Abe Segal stood on the other side. Abe was a beefy South African who could demolish his own bodyweight in food at lunch and had the most flamboyant sense of humour. Peppering my body with volleys would be amusement enough for him in this session.

I had quite a backswing on my forehand volleys and Lew immediately said: 'No, we've got to get rid of that.' When Lew and Abe hit volleys, they took the racket head back just a fraction and yet produced so much power that balls returned my way like missiles. I was being hit left, right and centre. Ducking and diving was not helping my bruise count. I had to learn and I had to learn fast. I put so much work in, my hands were bloody and blistered much of the time. But at the end of the six weeks, my backswing on my volleys had been knocked out of me. The genius Lew Hoad did that. It was one of the best times I ever had.

Roy Emerson, winner of 12 major singles titles and another 16 in doubles, was another wonder to come off the remarkable production line of Australian tennis talent. Born in 1936, 'Emmo' was still in the world's top 20 a full 37 years later. I was just 21 – he was almost twice my age and nearing retirement from the main tour – when I beat him at the Spectrum in Philadelphia. I played out of my mind to win in straight sets, but was under no illusion this was a champion who would have destroyed me in his prime.

Such was his aura and such was my awed respect, Emerson could have easily intimidated me during changeovers. Here was this impressionable young wannabe playing one of his idols. Instead, all I heard from Roy was 'great shot' and 'well played'. He was the perfect sportsman, raised in the old school. As we shook hands he said: 'Great match. You've got a hell of a future.' I will never forget how special that made me feel. He would equally have been at liberty to utter: 'I would have kicked your arse a few years ago.'

I was honoured to play other greats on my way up, when they were on their way out. I defeated 1952 Wimbledon champion Frank Sedgman in his native Australia when he was well into his 40s; I lost to a fiery 40-something Pancho Gonzales, twice US Open champion, at the South Orange Open when he was making more comebacks than Frank Sinatra. The night before these matches, I would have to pinch myself to realise the players I worshipped were now my opponents. I'm not sure how to sum it up in words. How about spine-tingling? That works.

Thankfully, I grew to know and appreciate these fine gentlemen through the years at coaching clinics and corporate events. Pancho had a reputation for not suffering fools gladly. He was volatile and confrontational. He mellowed, though, at least if the time I spent with him was anything to go by. He regaled me with countless stories of the good old days, with never a hint of that infamous temper. I found it all truly fascinating.

I spent similar quality time with Roy Emerson thanks to a company called Grand Slam Sports, created by Fred Stolle, another Australian major winner from the 1960s. I was allowed into the Grand Slam set courtesy of my three major mixed doubles titles but the true headliners were Emerson, Rosewall and Stolle. Other members included Owen Davidson, Marty Riessen, Sherwood Stewart and Bob Lutz, all major doubles champions.

We would hold tennis clinics, exhibitions, lunches and dinners for companies and their clients throughout the United States and sometimes globally. I would always tell our CEO John Lehman to get my introduction out of the way early, before he got to the stellar names. There's nothing quite so humbling as a muted round of applause after a series of rapturous receptions, as I found out the hard way in Las Vegas.

When I worked for American network HBO, I was given tickets for one of the channel's huge boxing nights in Vegas. I loved boxing and fondly remember the times my father would let me stay up late with him to listen to big fight nights on the radio, like in 1964 when Cassius Clay – as Muhammad Ali still was then – beat Sonny Liston in a classic.

I invited Jimmy Connors along to watch Evander Holyfield take on Michael Moorer in a world heavyweight title bout. We flew the short distance from LA on a private jet full of celebrities. Legendary actor Kirk Douglas was at my side.

The atmosphere before the fight was electric. Everywhere I looked, there was a famous face. Renowned ring announcer Michael Buffer, the man of 'Let's get ready to rumble!' fame, built the occasion yet more by introducing more of the gathered constellation. It went something like this.

'Ladies and gentlemen, we are joined by some of the great names of entertainment and sport this evening, starting with one of the biggest superstars in Hollywood. It's none other than Rocky himself ... Sylvester Stallone!' Sly got quite the ovation.

'Please also welcome one of the kings of comedy … a star of stage and screen … it's Eddie Murphy.' Cue the ear-ringing cheers. As the hilarious Barry Humphries said when portraying the outlandish Sir Les Patterson, they were all 'getting the clap they so richly deserved'.

Buffer ended with the starry sporting contingent, mentioning the biggest of heavyweight hitters Larry Holmes and George Foreman, before announcing: 'Welcome from ice hockey, the NHL's all-time leading scorer, the Great One, Wayne Gretzky!' The crowd went nuts.

'From the world of tennis …'

I thought at this point, 'Oh great, Jimmy's getting a mention. Quite right, too.'

'… an eight-time Grand Slam singles champion, one of the greatest players ever … it's Jimmy Connors!' Again, there was nothing but adulation.

Buffer continued: 'Also from the world of tennis …'

I glanced around to seek out another Jimmy Connors-type figure. Who had I missed? Had John McEnroe sneaked in? I was thinking: 'Please don't let it be me, please don't let it be me. Andre Agassi lives in Vegas. It must be him. Yeah, it'll be Agassi. Buffer has saved the local superstar until last.'

All this flashed through my brain in a nanosecond, until Buffer declared:

'… a warm welcome to the former British number one … John Lloyd!'

There was a polite ripple of applause. Exactly the clap I deserved, in fact. I could hear people around me saying: 'Who the hell is that?' That's where the celebrity introductions ended. I stared at my programme, mortified.

My HBO Ross Greenburg had kindly put me on the list. 'That's very nice of you to include me,' I said, 'but please don't ever do that again.'

Now you understand why I always insisted on being introduced first in our Grand Slam Sports company events. If anything, I was the mere appetiser for the marquee men of the main course, who were the serial major title collectors.

Making friends along the way was one of the joys of the organisation. Dave Bower was one such friend. He worked for financial services firm Cantor Fitzgerald, with whom we staged a number of events through the years. Dave became such a good friend that his family and mine went on holiday together.

During the 2001 US Open, we arranged another Cantor Fitzgerald get-together at the oldest grass court tennis club in the United States – Seabright at Rumson, New Jersey. As ever, we had tremendous fun and, much as we were handsomely remunerated, it seemed the farthest thing from work I could imagine.

Dave invited me to swing by his New York office, if I got the chance. He worked something like 120 floors up which, combined with my claustrophobia in lifts, was not the most appealing prospect. As it happened, work commitments took any decision out of my hands and I flew back to LA on the Monday after the US Open, believing I would next see Dave at ground level somewhere soon, possibly on a holiday beach.

The next morning, I woke early and switched on the television to witness the utterly shocking pictures of a passenger plane flying into one of the Twin Towers of the World Trade Center in New York. I realised that was the building in which Dave worked.

I called his wife Ginny, who quickly picked up, and through horrified tears said: 'I can't speak to you right now, John. I'm waiting for Dave to call me.'

He never did. Dave and all his Cantor Fitzgerald colleagues, who just a week earlier had enjoyed that fantastic tennis day in the sun, were murdered in the 9/11 terror attack.

Our Grand Slam Sports family shared in the grief. Disbelief quickly turned to devastation.

The support of friends counts more than ever in such harrowing times and there's no question the legends of the game taught me a thing or two about friendship and camaraderie. They had genuine love for each other – and that's no exaggeration.

But then they had come through the amateur and early professional days, when money was scarce, if not non-existent, and Wimbledon champions walked away with a gift voucher, for a sports store, worth a couple of hundred quid and not millions of dollars. There were no entourages, there was no grandeur. The on-court rivals would stay in the same digs and even cooked breakfast for each other on the morning of major championships finals.

There was no whiling away time on computers or mobile phones or taking yourself off to watch video footage of your next opponent. Win or lose, the locker room was the only place to hang out most of the time. Dinner was a group thing. Talk was about who was gonna get lucky tonight. Tennis friendships lasted a lifetime and we will not see the like again.

A Tennis Channel documentary entitled *The Barnstormers* illustrated just what the multi-millionaire generation owe these guys, explaining how the world's best like Rod Laver and American Jack Kramer would mark out their own courts inside gymnasiums and play in front of a few hundred people in appalling lighting, before moving on to another town and another badly lit gym. When the current crop moan about their lot on tour, they should be forced to watch this programme.

I wonder if some of the golden greats played on into their 40s to make money. There was a bit more cash flying around in their later years: still nothing compared to what's on offer today, but it was something.

Not that I have ever heard one ounce of bitterness from any of them. They begrudged no one and acknowledged, money or no money, they had the greatest time together, this wonderful band of brothers.

BRILLIANT BJORN

BJORN BORG arrived at the gates of Wimbledon as some kind of fifth Beatle. The hysteria that greeted him was shared in unequal measure by screaming girls and fascinated paparazzi. Tennis had its first global teen idol.

Sweden had no problem delivering the blond and the beautiful, but it wasn't a country known for its brilliance in tennis. Now the three Bs were brought together in one winning package by a 17-year-old with initials to match. Even now, it feels like a story created in the Hollywood script room. If I didn't know better, I would even suggest the Bjorn Borg phenomenon was created by some genius of a PR man way ahead of his time.

But this was no glossy campaign. This was very much for real. We have never seen its like again.

Borg mania was launched at Wimbledon 1973 without the internet and mobile phones. For it to spread so far so quickly was Bjorn going viral before that was even a thing.

And yet he was quiet and almost shy. All this sudden fame and attention: it wasn't like he invited it in. But it was there to stay because his arrival on the circuit coincided with the creation of the men's professional tour and the sport's growing television profile.

There was success and riches awaiting a player of Borg's talent, with Borg's looks.

Our relationship came full circle, from hanging out with him when we were both starting out on tour to hosting him at my place in Los Angeles when we played on the senior tour. It was through knowing Bjorn when I was just a teenager, when we were out in Australia for the first time, that I ended up engaged to a Swedish junior player named Isabelle Larsson. Bjorn had his Swedish girlfriend, I had mine. He wasn't so smitten as to propose to his partner. But Isabelle and me fell madly in love. I took her home to meet my parents in the UK. This thing was serious … or so we thought. Puppy love can cloud anyone's judgement.

We were too young and too naive to know a long-distance relationship while starting out in our tennis careers was destined not to work.

Bjorn would be the more consistent Swede in my life. He had this certain charisma. He wouldn't exactly light up a room when he walked in, nor would he start joking around to grab attention. There was just something about him, that intangible star quality that saw people gravitate towards him. The more you got to know Bjorn, the more you realised he had a great sense of humour. He was definitely one of life's good guys.

When all the Borg mania started, he didn't know what had hit him. I could relate to some of what he was going through because I was making regular appearances of my own in newspapers and girls' magazines like *Jackie*. I was Britain's tennis pin-up, with nicknames like 'Legs Lloyd' and the 'Blond Bombshell'. Though this was nowhere on the global scale of interest in Bjorn, it had its interesting moments.

Another nickname from the time, which I'm called to this day, is 'Flossy'. Americans ask me is it something to do with my teeth, thinking of dental floss. I point out it is actually in reference to my hair. Cotton candy in the US is candyfloss in the UK. In the early days, I did these modelling shoots when I was about ten stone wet through. I don't know what the heck any of us were thinking. I was such a lightweight, with no muscles to show off at all. They dripped me in gold jewellery. My hair was all over the place. Stanley Matthews Junior, son of the legendary English footballer, coined the nickname Flossy as a result. Like candyfloss itself, it stuck.

There was another photo shoot, a few years later, that landed me in a bit of hot water at home. The *Daily Mirror* had offered me big cash to write a column during Wimbledon, dishing the dirt from behind the scenes and posing for photographs with page three models. There was no way I was about to betray people I knew on the circuit, so quickly put an end to that notion. But I was all for posing with a few glamour models: as long as it didn't interfere with my work, of course. Heaven forbid.

The proposal was that on a daily basis I would appear alongside a model in a skimpy tennis outfit to titillate the readers. It was a major source of amusement in the men's locker room, where players cut out the pictures each day and pinned them on the noticeboard.

My mentor John Barrett, who was helping me out in a managerial role back then, accompanied me on the photo shoot and insisted we have the final editorial say on which pictures were printed. When he left, believing the shoot was over, the photographer persuaded me to do a few more poses with their leading page three model, claiming the paper wanted something extra special for the final weekend. I didn't need much persuading.

In walked the model … topless. None of the other models had gone this far. She pressed up against me as the photographer clicked away. I was sweating bullets, thinking of the Antarctic and world poverty as a way of keeping me under control. When the photos arrived for us to 'okay', John saw a few of the more risqué ones and said, 'No, no and no again' to the saucier selection. The ones with the model's boobs pushed up against me were missing. I thought nothing more of it.

The weekend of the Wimbledon finals arrived and I left the maisonette I had bought in Wimbledon to buy a newspaper. I opened up page three to see me in an uncompromising position with the topless model. They had double-crossed me. John rang to complain. The paper's reaction: 'So sue us.'

The first thing that sprang to mind was: 'Oh no! What's my mother going to say.' Sure enough, about ten minutes later I got a phone call. 'John, what on earth is all this,' she said. 'All my friends have been calling me. It's very embarrassing.'

I had to think quickly on my feet. I replied: 'Mother, do you really think I'd do something like that? That's not really me. They superimposed me on the photo.'

'Oh,' she said, with a sigh of relief. 'I knew you wouldn't do a thing like that.'

'Of course I wouldn't.'

My mother believed my explanation for the next 20 years until the beans of truth were finally spilled.

The photographer who stitched me up knew he owed me so passed my number on to some of his modelling colleagues. Did I ever hear from any of them? Just the odd one or two, maybe.

Bjorn's fame shot to new heights when he won six consecutive French Open titles and five Wimbledon Championships in a collection of summer spectaculars no one had seen before or seen since. Wherever he went, he was greeted like a tennis god.

His first Wimbledon in 1973 was the boycott year (when 81 top male players decided not to compete at the Championships in protest at the suspension by the Yugoslav Federation and International Lawn Tennis Federation of Niki Pilic). He reached the quarter-finals, losing in five sets to Britain's Roger Taylor. Three years later, he was champion – beating Romania's Ilie Nastase in the final. I remember saying, when I had first seen Borg play at the age of 17 – with his style of play, that grip and big backswing – that there was no way he could ever win Wimbledon. Grass courts in the 1970s, unlike now, didn't give you time for such extravagance. Borg found time.

He was fortunate not to have been born British. Coaches here would have tried to banish that unorthodox style like a priest exorcising a demon. When I was getting some training as a youngster with the Lawn Tennis Association, they tried to get me to change my grip because I sometimes flicked my backhand in an unconventional way. When I told my dad, he said be respectful, make the most of the court time, but don't listen to them. He was right. It was like they wanted to snuff out originality – and Borg's quirks would have been picked apart, too. Yet, to this day, there is no one true way to hit a tennis ball. If there's a fundamental flaw in a youngster's game, you change it. Otherwise, leave nature well alone.

Borg was actually quite mechanical, almost manufactured. Unlike John McEnroe, who could probably stop playing for months on end, pick up his racket and it still be a wand in his hand, Borg had to play for hours and hours to groove his shots. That's why he burned out so young.

Borg wouldn't play any warm-up tournaments between the French Open and Wimbledon but practised instead at the Cumberland Lawn Tennis Club in Hampstead. I joined him there a couple of times and he was so bad those first few days of practice it was unbelievable. I was thinking: 'Can we start Wimbledon now please and let me draw Bjorn in the first round.' He would find his groove eventually, but he could be vulnerable in the early rounds of Wimbledon. His first year as defending champion, he was two sets down to Australian Mark Edmondson and won in five; the following year of 1978 he was two sets to one down to American Victor Amaya in the first round on Centre Court and pulled out the victory; and again the next year he faced a similar deficit in a second-round match against India's Vijay Amritraj and came through. Once Borg was on top of his game, though, he was brilliantly brutal.

He was all the more fearsome to face because he was impossible to read. Bjorn admitted that as a kid he could lose the plot on court, throwing his rackets in temper. He quickly realised that was not only wasted energy, but gave his opponents the edge because they could see he was rattled. The demeanour of professional, adult Borg never changed. He was like my ex-wife Chris Evert in that way. You couldn't detect from their faces whether or not they were winning. I played Bjorn in Memphis and led 6-0, 2-0. I was killing him. His mind was probably on the argument he had had with his wife Mariana Simionescu. But there wasn't a flicker of anger, frustration or disappointment on his face.

That lack of emotion was unnerving. The only look I could pick up on was that of a man saying: 'You still haven't won yet.' You knew he would chase down every ball, you knew he would keep coming at you. He beat me 6-4 in the deciding third set that day. His face in victory was the same as it had been after losing the first eight games. This ice-man routine proved a perfect contrast to Jimmy Connors and later John McEnroe. Their rivalries wouldn't have worked had they all been created the same.

Bjorn would show emotion when his first championship point at Wimbledon was won, falling to his knees in tears on Centre Court. It became a familiar sight because the greatest clay-court player we had ever seen, before Rafa Nadal came along, had begun a historic run of five successive Wimbledon men's singles titles.

I believe the toughest feat to achieve in tennis is the 'Channel Slam': to win the French Open, then, just a few weeks later, triumph at Wimbledon. It's a supreme test to master the slower, higher bounce of clay at Roland Garros and then the faster, lower bounce of grass, as well as cope with the physical demands of such a quick turnaround between major championships. Just five male players have managed it in the Open era.

Rafael Nadal did it in 2008 and 2010, sandwiching a similar double by Roger Federer. More recently, the great Novak Djokovic has joined the elite club. But astonishingly, Borg did the improbable double three times in a row between 1978 and 1980 when the clay and grass were – unlike more recent times – as different as night and day. Rod Laver is the only other man to win the French Open and Wimbledon on such drastically contrasting surfaces. He did it twice in the

1960s as part of his phenomenal calendar Grand Slams, but only one came in the Open era, in 1969. Borg's place as one of the all-time greats would be cemented by that sensational treble-double alone, even if he had never won another point in his life.

It was success born of routine, superstition and his relationship with towering Swede Lennart Bergelin. Bjorn was the first top player to travel with this kind of coach: someone to ensure his rackets were strung, his practice courts booked, his massages arranged. They made a fantastic team. Bjorn refused to shave and abstained from sex during Wimbledon. He stayed in the same hotel, practised at the same club, asked for the same locker and so banished any extraneous thoughts. He was a superstar, making unbelievable sums of money, packing out venues just for exhibitions and continuously doing what he did best: winning. However, when he lost the epic fourth-set tie-break 18 points to 16 to John McEnroe in the 1980 Wimbledon final, Bjorn later revealed it was the first chink in his armour. Even though he went on to win a fifth straight Championship that day, he had allowed doubt to enter his mind.

In 1981, Borg lost the Wimbledon final to McEnroe and then succumbed again to the American in the US Open final. Bjorn left the court and would soon leave the sport at the age of just 26.

There are many tales of players amassing fortunes, quitting the sport, taking the wrong advice and losing the lot. Bjorn was a very trusting guy and generous to a fault. His clothing company was failing him and so, I suspect, were many of the business people around him. That was the inference behind his ill-fated comeback in 1991, although he denied it publicly and I never felt it right to ask him.

Bjorn came out to train with me in California and asked me if I would travel with him to a few tournaments overseas. It was soon apparent the comeback wasn't going to work. He failed to win even a set in his first nine matches back and, although he improved slightly in 1993, he was still without a victory when he called time on his return. That was the sad part of the experience for me: watching this great champion losing to players he would have swatted away left-handed in his prime. It was unfolding before my very eyes. I was doing my best with him and for him, but he just wasn't ready for it. Even Bjorn would later admit he knew he wasn't playing well, that he was aware it was 'madness' but said: 'I can't explain it except to say I wanted to play.'

The senior circuit wasn't an option for him when he decided on the comeback, but seniors' tennis was soon to flourish and allow Bjorn his time back on court. He could scratch his itch without being mauled in the process. Popular as he was with the rest of us on the senior tour, we were somewhat annoyed by the fact he still wore the same size shirt and shorts as when he played on the regular tour. He hadn't put on even a single pound in weight.

Bjorn could make a good living from tennis once again, while his name would emblazon underwear that helped restore his fortune. His undies are still big business across Europe. Only Calvin Klein outstrips him in Sweden, apparently.

This is where our friendship comes full circle. From those naive kids hanging out in Australia, we were now these more seasoned fellas hanging out at my place in Los Angeles. We had both been through so much since the innocent days of youth. In his heyday, Bjorn had his entourage and I moved in different circles, so we no longer socialised. But it was a pleasure getting to know him again. Bjorn was great with my two children and such a wonderful character to have around.

My second wife Deborah and I went to play tennis in our local park in LA's Pacific Palisades. We were warming up when Bjorn and his girlfriend appeared on the horizon, dressed in tennis gear. 'Can we join you?' he asked. People were walking by, looking over at the court and doing double takes. I heard one passer-by say to his partner: 'Oh, that looks like … nah, it can't be.'

Deb was about to serve to Bjorn. He was waiting … and waiting … and waiting. Deb just stood there, frozen. I sidled over to her to find out what was wrong. 'I just realised I'm serving to Bjorn Borg. I can't release the ball.' She had to serve underarm to him. That's the Borg effect.

It was during another stay in LA that I discovered Bjorn was some kind of bionic man. I already knew he was the greatest athlete ever to play the game of tennis and that he had a freakish metabolism that kept his weight constant. I just hadn't realised quite how superhuman he was.

Comically, there was some kind of survey in the *USA Today* newspaper listing the top ten tennis athletes. To emphasise, this was about athleticism not tennis prowess. Bjorn didn't make the list. Over a few beers one night, he modestly laughed it off. I was insistent on righting the wrong, declaring: 'But you'd beat any player in a sprint and there's no one better for endurance. I know how much running you must have done in training.'

'No, I never ran,' he said. 'In fact, I only bought some running shoes when this laboratory asked me to do some fitness tests. I hadn't played tennis for a while so I was interested to see where I was.' In other words, the always competitive Bjorn Borg was keen to know how the 40-something version was functioning.

They put electrodes on him – Bjorn's heart rate was ridiculously low – and put the breathing apparatus in his mouth and set him on his way on a treadmill. Two hours and 45 minutes later, this freak of human nature had completed a marathon. 'Have you got what you need?' he asked. His explanation of just how this was possible was a simple: 'I've always been lucky with my genetics, I guess. I never get tired.'

Another day, Bjorn asked if he could come along to see my trainer Greg Isaacs and me work out. He had never done weights and was intrigued. I told Greg: 'Be careful, this guy is competitive and I don't want you killing him.' Bjorn started on light weights and it wasn't long before Greg's eyes were bulging out of their sockets. 'I've never seen anything like it,' he claimed. 'His muscles are growing as I'm watching. This guy could have been a weightlifter ... he could have been anything he wanted to be in sport.'

That was further illustrated in phase two of the session when we went for a run at a nearby hiking park. We tackled a mile-and-a-half stretch, all uphill. On the way up, I could feel Bjorn breathing down my neck. 'Are you okay?' I asked. 'Yes – where's the finish?' I pointed to a bridge in the distance and off he sped. I got there as a sweaty mess. Bjorn was waiting for us, cool as could be. I told Greg he was going to have to try to tire him out, to make Bjorn feel like he had actually done something. The next half hour, Bjorn kept charging up and down the hill until Greg had to concede defeat. If I hadn't seen it with my own eyes, I would have said it was beyond belief.

And I suppose that sums up the man for me. Bjorn Borg: amazing tennis player, incredible athlete, with remarkable resilience, a wonderful heart and a kind soul. Beyond belief, if I didn't know it to be true.

DAVIS CUP DAYS

A WHOREHOUSE played host to my first team as Davis Cup captain. Ukraine was the country. Odessa was the city. The surreal episode on the shores of the Black Sea taught me that when leading your country, always be prepared for any eventuality.

Playing for my country in this prestigious team competition was always an honour. We made the final in 1978: the first time that had happened for 42 years. I then had the privilege of coaching the national team, when my brother David was captain in the late 1990s. When I was appointed to lead Great Britain in 2006, I had completed the set and my pride knew no bounds.

But I could never have envisaged starting my captaincy in a hotel with pink walls, mirrors on the ceiling and a sideline in prostitution.

There was usually a recce ahead of a Davis Cup tie overseas, to scout the best hotels and restaurants and check out the tennis facilities. The person on the mission in Odessa rang me to report back. The tennis country club and hotel we were to use had a small locker room. It wasn't ideal, but nothing we couldn't handle. Then he added: 'There's one other thing ... and this is on the level, I swear.'

'There's a what? Inside the grounds? Are you kidding me?'

He wasn't.

'So, you're telling me that if the club members lose at tennis they can go elsewhere for a happy ending?' My question was part joke, part disbelief.

The other facilities were such that it was the best option for the team. We would just have to overlook the garish colours, the mirrors and extra-curricular activity. It was booked.

We arrived in Odessa in the September of 2006. My team included the experienced Greg Rusedski and 19-year-old Andy Murray, who was already in the world's top 20. Andy was now under the wing of Andre Agassi's former coach Brad Gilbert. That summer, the Lawn Tennis Association struck a deal with the American, worth a reported £0.5 million a year or more, to coach Murray as well as work with the LTA's development programmes.

Taking stock of the surroundings, I still imagine the team thinking: 'Who's this classy new captain we've been landed with, bringing us to a tennis club attached to a brothel?'

In keeping with the predicament, I said to them: 'Be careful around here, boys. You never know what you might pick up.'

Greg asked: 'Like what?'

'Like crabs.'

'What are crabs? Not the things you eat?' Greg might have been a 33-year-old adult, but he often came across like a naive 15-year-old.

'No, Greg. The little things you get on your private parts if you've been a naughty boy.' He still hadn't worked it out, so I spelled it out. 'When you have sex with someone with crabs, you catch them too ... or you get them from a bed or sheets if you're really unlucky.'

'What do they look like?'

'They're tiny. They're lice.'

'That's disgusting,' was Greg's summing-up of the unsavoury discussion, still a bit bewildered. What was most bewildering was that this widely travelled 30-something bloke had never heard of a crab that wasn't a crustacean.

The president of the Ukrainian Tennis Federation ran a Challenger event – one rung down from the men's ATP Tour – that was renowned for its prize money, appearance fees and dozens of beautiful models. He was staying at our hotel and showed up with eight of these women in his entourage. Greg came to me and said: 'You've got to come downstairs with me.'

'Why?'

'The president has invited me to join him, but he's got eight women with him.'

I believe Greg knew this guy from playing in the aforementioned tournament.

'And the problem is?'

'If my wife finds out, I'm in trouble,' said Greg.

'Do you intend to do anything with any of these women?' I asked, knowing full well that Greg Rusedski was the last man on earth who would even contemplate such a notion.

'No, of course not. But it won't look good. What if word gets out?'

Paranoia was taking hold, so I joined Greg downstairs with the president and his female friends, but made sure the rest of the team were there, too. Call it safety in numbers. The women looked like they had thrown their clothes on and missed. No one knew quite where to look. Across the way sat Andy's mum, Judy Murray, and some of the LTA delegation. I told my coach Peter

Lundgren it might be best if I made myself scarce, so I made a sharp exit left as if declaring: 'This scene here, it has nothing to do with me.'

Thankfully, Greg was more switched on when it came to tennis. He had been a US Open finalist and World No.4 after all. His injured hip had been a concern but, fair play to him, he came from two sets to one down to beat World No.188 Sergiy Stakhovsky 9-7 in the fifth, saving a match point in the deciding set. Andy Murray won his match in straight sets against Alexandr Dolgopolov, setting us on our way to a 3-2 victory to avoid relegation. Nonetheless, we would have to wait until at least 2008 to have a chance to play in the elite World Group once again. There was a lot of work to do.

This was a far cry from the heady Davis Cup era of the late 70s, when we stood just one win away from a place in the 1978 final. Australia were our opponents in the semi-final. Unfortunately, I had a major distraction. Her name was Chris Evert.

We had started out that year practising in the glamour of the Monte Carlo Country Club, before beating Monaco 5-0. We later had a fantastic win over France on the Parisian clay. That was almost unheard of – a stunning result. With the Czechs also defeated, it was down to a leisure centre in Crystal Palace to host one of the biggest matches in Britain's Davis Cup history. The Monte Carlo Country Club it was not. There were people swimming in the pool next door as we faced the Aussies. This place could hold maybe 2,500 people when five times that many tickets could have been sold. The NEC in Birmingham had opened just two years earlier, while the Royal Albert Hall staged Wightman Cup tennis that year. So why we ended up in this cubbyhole, only heaven and the Lawn Tennis Association know.

The team were gathering at Crystal Palace on the Saturday before the semi got underway the following Friday. Chrissie and I had started seeing each other in the second week at Wimbledon that year and the romance was going strong. She was playing in a tournament in the States. Here's a quiz question. Did I a) join a bunch of guys to practise at a leisure centre in south London; or b) join my new love Chrissie for some fun Stateside, even though this could land me in big trouble with my Davis Cup captain and team-mates? The answer is, of course, b.

Controversially, I showed up in London on Monday night, with just three days of preparation left. It was totally unprofessional. I had let the team down, including my own brother David. He wasn't happy, captain Paul Hutchins wasn't happy, no one on the team was. With Chrissie, I had honestly been very happy.

There was an atmosphere at practice all week. Yes, I had weighed it up. Yes, romance had come out on top. But why should my team-mates understand that ahead of the biggest occasion of any of our careers? I got it. My mind was in a good place, though. I wanted to do it my way. Seeing Chrissie would help me, not hurt me – or so I assumed.

That first practice, I was all over the place. I was jet-lagged, I wasn't focused. The biggest match of my career to date was fast approaching. What had I done?

Friday came. Our captain Paul Hutchins and Mandy Ripley, a great tennis fan who has worked in the Wimbledon referee's office for many years, had just set up the British Association of Tennis Supporters, encouraging a bit of the jingoistic cheering and flag waving that's now part and parcel of the Davis Cup. BATS went nuts, creating a great atmosphere for us in which to perform.

I was up against John Alexander, a damn fine player from Australia. The pressure was immense, even more so for me after what I had done in the build-up. My team-mate Buster Mottram had done his bit, beating Tony Roche in straight sets. A perfect start. My parents were in the crowd. We were 'live' on national television. It was the most important match of my life.

The first ten points were played out. I lost them all.

At two-love and 30-love down, my brother was giving me the kind of look that would have made Medusa proud. If he could have turned me into a block of stone right there, he would have done it in a heartbeat: forget the sibling thing. I'm thinking: 'John, you've got yourself into a bit of trouble here, son.'

What I would now coach for such situations is to cut down on the margin for error, to not go for the lines, to hit the ball down the middle until you find some rhythm, play the percentages. That semi-final day, though, as my heartbeat was racing and I was trying to calm myself down, the percentage game was the furthest thing from my mind. 'Get a grip, John. Just connect with the ball.'

Suddenly, something went off in my head. From the nightmare start came the dream performance. I entered that magical place top sportsmen refer to as 'the zone', like a switch had been flicked. The tennis balls seemed huge before my eyes. I simply could not miss. I destroyed Alexander 7-5, 6-2, 6-2.

I have been in that kind of zone in other matches, but normally felt it from the warm-up. It was the weirdest thing. Balls would come so sweetly off the strings. I just knew that I would be difficult to beat on those days. The match against Alexander was not one of those occasions. The warm-up was average at best. I started horrendously then flipped it round in an instant. I also knew, though I didn't always show it, that I had a certain flair: a certain ability to do things with the ball that others couldn't do. When I got it right, I got it spectacularly right. This was one of those times. Even when I came close to winning, I didn't get tight. I kept smacking the ball … it kept going in.

The victory put us two-up in the best-of-five tie and the following day my brother David and Mark Cox teamed up to win the doubles. Britain was in the Davis Cup Final for the first time since Fred Perry's heyday in the 1930s.

If I had lost that match against Alexander, I have no doubt word would have leaked out about me turning up late to the training camp, about me choosing Chrissie over the GB team. I would have been public enemy number one, probably cast as some kind of unpatriotic loser. You know what, I would have deserved it. As it was, even if people had heard what I had done, they would likely have said: 'We won. What's the fuss? John knows what's best for him. He's happy in life and that showed in his game.' However, they wouldn't have been entirely accurate. Happy though I was, I didn't always know what was good or best for me. Most of the times when I took shortcuts like that I got bitten on the arse – and quite rightly so. This time, in the biggest of matches, I got away with it. It was pure luck it all clicked into place for me. Going AWOL was never mentioned again.

On the final day of the tie, Buster and I both lost the much-hated dead rubbers. There was nothing on these matches. We were already through to the final against the United States and yet had to go through the motions on the Sunday for the sake of television and the paying customers, both of whom were being short-changed by these frankly ludicrous reverse singles of no consequence. Why push yourself and risk injury when the job was already done? I loved playing for my country, with the exception of these 'nothing matches'.

I played in 23 Davis Cup ties from 1974 to 1986 and won 16 singles matches. But I lost 19 and many of those defeats were in dead rubbers. I also enjoyed 11 victories in doubles to five defeats. That illustrates I won more often than I lost in Davis Cup when there was actually something on the line. I mailed it in when there wasn't. Buster hated the dead rubbers almost as much.

Earlier in our run to the Davis Cup Final, we had played Czechoslovakia on the grass of Eastbourne for a place in the semis. I had a marathon match against Jiri Hrebec, beating him 12-10 in the fifth set. Buster defeated 18-year-old Ivan Lendl in straight sets and David and Mark won the doubles. Another tremendous performance. We were through to the last four. After my four and a half hours on court, a nasty lump appeared on my hip. The doctor said he could drain the fluid and enable me to play the next day, or I could rest and it would go down in a few days. I took the second option and reported back to the team: 'Sorry, I can't play tomorrow. Doctor's orders.' Buster could sense foul play. He wasn't best pleased he had to play a dead rubber, while I had wriggled my way out of it.

Mark Cox, ever the professional, stepped in for me and won in straight sets against Lendl. We were looking at our watches on the side of the court, thinking: 'Great. A quick win for Buster now and we'll beat the worst of the Sunday traffic back to London.' Mr Mottram had other ideas. As I have described elsewhere in the book, Buster was a quirky character, very much his own man, and not for toeing the line. He decided to scupper our travel plans and show me I couldn't have things all my own way.

Buster dropped the first two sets 7-5, 6-3 to Hrebec. 'He wants out of here,' I thought, knowing his dislike for dead rubbers. 'His heart's not in it.' Then he looked over at the bench: one of those looks I know well, which said he was up to something. Straight away I thought: 'This son of a gun is gonna start trying to win.' Buster won the next three sets and annoyingly kept us waiting. We wouldn't be beating the traffic after all. He had the last laugh on me.

That 1978 Davis Cup campaign was memorable in so many ways, although – as I document in the chapter on John McEnroe – the final in California left me with painful memories. Buster had not trained all week because of a bad back, although he still managed to come from two sets down to beat Brian Gottfried. But I was hammered by Mac, we lost the Saturday doubles and McEnroe then inflicted a heavy defeat on Buster to clinch the trophy for the USA. I lost the dead rubber to Gottfried. The end result: 4-1. We won BBC Sports Personality Team of the Year, alongside Britain's victorious Wightman Cup side. Sue Barker, Virginia Wade and co had beaten the Americans, my girlfriend Chris Evert included, 4-3 that year in their annual showdown. We men might have lost our face-off to the US, but we created our own piece of history just getting to the final. It wouldn't happen again for another 37 years.

The importance of the Davis Cup has been diluted by the absence of star players in recent years. It feels a bit like the FA Cup in football: once the showpiece event but now in the shadows of the Champions League and Premier League.

Trends develop like this in tennis. Bjorn Borg and Jimmy Connors were the first two major names not to play regular men's doubles matches alongside their singles. Others followed and now none of the top male players go anywhere near doubles tournaments. Roger Federer, Rafa Nadal, Novak Djokovic and, most recently, Andy Murray have all enjoyed Davis Cup success, but they refuse to play the competition year in, year out. It just isn't done. The trend is ingrained.

In fact, Andy was very smart in 2015, the year Britain won the trophy for the first time since 1936. He saw how few top players were committed to playing the Davis Cup that year – and certainly no one in his league – and figured he could bag two wins in singles in every round. That would mean it only needed a doubles victory to see the team progress, even if the second singles player lost his matches. With Andy's brother Jamie established as one of the best doubles players in the world, there was every chance of success.

When I was captain, I sat down for a chat with Andy about the importance of the Davis Cup in his career. The essence of his feedback was that he couldn't see why he should put himself out for the team when the work ethic of some of the other players was not in his league. My view was: 'Andy, let me tell you about the Davis Cup. When it comes to the end of your career, you are going to be remembered for Grand Slam and Davis Cup wins. You won't be remembered for winning tournaments at Indian Wells and Cincinnati. People will forget that. Yes, you might win millions in prize money, but these events won't define your career.'

No doubt the supporting cast around him grew stronger, none more so than his own brother. Maybe that made Andy want to commit more to Davis Cup tennis. Then he boxed clever in 2015, weighed up the opposition, saw an opening and knew history was there for the making and taking. So it proved. He was immense on that run to victory. No one could touch him. What I said to him was true, much as he didn't want to buy it at the time. He will always be remembered for winning the Davis Cup with Great Britain, as well as his remarkable Grand Slam achievements.

It always surprises me how the big names are given licence to opt out of the Davis Cup. I think the British public even sympathised with Andy for a while there, thinking: 'We're not in the elite group, he's got no one to help him carry the load, poor lad. Let him concentrate on the majors.' Even the British press cut him some slack.

Federer, Nadal and Djokovic have won the Davis Cup for their respective countries but have always put their Grand Slam preparations first. Some years, with the schedule being so overcrowded, they opted out of the Davis Cup. That has not been widely condemned. It has just happened.

I came out with the line: 'When has it not been a privilege to play for your country?' Twice US Open champion Pat Rafter had just become Australian Davis Cup captain when we ran into each other at Wimbledon, a few days after that quote made the papers. He said: 'I loved your comment. You're exactly right.' Rafter, like his compatriot Lleyton Hewitt, came from the correct school of thinking on representing your country. To them, it doesn't matter what group you are in, how poor your team is, whether or not you are going to win the overall match, the bottom line is: when is it not a privilege to represent your country? Hewitt always said, when the tennis schedule came out for the next year, that he looked at the Grand Slams first, closely followed by the Davis Cup dates. There was no way in hell he was going to miss the team event, no matter where the travel took him or how many miles he had to put on the clock. It was a done deal with him. With more Lleyton Hewitts, the Davis Cup would still be the great competition it once was.

The Davis Cup has seen changes in recent years, but they are not working. In my opinion, I'm not so sure enough players care about the competition to play it yearly and the only way to make it as appealing as it once was, perhaps, is to turn it into a biannual event or, like the football World Cup or Olympics, stage it once every four years.

When I started out, the Davis Cup was still huge. The big players knew it was big-time. The first time I got into the team, I didn't play but tried to take it all in: the anthems, the partisan atmosphere and watching how my brother David, Mark Cox and Roger Taylor competed as though their lives depended on victory. It was something I desperately wanted in my career.

My playing debut came when I was just 19 against Egypt in Cairo in May 1974. It was the Preliminary Round of European Qualifying Zone A. Not the catchiest title. And why Egypt played in the European group, with such nations as Nigeria, Iran, Morocco, you would have to ask the organisers. It would later become, more sensibly, the Euro-Africa zone. I had already had a bad experience in Cairo and vowed never to return. So much for that determined aim.

Why was I put off? Well, David and I were booked to play a tournament at the Gezira Sporting Club on the island of Zamalek in Cairo. My brother was travelling from another tournament abroad, so I flew from London on my tod. It was a big deal for a teenager like me, considering I had never travelled that far on my own. I was so green, so naive. All I knew for certain was that a tournament organiser was to meet me at Cairo

Airport. That was it. No hotel details, no directions to the venue – nothing.

The flight from London was stuck on the runway for hours, so, rather than an early evening arrival in Egypt, I got there in the early hours of the morning.

There was no one to meet me. Mobile phones were gadgets of the distant future. The sporting club would not be open. I was stranded.

I had a suitcase, my rackets, too many layers of clothing – including a raincoat for some inexplicable reason – and must have stood out like the sorest of sore thumbs. I at least had the nous to change some sterling into local currency, then found a taxi driver that spoke decent English.

'Sir, you are in a very bad situation,' the taxi driver told me after I had explained my predicament. 'Well, thanks for pointing out the bleeding obvious,' I thought.

'I can drive you to some hotels until we find yours.' What option did I have? So, the search began.

Hours and dozens of hotels later, I was none the wiser. 'Do you have tennis players staying here for this week's tournament?' I asked, endlessly. 'No,' came the reply, repeatedly. It was now about 6.30am. It was already baking hot and I was flagging.

'Why don't I take you to the Gezira Sporting Club,' the taxi driver suggested. 'It might be open now.' It wasn't. I sat on a stone block near the entrance, sweating like a pig and feeling sorry for myself. Finally, about 8am, a man who worked at the Gezira walked over to me – maybe thinking: 'Who's this raincoat-carrying idiot' – and asked could he help me.

'I'm playing in the tournament here, but my flight was delayed and I don't know what hotel I'm staying at.'

'Sir, it is that one over there.' He pointed to the Hyatt just across the road. So browbeaten and demoralised had I been, I had given up my hotel search before giving that even a second glance. Why I hadn't started there is beyond me.

The Gezira Sporting Club had been founded almost a century before my arrival and, in colonial days, had been for the exclusive use of the British Army. It was then one of the world's most elite sports clubs. There was evidence of its former beauty and glory, but it was now run down and in need of renovation. It held national and international tennis competitions from the early 20th century, the latest of which saw David and me playing doubles against a formidable Russian pair who were about twice his size. Built like sumo wrestlers, they were. It didn't stop him accusing them of cheating and promising to punch their lights out, with lines such as 'I'll do you two.' My brother could be a ticking time bomb. As if that trip couldn't have got any worse, there was this sudden vision of hospitalisation. 'Let them have the point,' I insisted, 'I don't care about the point … I do care about my future mobility.'

When a giant swooping bird took food from my hand and a wild cat jumped on to the table to swipe what was left on my plate, when sickness took hold so that my mouth hole and bum hole were kept way too busy, I knew I'd had enough. 'That's it! I'm never coming back to Cairo.'

Within a couple of years, we had drawn Egypt away in the Davis Cup and I was back. At least that second trip was properly organised. I knew where I was staying for starters. Plus, I knew to avoid feral cats, dive-bombing birds, ice in my drinks and to leave the raincoat at home. Still, there was someone, somewhere with a wicked sense of humour, pitching me into my Davis Cup debut, in Cairo of all places.

David and I played singles and doubles. It was Team Lloyd, captained by Stefan Edberg's long-time coach Tony Pickard. Egypt had a talented player by the name of Ismail El Shafei, who had won the Boys' Singles title at Wimbledon a decade earlier and would reach the quarter-finals of the Wimbledon men's tournament just weeks after our match on the red clay of Cairo. Losing to him was no embarrassment, although the same cannot be said of the second Egyptian player, Aly El Dawoudi. We had never heard of him. Had anyone outside of Egypt? But with diabolical temperatures reaching 100 degrees, hot winds blowing in off the desert and a maniacal crowd going nuts, this part-timer beat me. It was a terrible baptism of fire for me and a quick lesson on how local players, with this kind of backing, can raise their game to previously unseen heights. I panicked and froze. Freezing in that heat was painfully ironic.

Throughout my Davis Cup career as a player, coach and captain, I saw many men who rose to the occasion and played above their ranking. I also saw players who shrunk with the pressure and performed below their level. It did cross my mind after that loss in Cairo that this competition might not be for me after all: that I might be one of the 'shrinkers'. Thankfully, that was not how it turned out.

As for the overall result that punishing weekend, David lost to El Shafei, we then lost the doubles and it was 3-0 and out. An old British reporter Frank Rostron approached me and said my loss to El Dawoudi was the worst defeat ever for a British player. Tactful, he wasn't. He was in my face, slating me and my performance, and all I could think was: 'Hell, John, welcome to the Davis Cup.'

Africa brought me another bizarre Davis Cup experience in 1996 when I was coach to David's team, which contained an up-and-coming Tim Henman, for a tie in Ghana. The head of Ghanaian tennis stood to address the teams and gathered dignitaries on the eve of the match in Accra and declared to the Ghana squad: 'Boys, this is a chance to get one over on your colonial masters.' I was thinking: 'What the ...'

David was next to speak. He could be controversial at the best of times. The Ghanaian tennis chief deserved a rebuke. We were one wrong word away from a major diplomatic incident. Somewhat reluctantly, I suspect, my brother held it together. International crisis averted.

The changing rooms in Accra were disgusting. People could pee over the walls into the facility and it stunk of urine. So, inside, we had to deal with that horrible stench and we couldn't sit outside because it was swelteringly hot. Plus, we were swamped by young kids wanting t-shirts and tennis balls and asking us where we were staying so they could follow us and pester us some more. My heart went out to these youngsters, but we were told not to encourage them. One ignorant, ill-informed local told us to stay away from them because some had Aids. It was harrowing.

We had been concerned about where we should eat so as not to get sick and thought the British Embassy might welcome us for food on our arrival. But only when Britain had won the match was an invitation forthcoming from a snooty bloke saying: 'Well done, chaps. Come over tonight for dinner to celebrate.' Our physiotherapist at the time was a blunt and funny Yorkshireman who quickly replied: 'It's too late now, you can f*** off.'

I bumped into a former player from Togo in Florida not so long ago who told me he was in Ghana to watch that weekend.

He assured me facilities are much better now. You would hope so, more than two decades on.

There have been huge changes across Eastern Europe, too, since my playing days. Back then, everywhere was so colourless, so grey. The food was terrible. The hotels were rank. Practice facilities were poor. We were even warned our rooms might be bugged.

That was also the time of local umpires. Unlike nowadays, all Davis Cup officials and line judges were from the host country, except for the neutral referee. You would have them foot-faulting you for no reason and calling perfectly good shots out. If you questioned calls, a few-thousand screaming nut jobs were ready to pounce. I was pelted with coins in Rome on one occasion. It was so hostile. No referee had the balls to intervene. It was brutal at times, making winning away from home incredibly tough. It all makes today's away ties seem like a jolly holiday by comparison.

I was a non-playing member of the team for a tie in Barcelona, where Spain's US Open champion Manuel Orantes was forced into a fifth-set decider by our own Roger Taylor. To drum up support, some tickets had been given to football supporters, and there was a distinctly different feel to the atmosphere in the crowd that day. Roger was being abused throughout, but was a feisty fella and looked like he might win the match and the tie. It would have been a huge victory for him against one of the world's best. Somehow, Orantes turned the tide and took the victory for Spain. Roger then jumped into the crowd and went after someone who had been insulting him all match. That took guts, I can tell you. This crowd was full of lunatics.

It was getting ugly. I went into the tunnel near the locker room, peering over the wall to watch what was going on. Another British team member, John Feaver, was near me. British captain Headley Baxter led Roger off, but some of the crowd followed and were running towards where we stood. I saw one maniac with a clenched fist pull his arm back. He was coming straight towards me, ready to smack me in the head. My reflexes were better than his and I ducked. Feaver didn't and was punched square in the jaw. 'Ouch! Bad luck, pal.' Security was non-existent. We had to stay in the locker room for an age until the baying mob were bored of waiting.

Another away day, another international incident. My brother David was riled by the behaviour of Ilie Nastase in Bucharest, where Romanians worshipped their star players, both of whom were not to be messed with, certainly not on home turf. I was partnering David in the doubles, while Nastase was alongside the giant Ion Tiriac. A bit like that day against the bruising Russians in Cairo, David was up for the fight. The crowd were insanely hostile. The atmosphere was toxic.

David was staring down Nastase and Tiriac. I was looking for the exit signs while encouraging my brother to calm down. He did the exact opposite. David and Nastase got into another spat at the net. David was in his face. Nastase then patronisingly tapped him on the head with his racket. At that point, my brother was ready to rip Nastase's head off, shouting: 'I'll f***ing have you.' The crowd were going crazy. The neutral Spanish referee was doing nothing. The Romanian umpire was loving it. I thought: 'We're gonna get killed. If I sprint, maybe I've got a chance.' Never was it more apparent, I'm a lover not a fighter.

Just in case you are in doubt as to the beasts from the East that David and I were taking on that day, here's a snapshot. Tiriac used to take money from players in the locker room to perform his party trick of chewing and swallowing glass: the guy was an animal.

When he was managing Boris Becker, he was in the locker room at the Australian Open in Kooyong chewing the fat (not glass) with another former colossus of a player Slobodan 'Bobo' Zivojinovic, who became president of the Serbian Tennis Federation after retirement. Bobo was shoving Tiriac, just fooling around it seemed. Tiriac said: 'Do you want a fight?' Bobo replied: 'Yeah, let's fight.' He sounded playful, but I was watching on thinking: 'Are they for real?' I couldn't be 100 per cent certain it was all fun.

Tiriac, this moustachioed moose of a man, suddenly got hold of Bobo and headbutted him on the forehead. The noise reverberated around the locker room. Boris's face was a picture of shock. Bobo staggered back, saying: 'That's unfair.' Tiriac replied: 'There's nothing unfair in a fight.' I thought: 'Boris, be careful if you ever get rid of Tiriac. Maybe invest in a good helmet, sunshine.'

Nastase was nicknamed 'Nasty' and had a penchant for winding up opponents until they reached breaking point. More than once at the US Open at Forest Hills, I saw him goad opponents. Though there was no air conditioning in the horrible little locker rooms there, the players would gather – even if it meant sweating our nuts off – when Nastase was playing a potentially volatile opponent, just to see what would kick off when they came in after the match. Germany's Hans-Jurgen Pohmann was one such volatile character.

During the match, Nastase was so much better than him that he toyed with him and taunted him on his way to victory. Near the end of the match, I sprinted to the locker room, discovered where Nastase would be sitting and pretended to change my racket grip, all the while knowing I was about to have a front-row seat for the post-match dessert. Other players had done the same. Next thing, Pohmann had Nastase by the throat and up against the wall, with his fist cocked. Enter, right on cue, a solid Italian unit, who was Nastase's personal security guy. 'No!' he bellowed, grabbing Pohmann's arm. Nastase smiled. It was great theatre: entertainment money couldn't buy.

I had a few people taking swings at me during my time as Davis Cup captain. If you aren't well versed in tennis terminology, captain in this context is the equivalent of manager in football. England soccer bosses receive many more swipes than a Davis Cup leader ever does. But when you are in the job and on the receiving end, you are not counting the volume. The punches still hurt.

Taking over from Jeremy Bates, I inherited players of the calibre of Andy Murray and Greg Rusedski and was hopeful Tim Henman might return to the GB fold before his career was over, which he duly did.

I asked Australia's Davis Cup captain John Fitzgerald how he coped with giving star players advice. He told me: 'Less is best.' When he tried to instruct volleying supremo Pat Rafter on his best shot, Pat put his captain straight. 'Fitzy, don't worry mate – I know what to do.' John said he had got a bit excited and carried away with all this captaincy business. Of course Rafter knew what to do. John told me he was more tactful after that, offering praise and support, but advice only when requested. That was what I planned for my captaincy with our star players.

Also, I had seen first-hand how Andy Murray could hurl insults in Brad Gilbert's direction during matches, when Andy questioned his coach's tactical input. Brad was being paid a lot of money, having agreed a lucrative deal with the LTA, but a relative kid shouting at a grown man like that? I wouldn't have put up with it, whatever the cash incentive. I didn't want any of that flack coming my way. I wouldn't take abuse from anyone, let alone a young player. I was happy Brad was going to be taking the brunt of all that.

I told Tim Henman's coach Paul Annacone that I would act as a go-between with any coaching tips during matches, if that's what they both wanted. Tim and Paul were both fine with that.

Greg Rusedski liked plenty of reassurance during his matches, but in some ways, he was the easiest of the big three British names to work with on the court. He was very animated during changeovers, but I could slip in the odd piece of advice under the radar. Say he had missed a string of backhands when hitting over the ball and at the changeover said to me: 'I'm playing well, right? The backhand's working well, right?'

I would suggest: 'Yeah, but maybe you want to try a few sliced backhands to mix it up.'

'But I'm playing great, though, right?'

'Great, Greg. Just great.'

I had some euphoric moments in those early years of my captaincy, most notably beating the Netherlands in Birmingham and then Croatia at Wimbledon in 2007 to earn promotion back to the World Group, helped by the comeback-man Tim Henman.

It was great he delivered those triumphs for his country before signing off for good. Greg bowed out after the Dutch victory, announcing it live on BBC television to Sue Barker. I wish he had warned me.

Rusedski and Jamie Murray had just defeated Robin Haase and Rogier Wassen in four sets to give us an unassailable 3-0 lead and carry us through to the World Group play-off with Croatia, when Greg revealed: 'It was a proud moment considering this is going to be my last match. I'm officially retiring on a win today. I'm retired now, I can enjoy life like everybody else. Now it's time to move on.'

'I wish you'd move on a day later,' I'm thinking, listening to his bolt from the blue, 'because I had you bailing me out in tomorrow's dead rubbers.'

Now, I was in a bit of a bind – and this is why. Tim and Andy had won the opening day's singles. Greg had been frothing at the mouth to be involved in Saturday's doubles (because he had obviously made up his mind to retire at the end of the match) and his commitment to the cause made him a certainty in my eyes. I asked both Tim and Andy about their thoughts on playing doubles and both preferred to concentrate on being ready for Sunday's reverse singles if necessary – matches which could have proved pivotal. That was absolutely the right call and it gave me the pleasure of saying to Andy's brother: 'Congratulations, Jamie, you'll be making your Davis Cup debut tomorrow.'

Jamie's initial reaction was: 'Great. Am I playing with Andy?'

When I told him it wasn't Andy, Jamie was clearly disappointed. I could see the security blanket effect of teaming up with his brother, but he and Greg had practised well together during the week – and anyway, the singles pair weren't exactly pressing their case for inclusion.

Gilbert walked in and asked me: 'What's the team?'

I told him.

He said it was a bad decision and asked why Andy was not playing.

'He would rather prepare for Sunday if the tie's still alive,' I replied.

Gilbert came back at me again with 'Bad decision'.

'It's not a bad decision. It's my decision and it is final.'

At that time, Gilbert was probably regarded as some kind of coaching god by youngsters like Jamie.

Now, right in front of the team, he had given them licence to doubt me and my selections. It was a lack of professionalism beyond belief.

Of course, Jamie and Greg went out and smashed it. We were through to the play-off against Croatia and there was a general feeling of elation. I had to hope Tim and Andy were up for taking part in the dead rubbers on Sunday, but that hope was tinged with trepidation. I knew all too well from my playing days how difficult it was to engage in these meaningless matches. Nonetheless, there were thousands of people coming to watch and we were still on television. Rusedski had just retired, of course, and was out of the equation.

Gilbert declared, again in front of everyone, that Andy was not playing on the final day.

'Hold on a minute. Let's talk about this,' I said.

Gilbert suggested putting Jamie out there for the fourth match and defaulting the fifth.

'We can't do that. Brad, no one hates dead rubbers more than me – I lost about a thousand of them. But we've got a paying audience and television to consider.'

He reiterated: Andy was not playing. Tim, being the professional he was, agreed to fill the second singles berth so a potential embarrassment was avoided.

Against Croatia that September, Tim played and won his first-day singles match and the doubles to carry Britain back into the World Group before retiring. It was fitting it should be at Wimbledon, where he had given so many British tennis fans so much excitement and pleasure in his career. Do you remember how bad we Britons used to have it at the All England Championships until Tim came along? If Jeremy Bates got to the last 16 there would be street parties. Tim changed all that. Andy Murray picked up that Wimbledon baton and ran so gloriously with it.

After those early Davis Cup highs as captain, there came a succession of awful lows – culminating in the devastating loss in Lithuania in 2010, to fall within one defeat of the bottom tier of the competition. That was to be the end of the Davis Cup road for me.

Unfortunately, Andy Murray made himself unavailable for selection. Regardless of that, we were 2-1 ahead after the doubles and looked capable of finishing the job. Sadly, James Ward was defeated by Ricardas Berankis and Dan Evans then lost in five sets to Laurynas Grigelis, a player ranked 269 places below him at 521 in the world and who had never played a match on the ATP Tour. We lost 3-2.

All through that match, there was this obese guy in the crowd shouting: 'John Lloyd – you are getting fired in the morning.' If I could have taken him down, I would. The size of him, I would have needed considerable help.

Jamie Baker would have played and, I have no doubt because of the way he was hitting the ball, won on that crucial final day but for a sprained ankle in practice. Dan would not have been my choice to play the decider but for Jamie's misfortune.

I got stick from all sides. Greg Rusedski was burying me in his TV punditry role, I have no doubt with an eye on my job, and the press were laying into the LTA and questioning my future. It was an embarrassing defeat. There was no escaping the fact. The blame game was in full swing. The end didn't come immediately. There were too many discussions required for any swift conclusion. But my resignation would duly follow.

One of my mistakes as captain was getting too carried away with the success we had climbing back into the World Group. It had been a long journey back to the top. I said at the time: 'We're back where we belong.' That was only true as long as we had Tim Henman, Greg Rusedski and Andy Murray in the team. But both Tim and Greg retired, leaving me with just one world-class player on his way up and a group of inexperienced players that were, at the time, not World Group standard.

Leon Smith was the eventual choice to replace me. He was the man at the helm as Britain won the Davis Cup in 2015 and deserves huge credit.

The Davis Cup chapter of my life is a kaleidoscopic mixture: of treasured travels and hostile welcomes; of career highs and bitter defeats; of lifelong friends and fleeting foes. The constant factor is that it was never anything less than an honour to fly the flag for my country in whatever capacity.

Growing up in my family, this competition was right up there in importance alongside Wimbledon. To not only play in it so many times for Great Britain, but to coach and then captain the team is beyond anything I could ever have imagined when I was that little kid, hitting a ball against the wall outside my house in Leigh-on-Sea.

TRUMP

A letter from the John Lloyd of today to his former self as he goes into business with a certain Donald Trump.

Dear John,
Know your own worth as a tennis professional even after
your playing career is long over. There's a future president
of the USA ready to invest to the tune of six figures. But
beware a spy in the Mar-a-Lago camp.
   John

DONALD TRUMP always introduces me as 'the great John Lloyd, winner of three Grand Slam titles'. It's a bit mortifying. That's a deep-tissue massaging of my ego from a US president. It doesn't matter where, it doesn't matter when … Donald has intro'd me this way as long as I have known him.

One look at the bold businessman dealing in millions, one look at the force of nature that is the former leader of the free world, and you think of him as this super-confident guy who takes no prisoners. In certain situations, I am sure what you see is what you get. That's a full-on, no-holds-barred Donald

Trump. I have seen that side of him, too. But that's not the man in his entirety.

I believe this 'introduction thing' explains a great deal about the man's success and how he can make people feel. He does not barge in, announcing his arrival with 'Hey guys, how's it going?' in some kind of generic way. He finds suitable lines to ease into the flow of a conversation: sentences that involve some of the most special memory recall I have ever witnessed. He will have a line – like the one he uses for me – for pretty much everyone. It is a very personal thing and most flattering that he has taken time to know who you are and remember you. When a famous person does that and engages in a pertinent conversation with you, about you, it elevates you.

When we met at his golf club, the line Donald greeted me with was: 'Hey, the great John Lloyd, winner of three Grand Slam titles, how are you? Got any funny stories?' When he introduced me to guests it was with similar generosity. He knew every single member of his Trump International Golf Club in West Palm Beach, Florida. He was aware what each of them did professionally and had an introduction line for all 200 of them based on that knowledge. It is a clever device that can make the people he is talking to feel important, but also serves his purpose for overcoming any initial awkwardness that we can all be faced with in those situations.

Mind you, I did throw him once when he delivered my personalised introduction in the club restaurant. I was with family, visiting from England, and had pointed out Donald was sitting in the other corner of the room. Next thing I knew, he was at my side and saying to my guests: 'This is the great John Lloyd, winner of three Grand Slam titles.'

I said: 'She knows, Donald. It's my sister.' He stepped back. 'Oh, oh … okay … Have a nice day.' Then he was off.

There are many clubs in Palm Beach I cannot abide because of their bonkers rules and ridiculous exclusivity. Trump's club is not so restrictive. He doesn't care where you come from or what you look like. As long as you have got the money, you have got a way in. Mobile phones are allowed, unlike at some clubs, and you can freely do business deals there. Donald doesn't care.

I had played tennis and golf with him many times before he became president and he had always treated me tremendously well. His club was a place I could imagine joining. There was just one issue. Memberships ran upwards of $150,000 a year. I had heard of the potential for 'special memberships' that might come at a different cost. I also knew this: Donald likes a deal.

I rang Rhona Graff, Trump's personal assistant for more than a quarter of a century, to make the initial inquiry.

'I want to see about the possibility of getting a membership … of some kind or other, Rhona. I'd be honoured if I could be considered. If you'd be so kind as to mention it to Donald. Maybe there's something we could work out.'

'Let me get back to you on that,' she said, and I thought that may be the last I would hear of it.

The next day, Rhona called me and said: 'Will you be available to talk to Donald in one hour?'

'Of course,' I replied, wondering whether there was even the remotest possibility I might win his approval. I might not have been the best advertisement for golfing standards at his facility. I wasn't very good. When I had played golf with Donald he would often laugh at me, saying: 'With shots like that, it's a good job you've got tennis to fall back on.'

Some of it was down to the pressure I felt. Donald's golf cart was driven three times faster than anyone else's. He was a buggy maniac. He didn't take practice swings or line up putts, and he expected you to do the same thing. His golf partners were in constant fast-forward just to keep up with him. Anyone on the holes ahead would simply have to let his group play through. Rounds would last two hours, if that. I had always managed to keep up. My golf kept him amused; my stories, too. He loved athletes and their tales from the locker room or field of play. Maybe I had a shot at a cut-price membership after all.

'The great John Lloyd, winner of three Grand Slam titles, I hear you want to become a member of my club,' Trump said. 'That's great. Let's do a deal.'

That was music to my ears, before he added: 'You do me a favour and I'll do you a favour.'

'Okay,' I said with some trepidation.

Trump had purchased the Mar-a-Lago resort in Palm Beach in 1985 and held on to it beyond two divorces. It is a magnificent place, with a spa, hotel and marvellous facilities that come with a $200,000-a-year membership. Michael Jackson and Lisa Marie Presley spent their honeymoon there, while Trump's family has private quarters in a separate area of the resort, which he still often used after becoming president: his self-styled Southern White House.

Members of the Trump International course in West Palm Beach had reciprocal privileges at Mar-a-Lago. I had stayed at the impressive Mar-a-Lago many times when it hosted a prostate cancer charity event. At every turn, Donald's face was in your face: on the Trump shampoo and toiletries ... on bottles of water ... on pretty much anything you could attach a label to. This was his place and he wanted you to know it. Visiting regularly was something I could have grown to enjoy. Just about. After a twist of the arm, maybe. If you really forced me to lap up such splendour. But what of this favour?

Trump continued: 'There are a couple of things. As you know, we sometimes have very important people coming to Mar-a-Lago and some are keen on tennis. Maybe we could call you to go over and play with them.' There were pristine red clay courts at the resort.

'Sure. No problem,' I said, thinking this wouldn't hurt my current real estate work either. 'What's the second thing?'

'We've got a tennis director there and I've heard mixed things about him. When you've worked with him for a while, tell me if you think he's good or not. If he's not, I'll fire him.'

The *Apprentice USA* television show suddenly springs to mind. But while firing people might have been to Trump's liking – on reality TV or in reality – it wasn't my style. With a lucrative membership deal in the offing, though, I said: 'Agreed.'

Trump declared: 'Let's do the deal. How about $11,000 for the year?'

'Really?' I couldn't quite believe I was about to have more than 100 grand knocked off the annual fee.

'$11,000 ... and you do me a couple of favours a year.'

'Done.' I signed up soon after.

The first time I drove to the club, I was being greeted by name at every checkpoint. Whatever your politics, whatever you think of Donald Trump the former president, his golf courses are first class and the staff deliver a warm welcome. That is undeniable. I was driving a borrowed Mercedes, quite evidently the worst car the valet attendant had to park that day, surrounded as I was by Bentleys, Lamborghinis, Ferraris and Rolls-Royce beauties. I was embarrassed climbing out of my less-salubrious wheels.

Inside the club, I was told: 'Mr Lloyd, we don't have your permanent locker ready for you just yet, so for now we are going to give you this one.' To the left of my temporary locker was one emblazoned with the name 'Tom Cruise'. To the right was a locker reading 'John Travolta'.

'Wow. This is the Scientology row,' I thought. 'Have I signed up for that, too, and not realised?'

Neither Hollywood A-lister was a member. Nor were they particularly interested in golf, from what I could gather. The locker names were fictitious: designed to create buzz around the place. 'Hey, Tom Cruise plays here – did you know? Have you ever run in to him?' That kind of thing.

When I was required to entertain guests at the club, the young tennis pro would ring me and say, for instance: 'Regis Philbin is here today. Can you join us?' Regis was the American presenter of *Who Wants to Be a Millionaire?* and co-hosted a long-running morning TV talk show. He was the kind of special guest I was meant to meet, greet and play. It was no hardship, trust me.

About six months later, I took some of my own friends over there to play – a billionaire businessman among them. Donald didn't visit the tennis courts much. He had hung up his racket and stuck firmly to his clubs. But when there were heavy hitters at the resort, he knew it. He had eyes everywhere. Suddenly, he was courtside. The 'great John Lloyd …' line came out again and he was perfectly charming. I saw him take the tennis director to one side, before leaving us to our doubles knockabout.

The tennis director came over to me and said: 'John, I just want you to know, I've got your back.'

'You've got my back. In what way have you got my back?'

'You know you did that membership deal with Mr Trump,' he explained.

'Yeah.'

'He just asked me if you were fulfilling your part of the bargain and playing tennis with the people you're meant to. So don't worry, I've got your back.'

'Oh, that's funny,' I countered, 'because I've actually got your back.'

'What?'

'Part of our deal was that Donald told me to tell him if you weren't doing a good job – and if you weren't, he'd fire you.'

He almost had heart failure, the poor guy. The colour drained from his face. He knew one bad word from me and Trump would have fired him in two seconds flat. Of course, I didn't need to be a member of the club but this was the tennis director's job, his livelihood. It was classic Trump. Donald was playing us both off against each other. He wouldn't see anything wrong in that. He was simply making sure both ends of the deal were being met, while keeping us on our toes. How many more thousands of times has he employed that kind of play-off in his business and political dealings down the years?

The tennis director didn't need to worry because he was doing an excellent job and I made sure I told Donald that. I gave a rave review.

Trump has got balls but, at times, no filter. Many people dislike that about him, of course. But he couldn't care less and, honestly, some of the stuff he comes out with is bloody funny. Donald won the Prostate Cancer Foundation event at Mar-a-Lago one year by teaming up with the youngest, Olympic sprint-type professional on-site, while he hogged the net. Again, the man is no fool.

The night before, the amateurs who had entered this doubles tennis competition (that is, the wealthy bunch who had put up $20,000 each to team up with the professional players) were invited to a dinner party during which a Calcutta auction took place. That's where entrants bid on the team they think will win. They are also expected to back their own team. The winning amateur punter would be six figures richer at the end of it all, but – as they each had piles of money to burn – would give the prize fund straight back to the charity. It was just a bit of auction-room fun, intended to raise more money for a wonderful charity. Donald Trump was the MC for the evening. He knew everyone in the room and, more pertinently, their worth. One super-rich guy, who I believe made his money from underground car parks, was renowned as a Scrooge. His terrible, miserly reputation preceded him. Having already pledged 20 grand to play in the tournament, he didn't want to bet thousands more on his own team – even though that was the accepted protocol.

In a packed room of some 300 people, Donald spoke into the microphone and belted out words to the effect of: 'Oh for f***'s sake, are you kidding me? You've got more money than God, you cheap son of a bitch.' The billionaire in question went bright red with embarrassment. Trump didn't give a shit who this man was. He simply knew he was not abiding by the charity rules. Everyone in the room was thinking it. Trump was the only one ballsy enough to say it. The hand was eventually raised, leading Donald to sign off with, 'Don't wait so long next time.' With the future president to the fore like this, Mar-a-Lago did the Prostate Cancer Foundation proud for many years.

Back over at Trump International in West Palm Beach, there's a tradition of staging delicious and plentiful buffets for members. We're talking cold lobster and crab, caviar, oysters on the half shell and desserts to die for. When Donald's in town, he is known to put in an appearance. He had just caused a global tsunami by winning the US presidential election when I heard he was due back in Florida and would attend the amazing Sunday spread. My girlfriend Svetlana and I were invited by a friend, so we witnessed the arrival of the president-elect, who was greeted by rapturous applause. Trump was on a table with his wife Melania, campaign manager Kellyanne Conway and chief of staff-in-waiting Reince Priebus, among others. Secret service staff watched over them. Svetlana asked if we might get a photograph with the new president and we approached, ready with our congratulations.

Donald immediately introduced me as he always had: 'Ladies and gentleman, the great John Lloyd, winner of three Grand Slam titles.' I was beyond coy; more embarrassed actually. This was the next president of the United States. The introduction seemed stranger than ever. I introduced Svetlana to take attention off me.

'You're from Russia, then?' Donald asked. 'How long have you guys been going out?'

'About nine months or so,' she replied.

'Well, let me tell you, you're going out with one helluva guy. He's a very good friend of mine.' He could not have been more cordial or complimentary. Then click: we had our photograph.

Whenever I post pictures of the president on Instagram, my left-wing friends in Los Angeles don't like it and give me stick. I do it regardless because there is no hiding it. All politics aside, Donald Trump has always been good to me and I like him.

Dear Mr President,

I feel strangely honoured to have been a very small pawn in your miniature game of tennis espionage. All the time I was keeping an eye on that tennis director at your club, he was keeping an eye on me. One slip and we were toast. Classic Trump! By the way, I immensely enjoyed the fruits of our membership deal.

Who knew back then, least of all me, that you would one day be elected to lead the United States of America? That's simply staggering.

But I will always remember you, if you don't mind, as the pre-presidential Donald: the man who laughed at my golf strokes; the man with the flattering introduction lines; the man who holds tightwads at charity auctions to task.

Yours truly,

John

BIG C AND ME

A letter from the John Lloyd of today to his former self as he is about to undergo surgery for prostate cancer.

Dear John,

Your head is a swirl of thoughts. There's fear doing battle with hope, anxiety trampling on positivity, doubt eroding medical fact.

It's time to employ the technique you used near the end of your playing career and have since imparted umpteen times while coaching.

Remember how the night before a match you would picture stepping out on court with your opponent and would run a few scenarios through your mind? Most of them were positive, like hitting winners, moving like lightning across the court and ghosting to the net. But you also threw in a couple of crisis points. Maybe you were break point down, even set point down. But you visualised coming through those difficult times – hitting a great shot at the most crucial moment. And always at the end of the match, you would imagine hearing the umpire announcing: 'Game, set and match, Lloyd.'

284

Cancer is your opponent now. There are possible crisis points beyond the surgery. Prepare yourself for those, but don't be overwhelmed by them. Visualise coming through this huge life test healthy and victorious.

In this contest against cancer there must be only one winner: 'Game, set, and match Lloyd.'

John

NEVER IN my life did I expect to be compared to Mother Teresa. But the most improbable things can happen when you have a battle with a potential killer.

The four words you never want to hear are: 'You have got cancer.' There is no way to prepare for such news. It shocks you to your core and shatters those who love you.

The weird thing is, for a few years up to my diagnosis in 2016, I had been thinking my luck was going to run out. I'm not religious. I don't believe there's a grand plan. I do believe one's lot in life – if you're born in a great country like I was and had the opportunities that affords you – is purely and simply down to random luck. Some people become ill through no fault of their own. I can't accept that's part of a greater plan.

My life has been enriched beyond anything I could ever have hoped. Time and again through the years I've acknowledged I have been such a lucky man. Then that strange notion crept into my mind: 'Some shit's going to happen to me – it has to.'

Even though I was shocked in one way when I was told I had prostate cancer – because I felt so healthy – I was expecting it in another way. I figured: 'You know what, it's karma. I couldn't have all the luck all the time.' I know some of you reading this might find that difficult to understand. But it made perfect sense to me. I felt my luck had run out.

As my cancer story unfolded, I very soon realised, of course, that I was still one of the most fortunate men on earth. How could I believe my luck had run out completely when I had the most fantastically supportive children, an incredibly understanding girlfriend, a network of encouraging friends and, crucially, gifted experts with the confidence to fix me.

But cancer doesn't give a damn about any of that. It's invasive. It's ignorant. It's despicable. It's repugnant. Even with all the support in the world, there were no guarantees I would come through this ordeal with a winning outcome. Lying in bed, waiting for surgery, I was worried. How had it come to this, when just a year before I was fighting fit and oblivious to the fact there was anything wrong? My divorce from my second wife Deborah was going through and I had moved full-time to Florida. I had a few quiet days and thought it was a good time to sign up to a new doctor, dentist and dermatologist – the kind of medical cover I'd had in Los Angeles.

I wasn't someone who had regular check-ups with my doctor, as much as that is what's advised when you turn 50. Apart from one bout of walking pneumonia and my knee replacement surgery, I had happily avoided hospital stays. I was playing tennis every day, I had no symptoms of ill health and was generally feeling great. It was only signing up with a new doctor that prompted the health check.

Everything was tested. My heart was fine, my lungs, too. There was no problem with blood pressure. Blood was taken and tested. It was the normal routine for a medical.

A few days later, I was attending a corporate function in Palm Beach where former British Prime Minister Tony Blair was the guest speaker. It was about eight in the evening when my phone rang. The doctor I had just registered with had left me a voicemail asking me to ring him immediately. I thought it was a bit strange, but stepped outside to make the call.

The doctor said something to the effect of: 'I've got some news. Your PSA is 5.9. You need to see a urologist straight away. Don't take the reading as gospel there's something wrong, we just need to get this thing checked out.'

PSA stands for prostate-specific antigen and is a protein produced exclusively by prostate cells. Doctors regard a reading of 4.0 or less as normal. My blood test had revealed a high level of PSA: a possible indicator of cancer.

I immediately rang a friend in Palm Beach who had been through the whole prostate cancer trauma and he tried to put my mind at rest, saying: 'There can be other reasons for high PSA readings, like if you've just been riding a bike. Get it checked, but don't worry.'

I hadn't been riding a bike but I didn't overly concern myself after that conversation, hoping the reading was simply down to other factors than illness. After all, I felt so fit and well.

I found this great doctor in Jupiter, Florida – Dr Neil Borland – and set about undergoing more tests. Without going into graphic detail, it involved lots of bending over and a bit of rummaging, after which he said everything seemed fine, adding: 'We'll keep an eye on things. Come back in three months for another blood test.' I was only marginally concerned because I couldn't have felt any better in myself. If the butcher's dog was fit, I was even fitter.

The second blood test was taken. The PSA reading had gone up to 6.1. At this point, nothing was making much sense so an ultrasound was suggested. I'd had tons of those through my career, but never an internal one. It was unpleasant but necessary. The good news was that it showed nothing untoward. But to be absolutely certain, an MRI scan was recommended.

Now, I had once been stuck in a lift in pitch black during a hurricane in Honolulu. It had made me extremely claustrophobic. I was more worried about going in the coffin of an MRI scanner than any potential illness. 'Don't worry,' said the doctor, 'we've got scanners now that won't close you in.' The MRI results came back and the doctor said it looked clear apart from one tiny area, which again didn't seem to set all the alarm bells ringing for him.

In a few more months, I had my blood tested again. My PSA level had fallen to 5.9, but it was still too high. Now the only course of action left was to have a biopsy.

I had heard bad things about some biopsy procedures, so when I was given the option of being awake or put under for the test, I chose the latter. A few people said: 'Are you sure you want to have anaesthetic, what if you don't come round?' I replied: 'I'm not going to know anything about it anyway, so what's the problem? I'd rather be knocked cold than be aware of what was being shoved where.' As the biopsy took place, my doctor was still confident there was an 80 per cent chance I didn't have cancer.

Surfing the internet for more details on my possible condition is not my thing, but my girlfriend Svetlana did the Google research for me. Prostate cancer has a good survival rate if it's caught early enough. But the by-products of the condition can be impotence and incontinence. Obviously, neither of those were high on my wish list. She held back some of the finer details, so as not to worry me. But we knew the potential downside.

Awaiting the results of the biopsy, Svetlana – this beautiful woman with her life stretching out in front of her – told me that no matter what, she would stay by my side. I was overwhelmed she would say something like that when I honestly wouldn't have blamed her for heading for the hills.

We were in bed, it was 8.30 in the morning, when Dr Borland rang to tell me: 'It's bad news, I'm afraid. You have got cancer.' It was shattering. He requested I visit his office the next day.

As soon as he asked to see me in person, I knew I was in trouble. Svetlana and I were aware of the Gleason scale that predicts the aggressiveness of prostate cancer. The lower your score, the less aggressive the cancer. If I had a less aggressive form of the disease, the doctor would surely have told me over the phone.

I had been told how you could test a random selection of 100 80-year-old men and something like 80 to 90 per cent of them would have prostate cancer. Many wouldn't know it, nor die from it. The cancer could lie dormant for years. These men would have scores at the lower end of the Gleason scale, at absolute worst below six. I instinctively knew I didn't fall into this category. The doctor's visit confirmed my fear: I was at seven on the scale. This was not good.

Dr Borland said it looked like the cancer hadn't travelled to my lymph nodes but that it wasn't dormant and 'we need to get this thing done'.

He informed me there were two options. The first was radiation treatment: less invasive but with every chance the cancer could return. The second was to remove the prostate:

most invasive but, unless the cancer had already spread, the best chance of eradicating it permanently. The second option carried the possibility – maybe even probability – of damaging my ability to have sex and to urinate. To be honest, the thought of the side-effects of surgery affected me more than the thought of losing my life. I was distraught.

Telling my children was hard. Hayley and Aiden were extremely upset when I broke the news. I'm not a huge bawler, but I have been known to get tearful watching a TV commercial. I'm pathetic like that. I used to always have a handkerchief with me at the movies in case I needed to dab away a tear without anyone catching me. But this family emotion was on a different level. They asked what the next steps were, what the prognosis might be. They quickly switched from being upset to being energised, positive and caring. I can't tell you how much their support helped me.

For the previous 15 to 20 years, I had played in the Prostate Cancer Foundation event in America, never imagining for even a second the disease would one day floor me. When I first got involved, billionaire businessman Michael Milken fronted the event. He had been diagnosed with prostate cancer many years ago and devoted much of his time and money to research into the disease. Jimmy Connors first rallied the players to get involved for the inaugural event at Donald Trump's Mar-a-Lago resort, which is where I first met the former US president. There are several of these events a year – now entitled The Charles Evans PCF Pro-Am Tour – with a newer addition to the tour taking place at the prestigious Indian Wells tournament in the Southern Californian desert. Massive stars like Taylor Swift and Diana Ross perform at the fundraising parties, there's Calcutta betting and staggering amounts of money collected. We're talking millions of dollars. I have been part of the family since it all began.

Because of that, I knew all about Dr Jonathan Simons, president and CEO of the Prostate Cancer Foundation. He's an internationally renowned oncologist and has won global acclaim for his investigations into translational prostate cancer research. I rang him for advice immediately after my diagnosis.

Dr Simons examined my lab results and we had a frank discussion about the treatment options. He said that at my age, in my early 60s, he thought the best course of action was to have the prostate taken out.

When I asked his opinion on the chances of problems with impotence and incontinence, he explained there are parts of the surgery where trauma can be created to the nerve, that it can be problematic and it could leave me unable to function as I did before. Some people regain the ability, some don't. Dr Simons didn't paint a great picture, but this was the reality of my situation. He did say that the main thing was I had caught the disease early enough to beat it.

I was brutally honest with him and said that wasn't the most important factor for me. If I couldn't be the man I was before surgery, I'm not sure I wanted the operation at all. He thought I was kidding. I could not have been more serious.

'You will survive this, John,' Dr Simons assured me.

'I want to survive, obviously,' I responded. 'But I'm not interested in that side of things as much as whether I can avoid the after-effects of removing the prostate. I'd like a doctor who, if he can't get to it properly and there's a chance of damaging the nerve, just sews me back up and lets me have a few good years of being able to function properly. Then I can ride off into the sun knowing I've had a hell of a life.' Jonathan still thought I was joking, pointing out: 'I don't believe a doctor would really be allowed to do that.'

And I get why. This way of thinking probably wouldn't enter the minds of most people. It would be the sanctity of life above all else. I can hear people reading this even now saying I was taking the value of life too lightly. But this was my life and I knew what I could and couldn't live with.

This wasn't about whether or not I was married, in a relationship or on my own, this was about me and what I could cope with going forward. If there was an important part of my life taken away, I'm not sure it would be a life I could altogether handle. That was my reality. I wasn't being the remotest bit flippant or cavalier. I had to make the doctors understand.

Dr Simons knew of many gifted surgeons and outlined their attributes. One reminded him of a tenacious Jimmy Connors at his peak. If you had to put money on someone to win a match, almost as if life itself depended on it, Jimmy was top of the list. I could imagine no one better than a doctor described in his image. Before I had even met Dr Ted Schaeffer, acclaimed professor of urology, I knew he was the surgeon for me. Even more so because he could carry out the procedure robotically, which I believed was my best hope of success.

Only later did I learn that, just a couple of years earlier, in 2014, Dr Schaeffer had carried out the same surgery on film actor Ben Stiller, who, at 49, was very young to have his prostate removed. At that time, figures revealed one in six men in the USA would be diagnosed with prostate cancer in their lifetimes. It was one in eight in the UK.

Ben and Dr Schaeffer did some enlightening media afterwards, explaining what a success his procedure had been and encouraging more men to get tested. There had been – and continues to be – a certain amount of controversy over the PSA test, in particular that it isn't necessarily a sure indicator of cancer. Was my friend right when he was trying to reassure me after my initial PSA test? Could a high PSA level be recorded after a bike ride? What was the myth, what was the fact? Ben believed the PSA test saved his life. That was fact enough for him. The same test had brought me to my diagnosis.

In an essay published on the blogging site Medium, Ben, who had been tested from the age of 46, even though he had no history of the disease in his family, wrote: 'There has been a lot of controversy over the test in the last few years. Articles and op-eds on whether it is safe, studies that seem to be interpreted in many different ways ... I am not offering a scientific point of view here, just a personal one, based on my experience ... If he [the surgeon] had waited, as the American Cancer Society recommends, until I was 50, I would not have known I had a growing tumour until two years after I got treated.'

I had a conference call with both learned doctors. Dr Schaeffer saw my results and gave me the same kind of response as Dr Simons: 'You will survive this – that I know.'

'That's great,' I said, 'that's wonderful – thank you for that vote of confidence. But ...'

I told him everything I had told Dr Simons about my concerns, to which he predictably responded: 'Are you serious?' The after-effects of surgery: that was my main worry among many. More so than life itself. I couldn't get away from that.

Eventually, the doctors came to terms with my feelings and we proceeded with a shared understanding.

Dr Schaeffer instilled in me the confidence I needed to get my head around the surgery and the possible negatives. He allowed me to delay the surgery until after the holiday season, although Thanksgiving and Christmas that year were, to put it mildly, unusual. I was all too aware what was looming. Even after that, I wanted to work on the Australian Open in the New Year and had a few other projects on the go. Psychologically, I was pushing the inevitable back as far as I could until the doctor said: 'No more waiting.' The operation would take place in March.

I was honestly dreading it as the clock ticked down to the day of the surgery. So many things were running through my mind. Are they going to open me up and find out it's worse? What state will I find myself in afterwards? It was tough to keep on top of the negative thoughts, even though there was such marvellous support around me. Can I put it bluntly and say there were times I was crapping myself?

I called at least 12 people who I knew had gone through similar experiences, former Wimbledon champion Stan Smith and tennis writer Joel Drucker among them. Both had battled prostate cancer. There were good stories, there were bad stories and others somewhere in between. Where would I fall?

The operation was to take place at Northwestern Hospital in Chicago. It was emotional as I left my Florida home. Svetlana had wanted to join me, but I told her: 'Look, this is uncomfortable. I don't want you to see me sick, with tubes coming out of me.' She understood and was consoled, at least, that my son Aiden was to be with me in Chicago. My daughter Hayley wanted to be there, too, but I said that it 'felt like a guy thing'. Truth is, I didn't want her to see me that way either. My dear friend Chad Edelstein was wonderfully generous. He has a place just half a mile from the hospital and said it was mine for as long as I needed.

The day of the surgery came. I was in the best hands possible. But that did little to suppress the anxiety. Only the deep sleep of anaesthesia could take care of that.

When I woke, the first thing I wanted to ask the doctor was: 'Did you mess with the nerve?' That's not quite how it came out, but I certainly came straight to the point. He assured me that it had been a success, but I couldn't help but have my doubts. A piece of me had been taken away. Would I, could I, be the same man I was before?

Two days later, how remarkable it was that I could walk back to the apartment in snowy Chicago with my son. I had a catheter fitted. Being mechanically challenged, it was a good job he was there because I'm useless with that kind of thing. We had the odd accident, but I got used to how it worked thanks to Aiden's help and patience.

I felt like I had this ridge around my lower belly, as if I had a bad case of gas. Every time I ate something, it would create pain. My appetite was shot as a result. I walked up and down the apartment, changing my catheter bag every couple of hours. After a few days of this, I was going stir-crazy. I couldn't take it anymore so asked my doctor if I could fly home early. I needed to keep the catheter in for ten days but he said I could use a travel catheter, as long as I remembered to empty it regularly when I was on the plane. I did as I was told, booking into business class so I could have easy access to the toilet. When I arrived at the airport, Svetlana met me. I looked and felt like shit.

The catheter came out a few days later, I had a check-up with Dr Borland in Florida and was advised to take everything in my own good time. I have had to undergo more check-ups, of course, every few months and still had to bend over during the examinations. 'What's there to find up there, doctor? I thought you'd taken the prostate out.' It's routine, apparently. One of these days he's going to find one of my old school caps up there.

After having your prostate removed, your PSA reading on blood tests should be zero. Dr Schaeffer had done a superb job but did warn me that even though he was confident he had removed everything, microscopically he could never say he was 100 per cent sure. Thankfully, no signs of cancer were detected in my first two follow-up examinations. The news brought a wave of relief after a few days of edginess leading up to the tests.

There I'd been, not so long before, thinking my luck had run out. Obviously not. Not only was I fortunate enough to have access to these amazing experts and physicians, not only did I have a fantastic support system of partner, family and friends, but I came through the surgery with my cancer gone and no ill effects. This doesn't happen for everyone. I knew that from hearing other men's stories of post-operative problems and complications. The bottom line for me was nothing had changed.

Clearly, though, I can take nothing for granted. I will have to undergo regular examinations for years to come. With cancer, you should never claim you are cured, just 'in remission'. I'm thankful but not complacent. When Dr Simons gives talks about all his cutting-edge discoveries for treatment and procedures, there is no one listening more intently than me.

Dr Schaeffer and Dr Simons didn't put any pressure on me, but encouraged me to publicly share my experiences to help other men out there. Many don't want to think about getting checked or are scared of the very thought. But leave it too late and you could be handing yourself a death sentence.

I believed that if I could help just one person by talking openly about my situation then I'd have done something good. I was only too happy to help and have given many talks on the subject, hopefully taking away the fear of examinations. A simple blood test is all it takes to get a PSA reading. If you have misgivings, do your research. Speak to your doctor. Make an informed decision.

I have already received a number of letters from men who say that thanks to hearing my story, they now get tested. If the worst should happen after a test, I offer myself as the poster boy, if you like, of life beyond prostate cancer. You can not only defeat the disease but can also return to a fulfilling life.

Knowledge is power. Get armed with all the information you need to make the right call. Be aware of the possible after-effects of surgery, but don't be cowed. Be positive. Catch this thing early and you can beat it. I say this knowing full well that I have some way to go before declaring I have beaten cancer. Only the years to come will determine that.

It was in the spring of 2018, at the Prostate Cancer Foundation charity event connected to the Indian Wells tennis tournament, that I continued to spread the good word. I was sitting with my daughter, her boyfriend and some close friends when Dr Simons addressed the audience with this opening gambit: 'I'm going to surprise you now by mentioning Mother Teresa and John Lloyd in the same sentence.'

Hayley and my pal Joe Cipriano (Dave to his mates and an American TV voiceover institution) looked at me quizzically. I thought: 'Oh no, is he going to hold Mother Teresa and me up at opposite ends of the scale of virtue? She's a saint … he's … erm … not!'

But Dr Simons instead praised me for going public with my story and potentially helping thousands of people. He thought that worthy of a Mother Teresa comparison. Okay, so he might have been stretching it. But it did give me a chance to ring my sister Ann and brother Tony and deliver this revelation.

They are both quite religious. I have sometimes thought they must believe there's only one direction I'm heading when the final curtain eventually falls. Maybe, with Dr Simons delivering his Mother Teresa line, I had given them pause for thought: that I could yet press the penthouse button at day's end and not be resigned to the basement.

Thanks to my magnificent doctors, there's a whole lot more living to be done before I have to concern myself with the final destination.

LIFE LESSONS

THERE WAS a British clergyman who once wrote: 'We live and learn, but none the wiser grow.' Mr John Pomfret came up with that clever line centuries ago and, it is fair to say, we can probably all relate to it.

We think we will learn from our mistakes, never to repeat them again, only to fall into old habits against our better judgement.

That quote certainly holds true for me some of the time, but not always. There are also many occasions when I have learned a life lesson and employed it at every opportunity thereafter. That doesn't necessarily make me wise, just not eternally foolish. I can live with that.

Recollecting stories of my life to fill the pages of this book, you will detect I have learnt many a lesson from love and loss, fatherhood and family, friendship and camaraderie. But there have been less seismic lessons along the journey as well and they, in their own way, have been useful and welcome.

Lesson one: fame and celebrity, even by association, can carry you through some of life's trickiest tests.

I couldn't drive until I was 24. I had been in London from my late teens and did not need a car there. The rest of the time I was travelling abroad, making my way in my chosen profession. I never found time to take lessons. I was still without a driver's licence when I married Chris Evert in 1979 and moved to Florida.

'Do you want me to drive you around for the rest of your life?' Chris asked.

'That'd be nice, thanks.'

'John, living in Florida you've got to have a car and be able to drive it. It'll take you no time.'

I sat quietly, brooding: 'No time, she says. How about weeks and weeks of lessons and the tedious waiting for a date for my driving test. Then, if I were to fail first time, another long wait before my second test. I've known very good drivers who have not passed their test until the third or fourth time. No time, indeed. That's easy for her to say swanning around in her spanking new car.'

Chrissie could hardly have been more accurate. Okay, so it did take some time as opposed to no time. But it didn't take months on end. I was going off my knowledge of the British testing procedure, forgetting I was in America now. This was the land of opportunity. How opportune of me to secure my driving test after just four lessons. Oh yes, they did things very differently in Fort Lauderdale compared to London.

I was clueless at the start of my lessons and felt only marginally less so at the end of the fourth lesson, when my driving instructor – who had kept me to the quiet roads of suburbia – said: 'I think you're good to go. We can book you that driving test.'

I replied: 'When will that date come through?'

'I'm sorry, you've lost me.'

'Will it be another month of lessons before the test date comes through or what?'

'I think you're missing the point, John,' he explained. 'You are good to go NOW. Your test will be tomorrow.'

'But I've not even been on the freeway … I've barely seen any other traffic during my lessons … there's no way I can …'

'Oh, we don't concern ourselves with the freeway. Don't you worry about a thing. I'll take you round the roads they'll test you on.'

'What, you mean you already know that?'

'Of course. I'm one of the examiners. We use the same route all the time.'

We meandered around four of the sleepiest streets on God's earth. Apart from a few parked vehicles on driveways, there was not another car to be seen, nor a pedestrian to consider. 'There has to be a catch,' I thought, so by the morning of the test I slipped back into worrying, armed with my knowledge of British driving tests and how strict the examiners could be. 'The streets might be easy to negotiate here, but my driving skills are beyond basic. That's going to be so obvious.'

The female examiner lit up as we were introduced, blurting out: 'I'm a huge tennis fan! I just love you and Chrissie. You are such an adooooorable couple!' Maybe I had a chance of passing first time after all.

We talked tennis as I drove, somewhat carefully, around the very backstreets on which I had practised the day before. It was just as quiet. So far, so good.

To end the exam, I had to parallel park between two poles in the test centre car park without knocking them over. I had been fine reversing in my lessons, but the whole 'pole thing' threw me. I came in at the worst angle and started bending back one of the poles. If it had been a lamppost, the car would have been pranged. If the pole had been a person, they would have been nailed.

The examiner said: 'Stop! If you carry on and knock it over completely, I'll have to fail you because there are people watching.'

My scrambled mind was thinking: 'So if there was no one to bear witness to how crap I am at driving, I would pass ... just because she knows me?'

'Turn the steering wheel a bit more this way,' she said, almost doing the driving for me. 'Straighten up slightly. Good ... that's it. Congratulations you've passed.'

As my instructor joined us, the examiner said to him, while for once ignoring me: 'Tell John to be careful for the next six months.'

She might as well have said: 'He's your problem now.'

Brilliant! I had my first driving licence. But I was honest enough to know it was my current celebrity that had carried me through and told my instructor as much as we left.

'Good job she liked tennis,' I said. 'It's all a bit of a relief. I wouldn't have wanted to wait another month to do it all again.'

'Oh, you wouldn't have had to wait that long,' he explained. 'You could have taken the test again tomorrow and the day after that and the day after that, until you passed.'

America, the land of the free and, as it happens, the land of the free and easy with licences.

Chrissie was brave enough to let me drive her places, even when I kept veering off the exit lane of the freeway by accident. What can I say? The whole left and right thing was an issue. I would always get there in the end.

Lesson two: never swallow water in a public swimming pool, even at the ritziest of places.

My good friend Joe Cipriano – 'Dave' to me, and a celebrated voiceover artist in the US – flew over to England to watch the Masters event at the prestigious Royal Albert Hall. He was booked into the London Hilton on Park Lane where, on his first night, he entered his room to discover a man lying on the bed in just his underwear. He had somehow wandered in drunk from an adjoining room and was not for moving. 'I think you're in my room,' said Dave. 'No, I'm in my room,' he slurred in reply. 'In fact, I'll call down to reception right now to prove it.'

The nearly naked man dialled reception and asked: 'Am I in my room?'

'Erm, yes sir ... if you say so.'

He hung up and declared: 'See, I'm in my room.'

To make up for the shock and shenanigans, the hotel put Dave in a sumptuous suite and gave him his own butler for the duration of his stay.

It got better still for him when, later in the week at the Royal Albert Hall, Dave and I were heading out of the artists' entrance and bumped into legendary singer Tony Bennett, who loves his tennis and who I had met before. We said our hellos and Tony explained: 'I was hoping to run in to Mac (his fellow New Yorker, John McEnroe). I don't have a pass. Is this the best place to catch him?'

'I'll take you to him,' I said. 'Follow me.'

Dave chipped in: 'Mr Bennett, it's so good to see you again. I met you taking a pee in the Beverly Hills Hotel.'

Without so much as skipping a beat, Tony Bennett said: 'Oh, was that in the swimming pool?'

Lesson three: engage one's brain before opening one's mouth when addressing the greatest golfer of all time, Jack Nicklaus.

The Golden Bear won a record 18 golf majors and brought joy and excitement to millions. He is a great traditionalist, which means his favourite tennis tournament can only be Wimbledon. He loves the grass and is a regular visitor to the Royal Box.

Indeed, Jack enjoyed the surface so much he had three grass courts built at his amazing home in Lost Tree Village, one of the most exclusive and secluded communities in the North Palm Beach area of Florida. Jack lived overlooking the water on the south side of the boulevard – known by locals as Nicklaus Boulevard – and just a short walk from the main house is this simply stunning tennis set-up.

The main grass court looks as good as Centre Court at Wimbledon. The other two are used more often, so are not as pristine all the time. The show court comes into play when Jack and his lovely wife Barbara host friendly round-robin doubles competitions, which I have been honoured enough to be invited along to. The Bryan brothers, multi-Grand Slam doubles champions, have been known to join in the fun as well. Jack tries to play every weekend that he can.

After one match there, I said: 'Jack, it amazes me to think Wimbledon dig up the court after the tournament and have a year to get it back to its best, helped by loads of groundskeepers. And here you are, with this most immaculate of courts and just a few of you to keep it looking this way. How the hell do you do it?'

He looked at me like I had fallen from another planet. 'Well, John, you do know I build golf courses? And on those golf courses there are 18 perfect putting greens? Keeping a square of grass in shape like this doesn't seem quite so tough by comparison.'

'Oh yeah. Good point. Let's pretend I didn't ask you that question.'

Lesson four: it really is true what they say about no pain, no gain.

Australia not only brought me my Grand Slam singles high, when I reached the final there in 1977, but also saved my career. The serious elbow injury I sustained when I was 16 was causing me issues again a decade later. The elbow itself wasn't hurting that much, but I had increasingly lost power in my serve. The longer a match went, the shorter and shorter I would serve.

Former Wimbledon champion John Newcombe said a deep-tissue massage would help me and gave me the name of the man to help: Stan Nicholls. I had no concrete idea what a deep-tissue massage was or its incumbent benefits.

Stan was a former Australian weightlifting champion, who had turned four rooms and the garden of his suburban house into a gymnasium full of equipment. Tennis greats like Newcombe, Lew Hoad and Margaret Court trained there, along with professionals from other sports like Aussie Rules. But at any given time, you would also see housewives and regular Joes working out among the athletes. Stan was the go-to man for all and sundry. It was an extraordinary sight.

At our first consultation, Stan pressed his fingers into my dodgy elbow and I was immediately jumping around in pain. He asked me to do a few bicep curls with a dumbbell. It was a struggle.

Stan, I soon discovered, was a blunt-talking guy. 'Your arm is shot,' he declared. 'You've got less strength in your bicep and shoulder than most of the women who come in here. I can work out some of the calcium deposits in your elbow with a deep-tissue massage, but it will only be a temporary fix.'

I still wasn't sure what that deep-tissue thing was all about, but I soon found out. He got to work with his thumbs, kneading deep into my tendons and causing these mini vibrations that sent shockwaves of pain up and down my arm. I couldn't help but shout out, turning the air several shades of blue. I had to endure that for a few minutes at a time. After that, it was ice and rest, followed by more massage. That was the pattern over the next few torturous days.

We hit it off in that week, at the end of which Stan said he might be able to help me with a more permanent solution. It was coming up to the Australian Open in December. He said he normally closed the gym for Christmas, but would keep it open to work with me. 'But you have to promise to commit to this,' he insisted. 'There can be nothing half-arsed or you're out of here. Do you really want to fix this?' The answer was a resounding: 'Yes!'

By the time Stan was finished with me, I had added a good seven pounds of muscle and my strength in that troublesome arm had improved beyond all recognition. In my eyes, he was a miracle worker. He changed my whole philosophy on weights and working out. Arnold Schwarzenegger, I was not. But the work Stan tailored for me protected my entire body, not just my elbow.

I have never needed surgery on the elbow that almost ended my career before it had even begun back when I was a teenager.

Lesson five: sporting knowledge is one thing, insider knowledge quite another.

The BBC's *Question of Sport* is a British television institution, for a long time anchored by former French Open champion Sue Barker. I had been asked to appear on the programme for years, but told Sue that living in America had caused my knowledge to dwindle in most sports outside of football and boxing.

But there was to be a final invitation, for the *Question of Sport* tennis special in 2004. All the questions were to be tennis-based and the guests, except for regular team captain Ally McCoist, were tennis players. This I could manage, without appearing a total imbecile. Tim Henman and Martina Hingis were to be my team-mates; former Wimbledon winners Virginia Wade and Richard Krajicek were on Ally's team.

The day before the recording, I was at Queen's Club in London and ran into former British player Martin Lee. He told me he had been hitting a few balls recently with Peter Fleming, John McEnroe's long-time doubles partner and now an occasional BBC colleague. 'He's just filmed a mystery guest spot for *Question of Sport*,' said Martin. 'That's a coincidence,' I said, 'because I'm recording a Wimbledon special of that show tomorrow.'

When it came to the mystery guest round – where each team has to deduce from quirky camera angles who the disguised sportsperson might be – we were watching the screen intently when suddenly I realised the man in question looked suspiciously like Peter Fleming.

I was confused because one part of my brain was telling me it was definitely him: it looked like him and Martin Lee had told me Peter had recently filmed this segment. But the other part of my brain was thinking these film inserts were in the can months in advance, so it couldn't be him if it was shot as recently as Martin had described. The more images appeared on screen, the more I knew my first instincts were right.

'Does that look like Peter Fleming to you?' I asked Tim and Martina. They weren't convinced. We needed the two points to help us to victory, but could I really not say anything about my inside knowledge? Forget that. 'It's Peter Fleming, Sue.' Two points to us. I felt guilty for all of two seconds.

I think I might be the only person that ever cheated on *Question of Sport*. I never did tell Sue.

Lesson six: if you can't say something nice, don't say anything at all.

What Arthur Ashe did for tennis was remarkable. Not only was he a superb tennis player, but he put the gentle in gentleman. His wife Jeanne, who was also such a pleasure to be around, has a talent for photography.

Just before the French Open one year, she was showing me some of the photographs that were to be displayed in an exhibit of her work. One was kind of strange. It was of Arthur, naked in the shower. The cubicle's frosted glass mostly covered his modesty, but I couldn't help blurting out: 'That's Arthur's butt on show.'

Jeanne responded: 'You are the first person to notice that. I thought it might be a bit too obvious, but no one has said anything.'

'Until now ...' I said sheepishly, forgetting to tell her what I really felt about the body of work – if you pardon the pun. It was seriously good.

It wasn't the case that no one had seen the bottom on show. It was more that I was the first person to spot the obvious and not keep my big mouth shut. Jeanne was so lovely to me when I took over in the HBO commentary booth from her late husband that I think my faux pas had long since been forgiven.

In my early days with the BBC, I was a guest on Harry Carpenter's Wimbledon highlights show. Harry was a broadcasting icon, who asked the most pertinent of questions but was maybe not so used to receiving brutally honest answers from his pundits. After a certain British player had lost in the first round, Harry asked: 'John, if you were her coach, what would you ask her to do to improve her game?'

'I'd tell her to drop a stone and a half in weight straight away.'

The next day, I was slaughtered in the newspapers. One editorial said: 'Who is John Lloyd to think he can get away with that?' Another comment was: 'He's got a nerve. He doesn't exactly look sylphlike himself.' What's that got to do with the price of coal in Spain? The cheek of it. I was in damn fine nick.

They were missing the point. It wasn't me out there on court trying to make a living from the sport. I was trying to be honest and constructive.

I am not so insensitive as to realise there are not wider issues around body image in the world today, for both sexes. But if you are a professional athlete, man or woman, you should not be carrying excess weight if you are putting in hours of practice in the heat and burning up thousands of calories a day. That was all I was hoping to get across to the audience that fateful night, but was viewed instead as having put my foot in it.

I learned the hard way, from that angry backlash, that it is not politically correct to mention female players and weight in the same sentence. Former Wimbledon champion Lindsay Davenport told me the only way to get away with it is to say something like: 'She needs to work on her fitness', and let the public read into that what they will.

In punditry and commentary nowadays, I steer well clear of the weighty subject. Lesson learnt.

Lesson seven: learn how to navigate celebrity situations at starry dinners.

My friend Ron Samuels, a Hollywood producer and manager, and his then wife Lynda Carter, who starred as Wonder Woman, invited me to a dinner in Los Angeles in honour of Belgian royals – and it was strewn with celebrity guests. Before we were seated, we got talking to revered actor and pioneer Sidney Poitier who – I was told – loved tennis. I thought that made him a safe bet when it came to telling him one of my funnier tennis stories. I was barely halfway through when someone more 'important' and famous than me caught his attention and he just walked away, leaving me talking to an empty space. I continued my story to its conclusion, speaking to the vacant hole where Poitier had been, much to the amusement of Ron and Lynda. That taught me a lesson that there's a totem pole of fame and where you are on it matters to some people more than others. Even now, I despise when people are talking to me but looking over my shoulder, eyeing a chance to move on to someone they perceive to be 'bigger and better'.

When we sat down to dinner, I was opposite the brilliant British actor Michael Caine and his wife Shakira. Both were completely charming. Next to me was one of the most powerful women in American television, Barbara Walters. She was known for securing the biggest interviews with world leaders and Hollywood A-listers. Barbara quickly got on to the subject of my marriage to Chris Evert, saying: 'It must have been very difficult married to Chrissie, someone more well known than you. How did you feel on those occasions?' I was naive enough to answer with a little too much honesty. As more strange and probing questions followed, I suddenly realised: Barbara Walters was interviewing me. It was like she couldn't help herself, even with me. I may have crept up to the B list at the peak of my American fame, but I was never a candidate for a Walters Special. Yet I was getting a taste of exactly what that must have felt like. She was renowned for making people cry in interviews and, as I was talking about some deep stuff, it did cross my mind I might start bawling right in front of Michael Caine.

At a charity dinner in England, I found myself seated next to former British Prime Minister Harold Wilson. The master of ceremonies and guest speakers turned it into a roast of the elderly politician. They were basically slating him and he was expected to laugh along. A couple of times he leaned in to me, clearly feeling the need to defend himself, and uttered: 'What he just said isn't true.' It is strange what sticks in your mind from events like that. I remember distinctly that Harold Wilson had the dirtiest fingernails I had ever seen. They were black.

Later that evening, I had the honour of moving to sit next to the legendary British comedian Eric Morecambe. I adored him growing up, as did my father. Watching *The Morecambe & Wise Show* was a ritual in our house. Thankfully, I was not to be disappointed in one of my heroes. He was a true gentleman and incredibly grounded for such a valued national treasure. We talked about football – he was a Luton Town fanatic – and he asked was I taking care of my future financially. 'You are doing well, lad,' he said. 'But make sure you keep your eye on things money-wise. Don't get done.'

I'm not sure if that was a man from humble beginnings offering sage advice or if he was speaking from personal experience. Either way, I liked that this great man – who made Glenda Jackson corpse, had Shirley Bassey singing in wellies and corrected conductor André Previn with his famous 'I'm playing all the right notes, but not necessarily in the right order' – wanted to look out for me. Eric was a lesson in the humility of superstardom.

McENROE THE GENIUS

A letter from the John Lloyd of today to his former self as he's about to be introduced, in more ways than one, to one John Patrick McEnroe Junior.

> *Dear John,*
>
> *Get over to the South Orange practice courts ... quick! There's a 17-year-old kid out there from neighbouring New York and he needs to be seen to be believed.*
>
> *In a couple of years, you'll be playing him in one of the biggest matches of your career in the Davis Cup Final. Take heed: you'll get your arse kicked if you don't go into that match with belief. It will be no time to doubt yourself.*
>
> ***John***

WHEN I looked in a dictionary for the exact meaning of the word 'genius' it read:

'an exceptionally intelligent person or one with exceptional skill in a particular area of activity ... great and rare natural ability.' Impressive as that sounds, I'm not quite sure that definition does John McEnroe justice.

He had exceptional skill in a particular area of activity: of course he did. He had rare and natural ability: no question. But it was more than that. Yes, he was blessed with tennis touch we have seldom witnessed. But it went beyond rare. His mind worked in a different way from we mere sporting mortals. He saw pictures on the court that no one else could. He was extraordinary. He was unique.

Not satisfied with the dictionary definition, I started searching out quotes on genius. It's funny what writing your own book will make you do.

The Greek philosopher Aristotle once said: 'No great mind ever existed without a touch of madness.' That's apt for Johnny Mac. This from author Margaret Atwood's *The Robber Bride* is better: 'Genius is an infinite capacity for causing pain.' Mac inflicted a whole world of hurt on his opponents with his genius and, I suspect, was occasionally tortured by it himself.

It was 1976 when I first saw McEnroe play. He was having a hit on the practice courts, having been handed a wild card into the South Orange Open in New Jersey by *Tennis Week* magazine founder Gene Scott, who mentored Mac for a time. My reaction on seeing the 17-year-old McEnroe in action was simply: 'Wow!' I knew I was witnessing something and someone special. He was a phenomenon in waiting.

Just two years later, he was walloping me in the Davis Cup Final as he inspired the USA to glory in California.

Thinking back to that encounter at the Mission Hills Country Club in Rancho Mirage, my biggest problem was belief or, more to the point, lack of it. I didn't really believe I could win that match. McEnroe killed me. He made me look like a rank amateur. I ended up winning just five games. Two days later,

Mac came out and destroyed Buster Mottram – again for the loss of only five games – to clinch the trophy for the Americans.

I played McEnroe twice more after that and actually performed well against him, although neither were such big occasions. He beat me 7-6 in the deciding set of our Pacific Coast Championships match at Cow Palace in San Francisco – although he got lucky with a net cord at five-all in the tie-breaker – and went on to win the tournament.

Then, funnily enough, we met in the 1979 final of the South Orange event where I had first seen him play three years earlier. I won the first set on a tie-break, lost the second 6-4 and ran out of gas in the third, losing it to love. I had defeated Vitas Gerulaitis in a marathon match the night before and was running on fumes in the last set against Mac.

Don't get me wrong. McEnroe and me is a mismatch every time if he's at his best, even if I'm at the very top of my game. I just wish the player I became under coach Bob Brett when I was in my late 20s could go back and have a Davis Cup Final re-match with him. I'm not saying I would win, but a more mature, experienced me would deal with the occasion better. I regret not showing my true ability that day at Mission Hills.

But listen, McEnroe dismantled better players than me. He played one of the greatest matches I've ever seen when he trounced Ivan Lendl in the 1984 US Open final. I had a front-row seat in the President's Box, alongside my then wife Chris Evert. Seeing him at the peak of his powers up close like that was a whole new perspective for me on the genius of the man.

Lendl was serving big: 130–140mph. McEnroe was taking those first serves on the rise and coming in behind them. It was outrageous and brilliant, something akin to Roger Federer's modern day SABR (Sneak Attack By Roger), which basically involves the Swiss great charging his opponent's second serve to hit a half-volley return. When Americans were making such a big deal about that and Boris Becker was having a good old moan about its disrespectful nature, I was thinking: 'Mac was doing that kind of thing 20 years ago … and doing it in his sleep, too.'

That dazzling day against a bewildered Lendl, McEnroe was a tennis maestro. No player that ever lived would have beaten him on that form. It was a performance from a different planet.

McEnroe claimed seven Grand Slam singles titles, but he should have won another four or five at least. Mentally, he tapped out a few times and I don't think he was always in the greatest shape. He improved his fitness after he quit, getting into yoga and working on his flexibility.

The sport had seen bad boys before McEnroe arrived on the scene, but none quite so verbal, quite so willing to push the boundaries as far as humanly possible. Pancho Gonzales was fiery, Ilie Nastase sometimes had a little devil perched on each shoulder and Jimmy Connors knew how to work a crowd to rile an opponent. But Johnny Mac ranted most and cared least.

It went back to that infamous 'You cannot be serious!' tirade at the All England Club in 1981, which I expanded on in my chapter on Wimbledon and its referees. If Mac had been booted out or suspended because of that, maybe his temper would have been chastened moving forward. But I'm not so sure. I believe the McEnroe we saw, good and bad, was the McEnroe we were always destined to see.

The old school 'Oh, I say' way of thinking was that his angry antics had no place in tennis. More recently the sport has been condemned for its lack of characters. You can't have it both ways. Tennis is an entertainment as well as a sport and Mac on the edge made captivating viewing. It was never dull.

One of the most amazing things about McEnroe through all these years, with his outbursts and controversial straight-talking, is how he's not been laid out. I was working at the Australian Open for the BBC but also entered the seniors' event, thinking 'I'll play a few sets and hang out with a few old pals.' Pure fun. Nothing serious.

When my proposed partner pulled out, someone volunteered to fill the void like a bolt from a clear blue sky ... one John McEnroe, no less. Oh my God! Mac desperately wants to win, even if he's playing tiddlywinks. Suddenly, I had gone from a bit of obscure fun out in the boonies to teaming up with one of the biggest names in the sport, who was sure to be put on courts designed for high-profile types. Worst still, I hadn't been practising. I was crapping myself.

Our first match was played in front of a predictably packed house. Packed! And horror of horrors, I couldn't connect with the ball. Knowing that, our opponents hit it to me all the time. I kept missing and Mac was looking at me like 'are you a f***ing tennis player or what?' Finally, I said to him: 'I'm just gonna stand here and volley what I can ... the rest is up to you.' He replied: 'Leave it to me.' I did and we won.

Next match, McEnroe took it up a notch. He went nuts at the umpire, ranting like the Wimbledon title depended on his ballistic behaviour. It was a mood soon to be mirrored in the players' lounge.

I was having a cup of tea with former Aussie player Ross Case. There were wives and kids milling around. Mac walked in, looking dishevelled as if he had emerged from a bad night, and plonked himself next to me.

'Are you okay, Mac?'

I'm paraphrasing, but his response went something like: 'These f***ing Australians, they're giving me shit on TV because I said something about this little son of a bitch.' He was going crazy. Ross got up and left. Various children were hurriedly moved out of earshot of the colourful language.

Enter this big security guy, who approached Mac just as he was chomping down on food, some of which was spilling forth with the vitriol.

'What?' Mac said.

'You haven't got the correct accreditation to be in here. You'll have to leave.'

'What the f*** are you talking about?'

Knowing Mac had a TV pass but had not yet been upgraded to a players' pass – him being a last-minute entrant and all – I tried to intervene, saying: 'The accreditation place is right by the transport, so when he leaves tonight, he can get his badge. Problem solved.'

The security guard would surely see sense now and let it go. How wrong could I be?

'No, you've got to leave. Come with me.'

Mac hit the roof. This brave – make that foolhardy – security bloke was given several new nicknames by Mr McEnroe, none of them terms of endearment.

This guy was 6ft 4in and big all over. He was now extremely red in the face. He could have pummelled Mac into the ground right there, right then. But he was a professional, doing an important role. So, what was it to be? Punch John McEnroe, lose his job and maybe get arrested ... or leave and keep both his job and his dignity. Sure enough, the security guy turned on his heels and Mac had once again got away with his volley of abuse. It's unbelievable how many times he's done that and avoided a good hiding.

Thinking of how to end this chapter on Johnny Mac, I saved another quote for last, from *Alice in Wonderland* author Lewis Carroll. 'You're mad, bonkers, completely off your head. But I'll tell you a secret. All the best people are.'

Dear Johnny Mac,

I compare you to Rod Laver and Roger Federer in that you are all players who defied the nature of this sport, with the imagination and skill to create shots that don't exist in any manual I've ever seen.

Bjorn Borg and Jimmy Connors, two of your great rivals, of course, were amazing in their own ways. But you were the one player in that era I would stick around to watch, even from the stands if I could. Fellow pros, as you are well aware, are not renowned for doing that. In your case, I was delighted to make the exception.

In any profession, it is special if you can be around at a time when genius is to the fore. It was a privilege to witness yours ... even from the other side of the net in the Davis Cup Final.

Cheers,

John

REMARKABLE RECORDS

THIS IS not my take on the must-have vinyl in your record collection. No, this is about tennis records and the obsession players can develop for them. Moreover, it's an impassioned plea to stop the agony.

When the best in the business get within striking distance of a record, out will come the platitudes: 'I'm not thinking about that at all. I'm just focusing on the tournament, taking one match at a time.'

What a load of rubbish!

Players don't say out loud how much records mean to them because they don't want to invite in more pressure. But they think about it. Boy, do they ever. The best live for records. They thrive on putting themselves in the pantheon of all-time greats.

That I understand. Given the opportunity, why would you not want to create history? But what I don't understand is why any player is meant to be ever so serene and gracious as their record comes under threat.

Wimbledon is great at this. I use the word 'great' ironically. The All England Club just loves to invite former players along to the Royal Box to see their treasured records shattered before their moistening eyes.

Fred Perry was the only man in the 20th century to win three successive Wimbledon singles titles, ignoring the era of challenge rounds, until Bjorn Borg came along. He equalled Perry's record in 1978 and had the chance to beat it by defeating Roscoe Tanner in the 1979 final.

'Hello, Fred, Wimbledon calling. Fancy coming along to the men's final to see Borg break your record and your heart?'

'Er … okay.'

'Great, it's a date.'

Borg won in five sets, with 70-year-old Fred in attendance. I knew Fred well and he was a lovely man. But I can tell you here and now, there is no way he wanted Borg to break his record.

The next invitation of this magnitude went to Pete Sampras, winner of seven Wimbledon men's singles titles. The year was 2009.

Sampras had set the record for the total of Grand Slam title wins in singles at 14. Roger Federer equalled that incredible achievement at the French Open that same year. By defeating Andy Roddick in the Wimbledon final, Roger would break Sampras's record.

'Hello, Pete, Wimbledon calling.'

'Hey, how's it hangin'?'

'To the left actually, but that's not why I'm ringing you. How about a front-row seat in the Royal Box to see Roger Federer wipe you from the history books?'

'Well … I'm in California and kinda busy playing golf seven days a week …'

'Great, I'll take that as a yes, then.'

Poor Pete. He can't have imagined the torment he was signing up for. Let's once more establish, tremendous human being though Sampras is, he didn't want his record to be broken. No great players do, just to reiterate.

As the Federer-Roddick drama unfolded, I wouldn't go as far as to say Pete would have liked Roger to drop dead with a heart attack, that's going a little too far. But Roger breaking a leg wouldn't have upset him that much.

Federer not only broke Pete's majors record that day at Wimbledon, it took him the largest number of games ever played in a men's final to accomplish the deed ... across four hours and 16 minutes of Sampras torture. I don't think Pete had been back to Wimbledon since winning the last of his seven titles nine years earlier. No wonder, if this was how he was going to be treated.

Federer triumphed. Fifteen Grand Slam titles. A new all-time record. Sampras stood and applauded, just a little bit of him dying inside.

Federer then pulled on his new jacket, with the figure '15' embroidered on it in gold. 'Nice touch,' thinks Sampras – never!

Pete was gracious in the immediate aftermath of losing his record: 'Roger is a great champion. He fought hard ... it was fun to watch.' Nonsense! Not the great champion bit; the fun to watch bit.

Bear in mind Pete had television cameras pointing at him the whole time, waiting for his reaction. He could hardly cheer wildly when Roddick won a set or mouth an expletive as he missed the line by two inches. He must have felt like actors do at the Academy Awards, when someone else's name is read out as the winner and they have to fake the smile. Inside they're thinking: 'You son of a gun' – or something vaguely similar.

And what of the opponents in all of this? Roscoe Tanner and Andy Roddick? They might as well have been told: 'Well done getting to the final, chaps, but if you don't mind losing. We've got some rather important historical tennis figures watching – and we wouldn't want them to miss their records being broken.'

I have never understood the British on this one: this expectancy of graciousness. I get it after the event. A player whose record has been taken can, sometime later, stand back and say: 'Congratulations. I know how damn hard you had to work to get that record.' That's absolutely the right thing to do.

But beforehand, there should be nothing wrong with saying: 'No, I sure as hell don't want anyone to break my record.'

I once had the record for the most first-round losses in a row. It stood at 16. Okay, it's not a great record: but it's a record, nonetheless. I was pissed off when an American player by the name of Vince Spadea broke it. I saw him a few years later and told him how I felt. He didn't get my sense of humour at all and jumped in with some of the big names he had been unlucky enough to draw. 'Vince, relax … I'm joking,' I said as he continued: '… and Jimmy Connors twice and …'; I think he was genuinely upset I had brought it all back to him.

I am part of a more-wanted record and don't want to lose that one either. My mixed doubles partner Wendy Turnbull only told me this last year and it's a gem. When we won the Wimbledon mixed doubles title for the second year running in 1984, it completed a repeat set of champions. That had never happened before – or since. John McEnroe won the men's title, Martina Navratilova the women's, McEnroe and Peter Fleming the men's doubles, Navratilova and Pam Shriver the women's doubles and Wendy and me the mixed. A record for the ages, I hope.

My ex-wife Chris Evert was born and bred a winner. She won 18 Grand Slam singles titles. Her great rival Martina Navratilova won 18 majors, too. Only Margaret Court, with 24, and Steffi

Graf, with 22, had won more, when another, younger American player Serena Williams started honing in on the big numbers. Indeed, she would draw level with Chrissie and Martina as the most successful female American player of all time with victory at the French Open in 2014.

I happened to be watching ESPN's coverage in the US and Chrissie was commentating as Serena warmed up. The lead commentator asked Chrissie: 'If Serena wins this title, she'll equal the 18 majors won by you and Martina. How would you feel about that?'

Chrissie replied: 'I'd be absolutely thrilled. Serena's great.'

I was looking at the TV screen thinking: 'This is horse shit.' I knew her too well. No way did Chrissie want more company in the record books.

'That's very gracious of you,' said the co-commentator. 'How does Martina feel?'

'Oh, she doesn't want Serena to do it.'

Chrissie had thrown Martina right under the bus.

Truth is, neither of them wanted it to happen. Serena would equal and then surpass their record and continued for years to try to overtake Margaret Court as the woman with most Grand Slam singles titles. But in that moment at the French Open, there was hope from one – probably two – tennis greats that they would not be out done or out shone.

There are some records that may never be broken; Rafael Nadal's sensational double-figures record title run at the French Open, for example. Mind you, when Bjorn Borg won six times in a row at Roland Garros, I didn't think that would be surpassed either. That's the beauty of records. They are always there to be shot at, however improbable.

Jimmy Connors has a record 109 men's tour titles in the Open era. Roger Federer, who reached a seemingly untouchable record 23 consecutive major semis, played a more selective schedule as age finally caught up with him. As time looks set to run out on Federer before he can overtake Connors, I know for a fact Jimmy is the happiest man in town.

Following Australian legend Rod Laver by winning four men's Grand Slams in a calendar year seemed improbable until the era of the 'Big Three' of Federer, Nadal and Novak Djokovic. Laver did it twice. That piece of history appeared as safe as any, until Djokovic put his own notions of history into action in 2021. He came up agonisingly short, losing in the US Open final having won the first three majors of the year. I had wanted him to do it and complete the calendar Grand Slam. I wanted that to happen again in my lifetime and witness it as an adult, acknowledging the astonishing feat it is.

Who was in the crowd that day to see Russian Daniil Medvedev end the Djokovic dream? An 83-year-old Rod Laver. See, the US Open organisers do it as well as Wimbledon. Laver had said beforehand: 'I don't own the club, I've just enjoyed belonging to it. If someone comes along to win all the four, I'd be the first to congratulate them.' And you know, he would do just that and would genuinely mean it. Rod is one of the tennis greats I actually believe wouldn't mind seeing his feats repeated or bettered. He's that good a bloke.

In the future, though, I would like to think Wimbledon might think twice about inviting former players to join the guests in the Royal Box in witnessing their records being broken. I'm not holding my breath.

THIS MARVELLOUS BREED

IT IS to my eternal shame that I did not join in the Wimbledon boycott of 1973. The day of the Association of Tennis Professionals (ATP) had dawned, but the importance and magnitude of it all did not hit me, this naive 19-year-old trying to make his way in the sport. To this day, I am hugely disappointed in myself that I didn't see it was the future.

In May of that year, Niki Pilic was suspended by his national federation for allegedly refusing to play in a Davis Cup match for Yugoslavia. Even when the initial ban was reduced by the International Lawn Tennis Federation, Pilic was still set to miss Wimbledon. The ATP – formed just the year before to help protect male players – decided after a vote that if Pilic could not play Wimbledon, none of its members would take part. Only three defied the ruling, while 13 men who would have been seeded in the top 16 that year missed the Championships, including reigning champion Stan Smith.

I wasn't a member of the ATP, nor was I yet of a standing in the game that anyone greatly cared one way or the other, I suspect. My fellow Briton Roger Taylor, on the other hand, was an ATP member and an established presence on the circuit. He still chose to compete at Wimbledon as one of the defiant three. Britain's Mark Cox, who didn't play even though he was a Wimbledon club member, was viewed as the bad guy. Roger was a hero. It should have been the other way around.

The press was very much on Wimbledon's side, viewing the boycott as an affront to Britain's precious Championships. The public came out in force to support the tournament, believing the ATP was the enemy. It was the equivalent of fake news.

The reality was that, before 1972, the players were in a time warp. There was no ranking system and in some tournaments no prize money. Players had to negotiate their fees – their so-called guarantees – and send letters with a list of their results to gain entry to competitions. I say 'so-called' guarantees because if a tournament didn't perform well financially, players would get stiffed by having their fees cut in half. If your face didn't fit or they had too many applicants from one country, you might not even be accepted in the first place.

There were events where I could earn more money from gambling with my fellow pros than I could from the tournament. Bourre was the card game of choice: a kind of poker favoured in the US state of Louisiana. Sometimes, the pot of money would grow and the tension would build to the point I had to delay going out on court, even when the referee was trying to drag me out. It wasn't right that the financial rewards from a card game were greater than the tournament incentives.

I am full of admiration for those players who stood up to be counted in 1973 and regret that I wasn't one of them. It was my fault and my fault alone. Some others that chose to participate claimed they felt sorry for Wimbledon or their associations. That is nonsense. They saw it as their big chance to win Wimbledon. When the cats are away, and all that.

The ATP changed everyone's life on tour for the better. No longer could you be judged on what country you came from, whether you were ugly, an idiot, dull to watch and unappealing to the tournament director. If your ranking on the new ATP system was good enough, you were in. It was that simple. The old subjective rankings, done by magazines and the press, were obsolete. Players could make their own call whether they played Davis Cup or not without fear of suspension.

It was certainly a novelty to have guaranteed pay cheques at tournaments. The understanding also grew among the players that the more work you put in, the better you performed, the higher your ranking, the greater the reward. My hard work paid off. I was soon able to buy my own maisonette in Wimbledon for £19,000. That was a huge amount of money for me and it was a struggle at first, causing me a few sleepless nights. But I managed and sold it a few years later for £42,000. I was on the property ladder, never to fall off. Another perk of stable earnings was that I could afford to stay in hotels rather than cheap digs and have my own room rather than share.

Television interest and sponsorship grew in our sport, especially as rivalries formed between Jimmy Connors, Bjorn Borg and later John McEnroe. Men's tennis had entered a boom time, riding on the wave of the ATP's creation. The Women's Tennis Association delivered similarly pivotal changes for female players. Billie Jean King take a bow. It is almost beyond words how much women's tennis owes this legendary lady. Nowadays, vast sums of money flow through the game, making millionaires of modest talents.

But I believe tennis is reaching another crucial crossroads, when only radical reform will keep the sport current and relevant.

Speeding the game up is essential. There are times I find myself shouting at the TV screen: 'Just get on with it!'

We are in an age of short attention spans. Tennis has to move with the times. That means a slew of changes. Cut back the warm-up to a maximum of three minutes: build up a sweat in the locker room before you come out instead. Quit the nonsense with towels, it has got out of control: no player needs to wipe their brow every point and certainly not after the first few points. Play on even when people are still taking their seats: a bit of movement on a show court should not make you take your eye off the ball when every practice, every match growing up, every outside court contest is surrounded by way more chaos. Ration toilet breaks: they have become tactical and par for the course and it's wrong. Revert back to 16 seeds for the majors: it devalues the early rounds and cheats paying customers to have 32 seeds. The introduction of the shot clock was just the beginning. Whatever Rafael Nadal says, you need no more than 20 seconds in between points. This development is to be applauded.

For me, it is only a matter of time before we do away with best-of-five-set matches. If you want to see a long, drawn-out test of endurance, watch a marathon race. Is anyone but a diehard tennis fan seriously sitting through an entire four and a half hours of a single match? That's not the world we're living in. We need to protect our game, not tradition. In the end, tennis has to change to thrive.

My fear for the men's game is what happens when we lose Roger Federer, Rafa Nadal and Novak Djokovic from the tour. While they have been in our tennis orbit, we have been truly spoilt.

Nadal is the greatest clay-court player ever witnessed. His unbelievable collection of French Open titles lays before him as bedazzling proof. What most impressed me with Rafa, though, was how he managed to adjust his game to become a Grand Slam champion on grass and hard courts as well, switching from a one-dimensional clay-court expert to a major multi-surface threat. Family has been at the heart of everything he has achieved. Uncle Toni coached him to umpteen major titles, while the rest of the clan – who lived together in one complex in Mallorca – gave him the supportive environment from which to launch his talents on the world. He was brought up to be respectful and appreciative of tennis history. There's much to be admired about the man he has become, let alone his champion pedigree.

Roger Federer is even more special and, for me, the king of the modern era. His inventiveness on court makes him my favourite player to watch – and it has been that way for years. He has these gems of shots inside him that defy the game. Even when he is trouncing an opponent, it is never boring because at some stage he will produce something extraordinary. He never disappoints. The crowd creates different noises when Roger is playing. There are thousands of people gasping in unison at his brilliance: a collective 'Oh my God! Did you just see what I saw?' He not only does things on court no one else can do, he does things no one else would think of doing. What a craftsman of the court.

The greatness kept on coming because he was always looking to add new elements to his game, like the forehand drop shot and the surprise introduction of serve-volleying on second serves. He could have kept his beautiful game on autopilot, but he saw the competition coming at him ever more fiercely so went in search of extra gears. He always found them. He has also been the ultimate professional, looking after himself so diligently physically that he moved as well in his mid-to-late 30s as he did when he was in his early 20s. He for so long laughed in the face of nature. I wrote him off a few years back, believing he didn't have another Grand Slam title in him. I could not have been more delighted to have been proven wrong. Knee surgery eventually slowed him down, but not before he had added to his major collection in stunning style.

Like Rafa, Roger has enjoyed the unconditional support of a wonderful family. I had met his mother Lynette a couple of times before we bumped into each other a few years ago at the Australian Open, where I was playing in the senior event and commentating for television. As we chatted, Roger's father Robert joined us. We had never met before. Lynette introduced me. Robert went straight in with: 'It's good to see that people like you are looking your age now.' Lynette scolded him: 'You can't say a thing like that when you first meet someone.' Too late; he had. I was only momentarily crestfallen.

Roger manages to be super-relaxed in the locker room, just like Andre Agassi was. If there was a rain delay and I found myself in the same locker room as Agassi, he used to like a gossipy chat, picking my brain for the latest scandalous tale or humorous story. His opponent was usually over the other side of the room staring at his racket and getting all uptight. Not Andre. Roger is the same. I have seen him before some of the biggest matches of his life, kicking back, playing cards, as if his next task in life was to take a stroll around the grocery store.

Roger is THE man in men's tennis. He is the Jack Nicklaus of his day ... the Muhammad Ali of his day. He's the bucket-list player: the one you have to see in person. Playing into his 40s, he has given many fans ample opportunity to do just that. There's no escaping the end game, though.

The end can come quickly when you make your mind up to stop playing. I packed in after Wimbledon in 1986 when I was ranked something like 60th in the world. I knew the training for the last two to three months had felt like drudgery. Then I lost from two sets up in the first round to South African Christo Steyn and just knew I was done. I told my coach Bob Brett when I came off court. He suggested giving it more time to think it over, but I didn't need more time.

Serbia's Novak Djokovic has taken his game to remarkable heights in recent years and threatens to rewrite records in his favour across the board, although his cause has not been helped by his controversial Covid vaccine stance. There was a time when his body – and mind – started to give in to the rigours of life at the top, a further reminder of just how remarkable Federer's trophy-laden longevity has been. But Djokovic came again, more determined than ever and stronger than ever, physically and mentally. He has been a modern marvel.

And on the subject of remarkable ... to witness a British player contending for Grand Slam singles titles in this rarefied era has been astounding. When Andy Murray broke through to win his first major at the US Open in 2012, then added a historic Wimbledon title the following year, he was achieving feats I was doubtful I would ever see from a Briton in my lifetime. With so many infinitesimals in the equation, the odds on such achievements are gargantuan. He is a special talent. I knew that the first time I saw him play in 2005. But it requires more than that to take on the tennis world and conquer it.

Andy's two Olympic gold medals, another Wimbledon crown in 2016, the World No.1 ranking and a Davis Cup triumph with Great Britain rightly earned him a celebrated place in the Fab Four alongside Federer, Nadal and Djokovic. To achieve what he has at a time the men's game has been touched by the extraordinary is special. Winning Wimbledon – the first British man to do so since Fred Perry in 1936 – when there was so much pressure on him as a serious British hope in the biggest tournament in the world would have been a stunning achievement on its own, without any of the other heroics.

The masterstroke in it all was the appointment of Ivan Lendl as his coach. Before Lendl joined his entourage, Andy had a character flaw – a weakness – in that he would get on his own case during matches when things were going wrong. More to the point, he would get on the case of his coach. I am not advocating players acting like robots. I like them to show emotion on court and I believe code violations for smashing rackets are just ridiculous. But there are ways of channelling anger and frustration. In my era, when John McEnroe or Jimmy Connors lost their temper on court, they were straight back to business the very next point. When Murray lost the plot, there was a negative effect on him that seemed to last for a few points. In major semi-finals and finals against the very best in the world, he could not afford to do that. It was a gift to his opponents. They could feed off his negativity.

More than that, it was out of order. To this day, that is the worst part of Andy Murray. When he looks back on it in years to come – maybe if his kids see that behaviour – he might realise how embarrassing it all was. I'm talking about the times he has smiled sarcastically and mouthed words to his team watching down on him like, 'Yeah – great tactics' or shouted abuse in their direction. It's not a great trait. Until he sorted that out, I always felt he would fall short.

It was a nonsense when his backroom team said they understood Andy and that was just how he got out his frustrations. Utter baloney. They understood it because they got big pay cheques to tolerate it. When Brad Gilbert was coaching him, he was being paid huge amounts of money to soften the blow of any public dressing down. But why anyone would take that is beyond me. Would it be acceptable for a younger person to treat an elder that way in any other walk of life? No. So why is it acceptable on a tennis court? It's not. If some young upstart did that to your face on the street, you would want to clip 'em round the ear.

Andy made the best decision of his career in teaming up with Lendl, who was not about to take any shit from anyone. There was definitely more respect there from player to coach. To paraphrase Lendl, the message was 'don't be such an idiot out there' – at least, that's what I'm told came from the former Grand Slam champion to a player still searching for his own major breakthrough. Whatever Lendl said, it worked, as major glory followed.

Andy reverted more to his old ways when Lendl left and new coaches joined Team Murray. Even when Ivan was back on board for a second stint, Murray had achieved so much by then that he continued to aim jibes at his box. His entourage was so big, you could never be sure who he was aiming his complaints at exactly. But I'm surprised Lendl put up with even one iota of that crap flying in his general direction. I thought he would walk out for certain.

That's the unattractive side of Andy Murray. But that should not overshadow his great achievements and his many appealing attributes as a player. I am full of admiration for all he has won and the entertaining style of play he produced to carry him to the top.

I was aware very early on that this was no one-trick pony. If plan A wasn't working, Andy always had a plan B or C ... and then a plan D somewhere up his sleeve if he really needed it. He could think on his feet, he had the ability to see what was going wrong and correct it himself. He had a certain presence on court, something I had first seen when I commentated on his Davis Cup debut, when Britain played in Israel. Andy was just 17, Britain's youngest-ever Davis Cup player, and joined fellow debutant David Sherwood in the doubles. Andy pulled off some amazing shots that day in a pivotal victory that helped Britain to a 3-2 win overall. His only technical weakness that I could see was on his second serve. But he could even back that up with superb anticipation and movement around the court. He was the real deal and everyone knew it.

There were no givens, though. Sublime ability does not come with a guarantee of major success. Years of hard work, application, learning and improving have gone into moulding the champion. The bottom line is that Andy Murray is a winner and we have been lucky to have him.

Any chapter on the modern era of tennis could easily start with the Williams sisters because I believe theirs is the greatest sports story in history. But in mulling it over, I thought it better to end on them ... to save the best until last, as it were.

When I make that kind of bold claim about their story, people message me with other tales – usually of siblings – that they believe rival and even surpass that of the Williams girls. I'm sorry, but you cannot compare anything in sport to this. It is other-worldly.

Venus and Serena's father Richard coached them. He had no tennis background, so had to watch videos and read books to glean some knowledge. The family lived in Compton, one of the toughest neighbourhoods in Los Angeles. They were not financially blessed and facilities in East Compton Park were poor. Richard decided that the girls were not to play junior tennis tournaments. Any tennis expert would have said this was ridiculous: that you have to get competition when you are young. Add to the mix, Venus and Serena have distinct personalities and different builds. Yet Richard predicted from the start that both these talented daughters would conquer the world of tennis. Not only did they each become World No.1, but Serena is the best female player of all time. This is beyond staggering. Just think about it for a second. Staggering!

I was among those to believe Richard Williams was deluded. If I hear parents make these predictions for their kids even now, I think they have got a few screws loose. His ambitions for his daughters seemed laughable. When I lived in LA, he called me to ask if I would hit with his daughters. I said I would be happy to as long as they came over to my side of town. There were stories of the girls' practice court in Compton being guarded by members of gangs. I don't know how much of that was true, but it was enough for me to want them to come over to my neighbourhood. It never happened.

Nonetheless, I always had a good relationship with Richard and enjoyed our chats, quirky as he could often be. When I saw him at Wimbledon, he always seemed to have cameras around him or one in his hand. He asked me if I could be interviewed for a video he was shooting. 'What's it about?' I asked. 'Me,' he replied. He did the filming and he asked the questions. We were near the press area at the All England Club, surrounded by a curious throng. Richard didn't care who was listening in. My sense of humour appealed to him and he chuckled throughout the interview. I could see the camera moving up and down as he laughed, so tried to move with it. Anyone watching the tape back might have thought I had some kind of ailment. What became of the material for *Richard Williams: The Video*, I'll never know.

Whatever you think about Richard, he got it right where Venus and Serena were concerned. They were allowed time away from tennis to follow other interests. Richard said it would help their tennis longevity. Again, onlookers said: 'You can't do that and continue to stay at the top.' Again, Richard and his daughters proved everyone wrong. They got the balance right. In fact, both women are far better prepared for life beyond tennis than many other stars that have gone before them. I know of some former players who have been so insulated from the outside world that they are socially insecure post-tennis and need someone with them at all times to steer them through everyday life. The only problem for the Williams sisters will be how they fit in all their hundreds of projects.

Richard's family mission went from seemingly delusional for many to aspirational for parents of junior talent. But the Venus-Serena story is a never-to-be-repeated one-off. Coming from nothing to achieve what they have is like winning the lottery twice. But there were no shortcuts. I saw them in the early morning at the US Open, then again under the lights at night, pounding ball after ball, completing drill after drill. They had the work ethic and discipline as well as the abundant talent.

Venus and Serena have not had the credit they deserve. They have been taken for granted and I don't know where the women's game will go without them. It was only a matter of time before a major film was made about their lives with Will Smith, no less, starring as the coaching dad in King Richard, bringing to the big screen the greatest sports story ever told.

PANDEMIC PLUS

THERE IS a line from the Rudyard Kipling poem *If* above the doors on the way from Wimbledon's clubhouse to Centre Court. It reads: 'If you can meet with triumph and disaster and treat those two impostors just the same'.

It is a line intended to keep you level-headed, I suppose: in some kind of happy medium ground. Don't get too high if you enjoy life's triumphs. Don't become too low if life's disasters strike. That's my interpretation, at least.

The thought is a good one. Putting it into practice not quite so straightforward. During a worldwide pandemic, it was pretty much impossible. None of us had experienced anything like it. Good luck with finding middle ground when such a hideous and horrendous disease as Covid-19 is running wild.

Life's negatives are never starker than in times like this, during which I lost one of my oldest school friends Trevor Stone and two of my former coaches, Bob Brett and Dennis Ralston. News of each death was a shock to my system.

Dennis was the 1966 Wimbledon men's singles runner-up, who won five major doubles titles. He was a Davis Cup captain of his native USA and also coached my ex-wife Chris Evert, as well as Gabriela Sabatini, Roscoe Tanner and Yannick Noah. He died from brain cancer aged 78 on 6 December 2020. I learned a lot from him, but he never got the best of me. We were together at that time in my career when I was not as committed as I should have been. My results were no reflection on Dennis. It was all down to me.

By contrast, Bob Brett coached me when I was at the bottom and ready to put the work in to battle my way back up the rankings. He got the best of me, when I worked to the full capacity of my capabilities, and he was the perfect coach for me. He pushed me into areas I didn't think I was capable of going.

Bob told me: 'I don't need your money. If you don't work 100 per cent, you are out of the door.' We had such a great relationship after that, one which made me feel like I had let him down if I lost. I needed that.

Bob was a fighter. It was that fight that saw him tackle a rare form of cancer head-on. His daughters called me from Australia to tell me it was not looking good for their father and he might not have long to live. I hadn't realised he was that ill. I sent a video message to him, all the time recalling just what a big influence he had had on my career. He had been so very calm, always offering good advice. Bob was older than his years. He was about the same age as me, but in his knowledge and way of life he was far wiser.

Expecting the worst, I was surprised and delighted to hear Bob and his family had boarded a plane to Paris in the hope of finding new treatments. There were apparently just two places in the world that could help with Bob's rare condition: Paris and Strasbourg. He had a couple of surgeries and, for the next month, I received videos from them of Bob walking with his grandchildren and generally looking pretty good, all things considered. There was optimism. I knew he was going to fight – and here was the evidence. Once a fighter, always a fighter. I thought: 'He's got a chance here.'

But cruelly, Bob quickly took a turn for the worse and within 24 hours – on 5 January 2021 – he had been taken from us way too early, way too young, at the age of just 67.

Tributes poured in from around the tennis world. This was a man who had touched so many lives, including the fantastic array of players he coached: Boris Becker, Goran Ivanisevic and Marin Cilic among them. Just two months before his death, Bob had unanimously been chosen by his peers as the recipient of the Tim Gullikson Career Coach Award. For the word 'coach' in that award title, read lifelong mentor, trusted guide and treasured friend.

Just a month before Bob died, only two days after Dennis's passing, I was hit by another saddening blow as my dear old pal Trevor died from pancreatic cancer at the age of 70.

Trevor was quite the player for Essex Seniors and Westcliff Hard Court Tennis Club, where my dad coached for all those years in Leigh-on-Sea. Trevor also contributed so much to the county's fundraising campaigns. His wife had hoped to hold a grand celebration of Trevor's life at the tennis club so close to our hearts. It would have been full to capacity and we would have shared such great memories. But Covid robbed us all of that. There were just a handful of people at his funeral. To not have the send-off he deserved is a tragedy upon tragedy.

Travel restrictions meant I couldn't fly over to see him in his last weeks or days. Coronavirus has stolen so many precious moments from so many people. It is one of the singular most harrowing parts of the pandemic.

During it all, it was tough not seeing my kids for such a long time – probably around a year in total. They were in California, where restrictions were much tighter than where I was in Florida. There was Zoom, of course. My daughter Hayley even had a Zoom wedding, by which point I was able to travel and be there as one of the small group of about 15 in-person guests, while more than 100 joined us virtually. This was brilliant light at the end of a dark tunnel.

There was so much uncertainty and confusion in the first six months of the pandemic. When Covid was at its worst over here, I didn't know anyone with the illness and that gave me a false sense of security. Only later, when I heard stories of athletic people with no underlying health conditions getting seriously ill, did the reality start to hit home. It was – and is – a scary thing.

After a while, though, I adopted a different philosophy. Covid was not going anywhere. We had to get on with our lives, helped by the vaccine roll-out. Once vaccinated, I believed that, even if I caught it, the chances were very good; it was not going to kill me. There are exceptions, I know, but I felt more protected. Life could go on.

Getting the vaccine in the first place was key, of course. Vaccinations were not yet available in my area, when I happened to see a friend of mine on Facebook who had just been given his shot. When I reached out to him, he said that as I was a Florida resident he could help me get mine ahead of time. A couple of days later, a message popped up on my phone informing me of my Covid jab appointment for the very next day. At first, I thought it was a scam, only for my pal to call me, saying: 'Did you get your appointment?'

'Oh. That was you. How did you manage that?'

'Don't ask questions.'

'Just one more. Is it legal?'

'Yes. Fill out the forms I'm about to send you and you're good to go.'

When I arrived at the vaccination centre about a half-hour drive from home, there was a huge line of cars. It took me about two hours to turn into the park, where the jabs were being given in an outdoor setting. I drove up to the first hut, where a woman asked to see my driving licence and completed forms. That was all fine. Then, she asked for evidence of my appointment. I showed her the appointment message on my phone.

'It hasn't got your name on it,' she said.

'That's not my problem,' I replied, thinking it actually might be.

'I'm checking the system,' she added. 'You're not in the system. Go to the next station, explain the situation, but I don't think you'll be allowed your vaccination today.'

She drew a big red question mark on my car windscreen with a Sharpie and sent me on my way. I had been there for two and a half hours at this stage.

I had driven just 50 yards from her when a rainstorm suddenly hit, seemingly from nowhere. The rain washed away the red question mark. I pulled up at the next hut, no questions asked. I got my first vaccination right there and then and was double-jabbed within the month. When it's just meant to be …

Keeping active amid this strange time was a way of maintaining some sanity and this is where I once again struck lucky. Tennis clubs were closed for long spells and, even when things started to open up, many remained shut or allowed you to play only if you numbered, say, four tennis balls. One player could touch just the 'number one' balls. The opponent could only touch the 'number two' balls. The belief was the virus could spread from cross-contaminated balls. Insert your own joke here.

There was a house up for sale nearby with its own private tennis court. It could not be shown by realtors for obvious reasons, so I asked for – and was given – permission to play there with my partner Svetlana for two hours a day. I talked to some envious friends on tour, like the doubles guys Jonny O'Mara and the Skupskis, who couldn't get any proper court time and yet here we were playing daily in the Floridian sunshine, working on a John Lloyd forehand that is way past its sell-by date. It prevented me from going stir-crazy during the whole ordeal of the pandemic.

How the professionals kept on going was remarkable. Most athletes found a way to maintain fitness levels. Many of the new routines were captured on social media, including tennis players hitting balls against mattresses propped up against hotel bedroom walls in the almost unbelievably restrictive build-up to the 2021 Australian Open. Lockdown never looked so lonely.

I can only imagine what would have happened back in my day. The mattresses might have been used in other ways, perhaps to deaden sound from neighbouring guests as players sneaked from room to room at the dead of night, dodging security. I can't imagine back then that for two weeks there would not have been parties going on, with all kinds of impromptu soundproofing. Not that I would have been in that category of player, of course. Not a good boy like me.

The modern-day players – far more professional and prepared, no doubt – found themselves playing on some of the biggest tennis stages with no crowds, no atmosphere and no encouragement. It was an eerie and weird scenario. Yet they put on some amazing shows. Wimbledon did not take place in 2020 (typical of the All England Club to have pandemic insurance cover), which was a huge miss for the game, but other tournaments found a way to take place. Slowly, fans were allowed back and, even with certain restrictions still in place, our great game started to resemble something like normal.

The pandemic and all its inherent problems for an athlete could have been the time Andy Murray called quits on pro tennis. After injuries had taken their toll on his glittering career, Andy had radical hip surgery and fought his way back to the tour with a determination I can only applaud and admire. His triumph was being able to play at that level again. But you could not have blamed the man – a husband, father, multiple Slam and Olympic champion, who will never want for a square meal the rest of his life – had the pandemic brought him to the point of retirement. After all, he was now being defeated in matches he would never have lost just a few years ago.

There is a sentimental school of thought that when top players start to lose to opponents they would have swatted aside in their prime, it is time to bow out and leave everyone with enduring memories of their greatness not their fragility. I feel the opposite. An athlete knows when his or her time is up. That has to come from inside the player, not from outside pressure. Andy has endured some tough losses since his return, but he has had some tremendous wins as well. Even during the defeats, he will have played points here and there just like he did when he was at his peak. That high cannot be compared to anything else in life. It is hard to stop that: to give that up forever. I understand 100 per cent why he wants to play on. And from what I am told, he still completes the toughest training blocks and never misses a repetition. I have nothing but admiration for him and his attitude.

Andy has done so much to inspire the next generation in Britain. Now I wonder whether it can be taken to an even greater level by the adventures of a teenager by the name of Emma Raducanu. Coming from nowhere – ranked in the 300s – to win three rounds at Wimbledon and then going on to win the US Open as a qualifier, without losing a set, is one of the most remarkable tennis storylines of all time.

On both sides of the Atlantic, Raducanu's fairy tale captured the imagination of millions. As she is British, you would expect that in the UK. But she conquered America, too, and in more ways than one. She was on television news and the front and back pages of endless publications. Massive endorsement deals came flooding her way. She was the belle of the Met Gala ball in New York. One industry expert, having seen Emma give an interview in fluent Mandarin Chinese, said she was the most marketable athlete since David Beckham.

Her US Open final with another teen sensation, Canada's Leylah Fernandez, was more eagerly anticipated than Novak Djokovic going for the historic calendar Grand Slam in the men's final. Simply astounding. The TV viewing figures here in the States were huge and I know Channel 4 in Britain had record numbers for a women's final of more than nine million.

Raducanu needed to win three rounds of qualifying just to make the main draw – then didn't lose a set in her march to the final. That's almost beyond belief. Fernandez was ranked world number 73 when she started out in New York, but was superb in beating such highly rated players as Naomi Osaka, Angelique

Kerber, Elina Svitolina and Aryna Sabalenka to reach her first major final.

On the morning of the final, I wondered if one of the terrific teens would wake up and realise what they had done and where they were: if it would finally overwhelm them. But there was no fear or hesitation from either of them. From the start of the final, they decided to blast the ball, compete hard and have fun.

The first game they played was like the tennis version of the boxing slugfest between Marvin Hagler and Thomas Hearns. The calibre of tennis was exceptional. So much for gradually easing into the final. They were biffing the ball at 3,000 miles an hour. No holding back. It was a pleasure to watch.

There was no telling exactly how their respective careers would pan out beyond the final. They were still learning, while other players on the circuit would go on to discover more about them and figure out how to contend with their skills. But watching that final unfold – and with thoughts of such enormous young talents as Osaka and Coco Gauff springing to mind – I genuinely believed the women's game had a chance to surpass the men's game as the big drawcard and rekindle an era of Evert-Navratilova or Graf-Seles-Sabatini. After all, Federer, Nadal and Djokovic were not going to be around together forever. Serena Williams carried the role of headline act in the women's game on her own for too long. Now we could see a few female stars share the load.

When Raducanu became the first British woman for 44 years to win a Grand Slam singles title, I ate some humble pie. I always said those *Rocky*-style tennis films scripts, in which an unknown player comes from oblivion to win the biggest of titles, were laughable. Not anymore. Emma was Rocky.

When I was married to Chris Evert, we were household names. Chris had long been a global tennis superstar. Suddenly, Raducanu was fired into that kind of orbit. Paparazzi camped outside her house. She was on multiple television shows and international news bulletins. Everyone wanted a piece of her.

That is when you need good people around you, to guide you and ground you and keep you from the kind of situation Naomi Osaka found herself in, when she admitted to depression and losing the joy of playing the sport she could and should illuminate.

Osaka voiced her displeasure at having to do press conferences straight after matches, which didn't go down well with tournament organisers who rely on player publicity to help put bums on seats and promote the game. No press conferences equals no reporters equals no coverage. Only when Naomi explained more fully about her depression was there more sympathy for her.

My first thought was: 'How do the people closest to her not know she is depressed? If they do know, how can they let her play.' Depression is not to be trifled with.

When Osaka spoke openly and eloquently about the Black Lives Matter movement, my second thought was: 'Why is she putting herself front and centre like this when she supposedly doesn't like publicity?' With all due respect, if Osaka does not like to be in the spotlight, she should not be getting involved politically.

I have no problem with any athlete making statements. It's a free world. If you have a certain profile, you can make a certain impact. But you cannot then turn around and say, 'I don't want to do press conferences.' You cannot have it both ways. The same applies to the world of multimillion-dollar endorsements. If you don't sign up for so many commitments, there is a chance to take a break from the glare of publicity. The player is in ultimate control – or, at least, should be.

My advice to Osaka at that time would have been simple: cut back on your endorsements and do your press conference duties, but deflect any subject you feel uncomfortable talking about. Reporters will soon have to make do with asking questions about your forehand, backhand and next opponent. The most 'controversial' it might get is when they ask you about your boyfriend.

Raducanu will learn all about this in her own way. She appears bright and intelligent. My concern after the US Open triumph was how rapidly she was changing coaches. That said, I don't think she made those decisions – with either Nigel Sears, who was with her at Wimbledon, or Andrew Richardson, who was with her at the US Open. She was very close to both of them and both did phenomenal jobs. So, the decision to get rid came from somewhere else. It was not a good sign.

What the hell does a new coach get told he has to achieve when signing up to work with Raducanu? Nigel got bumped after Emma came from nowhere to win three rounds at Wimbledon. Andrew got bumped after she won the whole damn thing at the US Open. The Raducanu camp could say these were only ever meant to be temporary arrangements, but that doesn't mean they could not have been made permanent – and with those successes, both should have been.

I am not a believer that you can learn from this person and learn from that person every few months, taking little nuggets of information with you. Not when it's at this level. I know the player does most of the work, but the coach has to have a relationship of complete and utter trust. Many things go into coaching players and it is not just hitting forehands and backhands. The mind, the mental side of things, is 75 per cent of it. Raducanu is strong mentally. She would not have won the US Open otherwise. But there are still things that players need to be able to tell their coaches: things that go on in everyday life that affect performance. Your business is your tennis and you need to be able to tell a coach very personal information and feel confident what you say stays within. You don't build trust dismissing people every three months. At some stage, it will bite you.

Of course, there are different ways to build a tennis career. No one knows what the exact winning formula is. There are exceptions to the rule on everything. Richard Williams went against the norm by not putting Venus and Serena on the junior tennis circuit and by giving them plenty of breaks to have more of a varied life off court. But at least the Williams sisters had consistency and a level of trust in their father that Raducanu was not afforded on the back of her US Open success.

I had a high opinion of Emma as she shot to prominence at Wimbledon. I had spoken to people who have been around her and know her and they told me in no uncertain terms that she was the real deal. There are tons of players on the circuit who hit the ball well. But if you hang around with them day in day out for a few months, maybe sometimes only a few weeks, you get to know what they are like mentally: what their dreams are, what their fire is inside, whether they are liable to choke or not. Many, many players are decent enough and look good much of the time, but when it comes down to it, they are not quite there at that very top level. There needs to be that extra something to become a major champion. I don't think you can teach that. You can definitely help nurture it by working on the mental side of things, but mostly it comes from what you were born with. I have alluded to that in this book when talking about Chris Evert. She had champion's blood running through her.

When experts say 'this girl is the real deal', they are not just talking about the way the player hits the ball, although that is, of course, crucial. The 'real deal' is when they are ready for the top. They have got it inside themselves to achieve great things. Emma Raducanu was and is the real deal.

Of course, we almost didn't get to see this particular real deal at Wimbledon. When the All England Club panel made its initial selection of wild-cards, Emma was not among them.

The experts on the panel, according to what I have been told, did not think Raducanu was ready.

Nigel Sears, who was working with her every day, said that was a total and utter joke. She was ready. He didn't know she was going to win three rounds, of course, but that wasn't the point. The point was Emma was ready to play her first Wimbledon – to go out there, shoulders back, head held high, attack the ball, seize the moment and embrace the challenge. Nigel knew it. The panel did not believe it.

The first thing Emma said when Nigel told her she had not been given a wild-card pass into the main draw wasn't, 'It's ridiculous I've got to play qualifying.' Instead, it was, 'What do I have to do to convince them to change their minds?' Nigel told her she would probably need to win a couple of rounds at a pre-Wimbledon event to convince the panel. She did just that and suddenly a wild-card invitation to the main draw at Wimbledon was forthcoming.

Herein lies the difference between a real winner and your average pro player. If it had been me, I would have been pissed as hell. 'It's a bloody joke I've got to plays qualifiers – I deserve this wild-card.' I would have had a big old chip on my shoulder. That would have been my attitude. Hers was so much better. 'Win a couple of rounds? Okay, if that's what I have to do, that's what I'll try to do.' That, you cannot teach.

The Wimbledon panel did not know enough about her and that is why, in my opinion, they are not qualified to make those decisions. If they respect the coach – and certainly Nigel Sears is one of the most trustworthy names around – and have faith in the LTA's head of women's tennis, they should bow to their knowledge.

The vast majority of wild-cards are easy to call, but there are occasions when someone like Raducanu comes along who is ranked in the 300s and is open to debate. However, she was 300-plus for a reason. She had barely played because of the pandemic and was studying for her A levels. The panel did not get the big picture. Sometimes, Wimbledon have got to suck it up, take sound advice, relinquish some control and not be the be-all and end-all. If you are handed a dossier which states a player is ready, trust in it and those that created it. When you are wrong, at least own up to your mistake.

They got there in the end and this dazzling new talent was introduced to the nation. And didn't Raducanu just embrace the occasion? She wanted it. She was not overawed or scared. A star was born: another light emerging from a dark time.